Teaching a Child to Read

Teaching a Child to Read
Just the Bones

Sheryl O'Sullivan

Bridges of Ross Books

Macon, Georgia

Ross, Co. Clare, Ireland

Teaching a Child to Read

Cover design: Jessica Cook
Editing: Pat O'Sullivan

Bridges of Ross Books

2720 Riverside Drive #7435
Macon, Georgia 31209-7435

Ross, Kilbaha, Kilrush
Co. Clare, Ireland

The Library of Congress Cataloging-in-Publication Data

O'Sullivan, Sheryl L.

Teaching a child to read: just the bones/Sheryl L. O'Sullivan

p. cm.

Includes bibliographical references and index.

ISBN 978-0-615-98881-8

1. Literacy. 2. Teaching. I. Title. II. Series.

2014

Printed in the United States of America

To the original Collin and Whitney,

who taught me so much about reading

and everything else

And to James Green, mentor extraordinaire

Table of Contents

Forward

Teaching a Child to Read: Just the Bones

Reading is undeniably a complex act involving numerous integrated skills and abilities. And increasingly the *teaching* of reading also has been portrayed as a complex act. Certainly teachers of reading must know many things and must be adept at matching their reading instruction to the variety of reading needs found in their students. Certainly reading has been intensely studied over the years leading to a vast body of sometimes conflicting research addressing best practices in reading instruction. And certainly teachers of reading, or anything else, must be constantly examining their practices and improving with experience.

No one would deny these certainties, but the knowledge base is so vast and the recommended best practices so numerous that beginning teachers often despair that they will ever be able to teach children to read. Beginning teachers need the act of reading and the teaching of reading to be brought down to their most essential elements. The "bones" of reading instruction, so to speak.

This text is an effort to do just that. All the general topics included in most reading textbooks are covered in this text, but the format is trimmed down to "Just the Bones". What are the truly essential aspects of reading that must be addressed? What are the seminal pieces of research that guide our practices? How can we translate this research into just a few best classroom practices? This text answers these questions. It is designed to help relatively inexperienced teachers of reading—either in the classroom or in the home—to focus their efforts on what really matters in reading instruction.

The text is organized into five sections: Background Knowledge, Cracking the Code, Becoming Literate, Meeting Diverse Needs, and Literacy as a Skill. The chapters within each one of these sections briefly discuss customary reading topics, such as emergent literacy, fluency, phonics and comprehension. And, each chapter provides a short vignette in which these topics are further illuminated through application with real children who are learning to read. Additional features, such as key terms, book and electronic resource lists and lots of teaching ideas flesh out the topics a bit.

Reading *is* a complex act, and the teaching of reading can also be overwhelmingly complex. Yet you can begin to be a credible reading teacher by focusing on just the bones. The bones, after all, are the skeletal structure and foundation of the whole endeavor. So begin here, and enjoy the act of bringing literacy to life for a child.

Section One

Literacy as a Skill: Background Knowledge for Teaching Reading

Section One consists of two chapters:

Chapter 1: Background Knowledge:

How Does this Reading Thing Happen?

And

Chapter 2: Methods and Materials:
How Do I Teach Reading?

Chapter 1

Background Knowledge: How Does this Reading Thing Happen?

Babies apparently arrive on earth bent on communicating. Their early attempts, consisting of various cries and coos, are effective only to a limited extent, so toddlers move on rapidly to more and more sophisticated use of oral language. In today's modern print-rich world, though, it quickly becomes apparent to children that facility with the written word is going to be necessary for efficient communication. As oral language becomes more solid for children, they increasingly focus their motivation to communicate on becoming literate. Becoming members of Literacy Land will occupy a great deal of children's intellectual energies for many years. Yet how exactly does this transition from oral to written communication come about? How does this reading thing happen? Let's look at the journeys of two young children as they navigate this transition before we consider what experts have to say about the act of reading.

Collin Learns to Read

Apparently the whole act of reading for Collin hinged upon French fries. As his mother was driving down the street one day with Collin, the excited ruckus from the car seat meant with certainty that the word "*McDonald's*" had been read. But was this really reading? Wasn't Collin just recognizing the symbol of the Golden Arches and reacting to that? Yes, of course, this is how it began, but soon enough he could recognize the word even without the Golden Arches, and increasingly he could recognize other words of great importance, too, such as "*Toys R Us*" and "*Wendy's*."

Collin moved on smoothly from this use of environmental print to finding words he knew in books. The bedtime story hour now became a quest for accuracy where Collin would quickly correct any reader who tried to skip a page, or even so much as a paragraph, in a favorite story. Once the idea formed in Collin's mind that oral language can be represented consistently by written squiggles on a page, it was as if a dam of words had broken free.

Every day, endless times each day, Collin asked any grown-up nearby to write down a word or phrase for him. First he wanted his own name and the names of those close to him. But very soon he moved to building a large bank of the words and phrases he needed most in order to communicate. Following Sylvia Ashton-Warner's (1963) organic reading approach without ever having read her work, Collin followed the path of his own need to communicate to become a relatively competent early reader before he ever learned the name or sound of a single alphabet letter.

Eventually, though, Collin did begin to notice that the words and sentences he could read contained a consistent set of squiggles. Focusing his laser-like will on this new code to crack, he followed his previous method of asking any grown-up at hand to name this letter or tell him how that letter sounded. Slowly the phonetic code of English was revealed, along with many of its rules, and Collin became able to read much more widely and more independently.

Whitney Learns to Read

Perhaps all children just want French fries because Whitney's journey into literacy began the exact same way as Collin's. She recognized the word *"McDonald's"* and other words important to her, early on. She also began to understand, just as Collin had, that written language can consistently represent oral language as she happily corrected the bedtime story reader's slightest mistakes or omissions. Yet Whitney's way of figuring out this written language code turned out to be completely different from Collin's.

Whitney focused her own laser-like will on the smallest building blocks of this written code—letters. She sang the alphabet song and played the alphabet game. She happily collected objects that began with the letter B to place into a Big Bag. The words in her word bank, while meaningful to her, also tended to represent her devotion to the alphabetic principle in that they were often phonetically regular or began with the recently studied initial consonant.

Since Whitney focused so much of her attention on letters and sounds, her writing came along nearly as quickly as her reading. While her journal entries were done in invented spelling, and were therefore filled with numerous indictments against conventional English, her strong sound/symbol comprehension meant that most of her entries could be read and understood by an adult. Eventually, as her literacy skills increased, the need for such intense focus on the small building blocks of written language was no longer paramount for Whitney. She moved on to focusing on larger chunks of text, but never lost the ability to fall back on phonics if she met an unknown word.

Everybody Learns to Read

It is important to note that both Collin and Whitney became competent readers. In fact, they are much older now (Collin is in fifth grade, and Whitney is in third), and you will meet them again later in this book as we discuss various stages of reading. It is also important to note that both Collin and Whitney undertook learning to read with energy and intensity because they wanted to be able to communicate more completely with the world around them. Meaning and communication, then, were the motivating factors in their learning to read.

Beyond these likenesses of eventual competency and similar motivations, however, Collin and Whitney went about the act of learning to read in startlingly different ways. In fact, they almost seemed to approach the task of reading from opposite directions with Collin focusing on big chunks of meaning and looking at letters and sounds very late in the game, and Whitney placing all her attention on those same letters and sounds before she worried too much about the bigger chunks of text. As one might expect, experts in the field of reading have noticed these two different approaches to learning to read and have studied them intensely. They have given these two models the straightforward and charmingly descriptive names of **Top-down** and **Bottom-up**. Let's look at what experts have to say about these two very different ideas about how reading happens.

The Top-down Reading Approach

The Top-down approach to reading takes the view that reading begins with the prior experiences (or schemata) of a reader who uses that background knowledge to find meaning in the written word. This theory of reading is in agreement with Piaget's (1955) viewpoint that says children construct their own meaning and learning based largely on what they bring to the learning environment. The Top-down approach to reading depends that children, far from being blank slates, are actually teeming with relevant information and are active participants in constructing their own learning.

Since meaning is the main point of learning to read and children bring much of what they need to the learning situation, Top-down advocates emphasize comprehension of chunks of text as the place to start. Good children's literature is the primary material for this method. Teachers who follow a Top-down approach stress meaningful chunks of text over sub-skills, advocate lots of student-selected free reading, teach the language arts in an integrated, holistic way, and want assessment of reading skill to take place using authentic literacy acts. Collin, the child you met at the beginning of this chapter, is an example of a student following a Top-down approach to learning to read.

Terms often associated with a Top-down approach to reading are: (See Sidebar 1.1)

- **Whole language instruction**
- **Literature-based instruction**
- **Language Experience Approach**
- **Reader response theory**

The Bottom-up Reading Approach

As opposed to the Top-down model which begins with what the reader brings to the text, the Bottom-up model begins with the text itself and seeks to reduce the reading of this text to manageable bites. The Bottom-up approach to literacy takes the view that reading is made up of well-known discrete sub-skills, and any complex act is more readily learned if you start with the smallest skill and build upon that. Advocates of this approach stress the importance of reducing reading to its smallest component parts and then

Sidebar 1.1 Terms for Top-down Reading

Whole Language: The theory that advocates that all the language arts (listening, speaking, reading and writing) be taught in a holistic, integrated fashion rather than fragmenting each act into discrete sub-skills to be taught in isolation.

Literature-Based Instruction: This term describes the reading instruction using authentic children's literature rather than basal readers or other materials written for the sole purpose of teaching children to read.

Language Experience Approach: This method advocates using children's own language as the material for reading instruction. In this method, the child writes (or dictates) a story then the teacher uses this writing to teach the skills of reading.

Reader Response Theory: This theory presumes that children bring their own background knowledge to the materials they read and that it is the interaction of reader with the text that produces meaning.

teaching these skills in direct and explicit ways in a logical sequence. Phonemic awareness, the alphabet and the sound/symbol relationships known as phonics make up a large part of the instruction in Bottom-up classrooms.

Numerous experts, from the early work of Chall (1967) to the more recent work of the National Reading Panel (2000), have emphasized the importance of phonics instruction for young readers. All of these Bottom-up proponents reason that young children will learn to read more easily if the act is simplified with letters and sounds leading to words, leading to sentences and finally leading to larger meaningful units of text.

The materials used in Bottom-up teaching reflect the desire to simplify the act of reading, too. Basal readers are the most common textbooks used. These come with workbooks, worksheets, and other materials that can be used to practice the discrete skills of reading. Assessment in the Bottom-up classroom also focuses on small skills and is usually done through objective, written tests given to groups of students. Whitney, the second child you met at the beginning of this chapter, followed a much more Bottom-up route in her quest to become a reader.

Terms often associated with the Bottom-up approach to reading are: (See Sidebar 1.2)

- **Skills-based instruction**
- **Decoding**
- **Basal or Core readers**
- **Automaticity**

The Top-Down and Bottom-Up theories of reading both have as their goal the smooth reading and comprehension of a text. The two theories just approach this goal from different directions. Figure 1.1 illustrates the way the two philosophical reading triangles meet to agree about the act of reading.

Sidebar 1.2 Terms for Bottom-up Reading

Skills-based Instruction: This method assumes that reading consists of a set of small sub-skills that can be taught in an orderly sequence to readers. Early skills are the base for later skills.

Decoding: This is the act of processing written language so that a reader can recognize and pronounce a printed word. The most common decoding skill is phonics.

Basal or Core Readers: Materials specifically written for the teaching of reading. These books are leveled according to grade, have controlled vocabularies and follow an organized scope and sequence of skills introduction. Basal or Core Readers also include numerous additional materials, such as workbooks, worksheets, computer applications and assessment packages.

Automaticity: In relation to reading, this term refers to the rapid, and largely unconsidered, act of integrating all the various sub-skills into the act of reading. Until automaticity is reached, the sub-skills remain abstract and laborious tiny pieces of knowledge that do not translate easily into meaning.

Figure 1.1: Two Theories of Reading

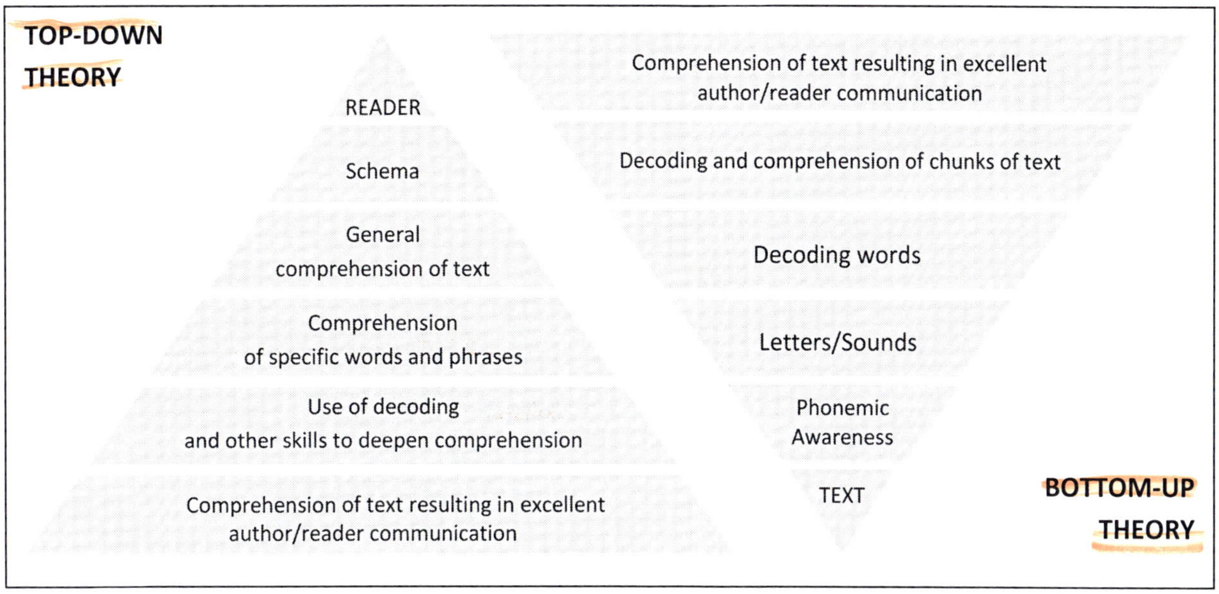

The Reading Wars

For at least 150 years, reading theorists have been willing to go to the mat about the best way to teach reading. Some advocate whole language and holistic teaching (a Top-down approach) as the only way to teach children that reading is a meaningful and enjoyable task. Others are so committed to skill-based teaching (a Bottom-up approach) that whether we teach consonants or vowels first is cause for battle. Public sentiment and governmental policies have moved back and forth with alarming frequency between the two poles of reading instruction for more than a century.

Luckily, good teachers (and countless children like Collin and Whitney) are more interested in teaching (and learning) reading than making war. While the so called Reading Wars continue to rage and find new, vociferous proponents and opponents, most teachers have found a middle ground in the teaching of reading which recognizes the benefits and pitfalls of both polar positions and integrates the best of both. This middle ground is variously called the Interactive Approach, the Eclectic Approach and the Balanced Approach. In this book, we will use the term Balanced Reading to refer to this conciliatory approach bent on making Reading Peace.

The Balanced Reading Approach

Balanced reading, as the name implies, seeks to find a balance point between the two polar approaches to the reading act described above. In the Balanced approach, attention is given to comprehension and reading enjoyment so important to Top-down proponents, *and* attention is given to discrete skills of reading, like phonics, which are stressed by Bottom-up advocates. The famous Eagles' song, Life in the Fast Lane, says, "Everything—all the time." And this slogan characterizes the "both/and" philosophy of the Balanced reading approach. Advocates of this approach do "Everything—all the time" when it comes to teaching reading. Numerous reading experts (Allington 2002, Routman 2003, Krashen, 1993) subscribe to this inclusive approach to teaching and learning to read.

One way to visualize this "Everything—all the time," balanced approach to reading is to think of reading instruction as a three-legged stool. See Figure 1.2. One of the legs of the balanced reading stool is the decoding skills leg, a second leg is comprehension and the third leg is reading volume. The seat of the stool is children's literature. In order for a three-legged stool to be of any use at all, its three legs must be very close to equal in length. Analogously, a balanced reading approach must give equal attention to skills, comprehension and reading volume.

Figure 1.2: Balanced Reading

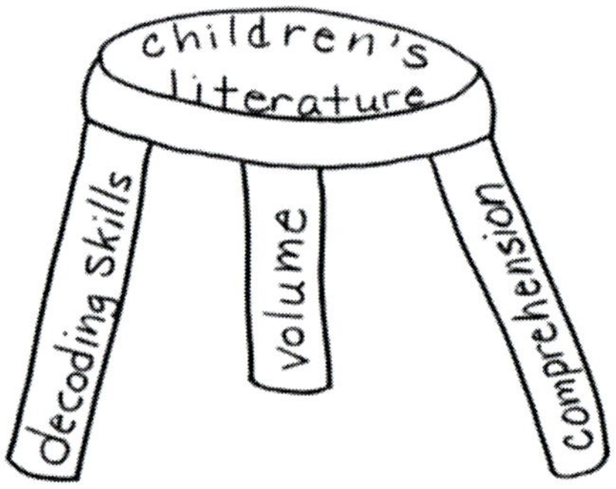

The skills leg of the balanced reading stool will necessarily contain different skills as readers gain in competence. For example, beginning reader skills would focus on phonemic awareness and the alphabetic principle while later readers would move on to more complex reading skills like morphemic analysis and informational text strategies. Similarly, the comprehension leg would focus on understanding smaller, simpler chunks of text for early readers and progress to deeper understanding of longer more complex texts as students become better able to deal with abstraction and different points of view. Finally, the reading volume leg will also change as readers progress, but reading volume must begin no later than first grade because this leg provides the practice for students to develop automaticity and fluency in their reading. (All of these new reading terms will be discussed in detail in later chapters.)

The whole stool is held together by a seat made of good literature for children. In thinking about this model, it is obvious that even exceptional literature will not be enough to overcome a shaky, imbalanced base. Literacy programs which have a weak skills leg may produce readers who cannot go forward independently because they have not been given the skills to do so. Programs that focus too keenly on skills while slighting the comprehension component may produce readers so focused on skills that they can sound out an entire story but not know what that story is about. And programs that shorten the reading volume leg on the balanced reading stool run the risk of producing readers who *can* read but never *do* read because they have failed to develop the fluency needed to use reading in daily life.

If, however, the three legs of the reading stool are strong and balanced, then children's literature is the platform that joins these three disparate legs together into a unified entity. Children's literature provides the material for children to read for reading volume, the grist for children to understand during comprehension activities, and examples in use of skills to address during skills instruction. A balanced reading approach, then, will include fairly equal parts of sub-skill teaching, comprehension instruction and time for free reading to build reading volume. All of these activities will take place using high quality examples of text like those found in fine children's literature. Figure 1.3 details how the three theories of reading we have discussed so far compare.

Figure 1.3: Three Theories of Reading

	TOP-DOWN READING	BOTTOM-UP READING	BALANCED READING
PHILOSOPHY	Reading is about the reader making meaning from the text	Reading is about cracking the code of written language	Reading is about comprehension of text and decoding skills make this possible
PREVALENT METHODS	Whole language Language Experience Student Choice Implicit Instruction	Explicit teaching in skills Controlled vocabulary	Implicit and explicit teaching of skills and comprehension Student choice for reading volume
PREFERRED MATERIALS	Authentic literature Language of the child	Basal readers Workbooks	Any printed material, including basal readers, children's literature, environmental print and child's language
INSTRUCTIONAL EMPHASIS	General meaning of text Semantic Cues primary	Accuracy in letter-sound relationships Sight words Phonic Cues are primary	Reading for accuracy and meaning All 3 cues are employed
ASSESSMENT TECHNIQUES	Retelling Comprehension tasks	Worksheets with skills Objective tests of skills	Objective or subjective assessment depending on purpose
STRENGTHS	Individualized Enjoyable Integrated Authentic	Organized Sequential Easy to assess	Inclusive Creative Matches teaching to child

Other Experts Weigh In

There are two other theoretical positions on how reading happens that are important for the beginning teacher of reading to understand. These two theories are the psycholinguistic theory of reading and the sociolinguistic theory of reading. Let's look at each one separately.

Psycholinguistic Theory

Like Reader Response Theory (Rosenblatt, 1978), psycholinguistic theory also believes that reading is the act of readers bringing their prior knowledge to the text and making hypotheses about what they will find in that text. Goodman (1973) labeled this interaction between reader and text as a psycholinguistic guessing game. Three types of information, called cues, are generally recognized as being used by students as they read. These three cues are: Miscues, not mistakes.

- Graphophonic cue—Using this cue, readers combine sound and letter knowledge to be able to sound out or pronounce an unknown word. If the word, then, is in the reader's oral vocabulary, knowing the pronunciation of the written word may be enough to lead to understanding.
- Syntactic cue—Using this cue allows readers to use their knowledge of the structure of language to consider an unknown word. This cue most often refers to grammar or word order. Readers using this cue, for example, will be able to anticipate whether the unknown word is reasonably a noun or a verb.
- Semantic cue—Using this cue, readers focus on the meaning of the unknown word using comprehension of surrounding words and their own background knowledge. A reader focusing on semantic cues, for example, would reject the sentence, "the house ran down the road," even though phonetically house is very close to horse and either word would make grammatical sense. However, semantically, house does not fit into the meaning of this sentence, and the reader focusing on semantic cues would reject house and replace it with horse.

The example in Figure 1.4 further illuminates the three cueing system of psycholinguistics. In this illustration there is an unknown word, *bootruncament.* Try to watch the way your mind works as it figures out this new word. Then read the explanations in each cue. While the explanation is divided into the separate cues so that you can understand each one, your brain does not divide up the work in this way. In fact, your brain uses all of the cues together with lightning speed, decides what it thinks, and moves on quickly.

Figure 1.4: Illustration of the Three Cues

First, try to read this sentence: **John opened the *bootruncament* as widely as possible and prepared to begin his vacation with some heavy lifting.**

Next, try to decide how to pronounce the unknown word, *bootruncament*.

Graphophonic Cues—You notice that there are probably 4 syllables, that the first syllable has the *oo* diphthong which will make a special sound, that the vowel (u) in the next syllable will probably be short, that the c will have the hard sound because it is followed by an a, and that the suffix *-ment* is a common one known to you. From all this, you come up with a credible pronunciation. Unfortunately, this does not tell you what the word means because this word is not in your oral vocabulary.

Finally, try to figure out what *bootruncament* means.

Syntactic Cues—Now you would like to know what part of speech this word is. It is fairly easy for you to decide it is a noun because it has a noun marker (the) before it, and the suffix *-ment* usually signifies a noun. So *bootruncament* is a noun, but that still doesn't tell you exactly what it means.

Semantic Cues—So now you try to decide what *bootruncament* means. First you use the words around it. Since you know every other word, you can narrow the unknown word to something that can be opened, something you might have with you on a vacation, and something that somehow involves lifting heavy objects. Looking at the word itself, you notice that the word trunk is almost there, and the word boot, which you know to be slang for trunk, begins the word. You hazard a guess that a *bootruncament* is a fancy way to say the trunk of a car.

Sociolinguistic Theory

Some theorists extend the three cues explained above to include a fourth cue. This cue is sometimes called the schematic or the pragmatic cue and has to do with the social and cultural backgrounds that readers bring to any text. This fourth cue is really at the heart of sociolinguistic theory which is based upon the work of Vygotsky (1986), and of Halliday (1978). Both of these theorists considered the impact of our cultural background on language development. Since language is unique to humans and has as its purpose communication with other humans, sociolinguists reason that oral and written language learning will be best undertaken in a social environment which accommodates the cultural backgrounds of students.

One important concept in sociolinguistics is the zone of proximal development, a term coined by Vygotsky (1986). Vygotsky reasoned that students learn best in the zone just above (or proximal) to the developmental level they currently occupy. With the support of someone (a teacher, mentor or older student) from that higher developmental level, the zone of proximal development provides just enough challenge without overwhelming a student. Figure 1.5 provides a visual for considering the development of a child on a continuum and seeing the zones of development surrounding the child's level.

Figure 1.5: Visual of Vygotsky's Zone of Proximal Development

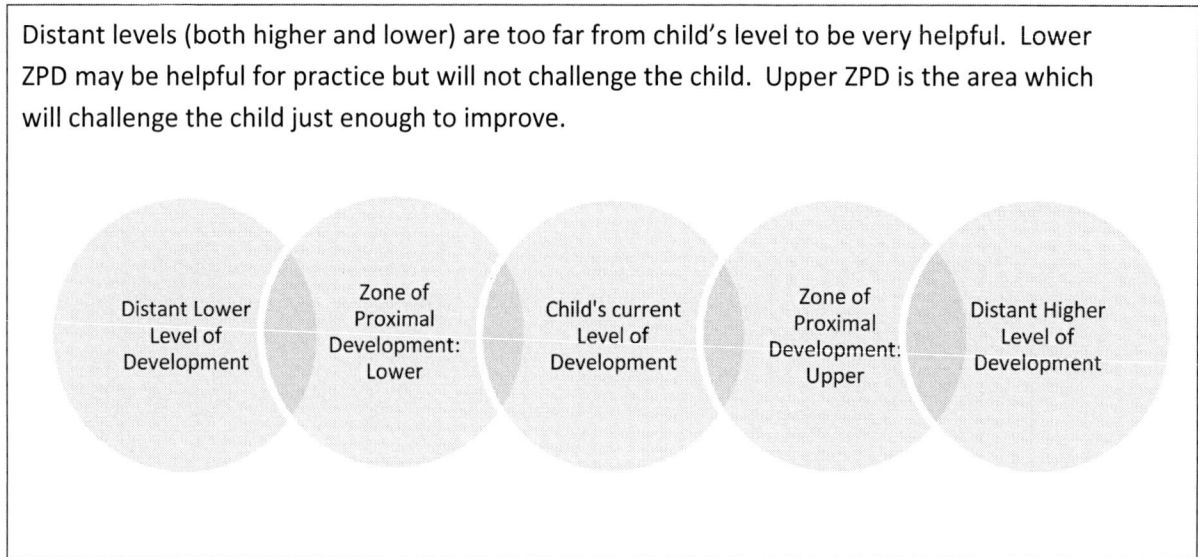

Distant levels (both higher and lower) are too far from child's level to be very helpful. Lower ZPD may be helpful for practice but will not challenge the child. Upper ZPD is the area which will challenge the child just enough to improve.

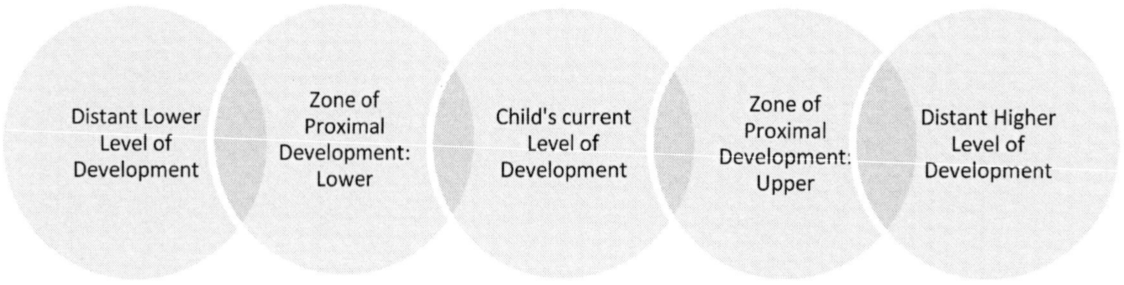

A second important concept in this theory is the importance of community to the act of communication. Readers bring cultural and other background knowledge to any reading task and are best supported in their literacy work by social interactions with peers and teachers. Reading, then, is a shared endeavor rather than an individual one. It is enhanced by diverse reading materials and by discussion in small and large groups.

Beyond Theory—Other Influences on the Teaching of Reading

Even the most expert of reading teachers does not teach reading in a vacuum. She uses knowledgeable sources to inform her teaching and she teaches within a political and legal context. Two of these other influences on the teaching of reading are particularly important for today's teacher to understand. These are the standards movement and the impact of current political policy on classrooms. The two are connected, but will be dealt with separately here.

The Standards Movement

Beginning at least with the publication of A Nation at Risk (National Commission on Excellence in Education, 1983), public schools have come under increasing attack. Much of this attack is unfounded. For example, National Assessment of Educational Progress (NAEP) data reveal that between 1971 and 2007 thirteen-year-olds and nine-year-olds have increased, not decreased, their reading scores slightly (Lee, Grigg, Donahue, 2007). In international comparisons, United States fourth graders are a respectable 14th in the world in reading achievement ahead of such countries as England, Austria, New Zealand and France (Mulles, et al., 2007). Yet, deserved or not, public outcry against achievement levels in schools has led to the present-day standards movement (Watt, 2005).

Standards are statements about what children should know and be able to do in different subject areas at different grade levels. Once the standards movement gained traction, standards proliferated. It will be important for any reading teacher to know the standards by which her students will be judged. Some of the most important standards in reading instruction are:

- The International Reading Association Standards for Reading Professionals. These standards detail what a reading teacher should know and be able to do. These standards may be found at the IRA website (www.reading.org).
- Common Core Standards. A 2010 initiative of the National Governors Association Center for Best Practices and Council of Chief State School Officers, this list of common standards in various content areas has been adopted by a majority of the states. The English Language Arts standards are divided into the areas of reading, writing, speaking, listening and language. A detailed copy of the Common Core Standards can be found at www.corestandards.org.
- State and Local Standards. Each state and sometimes even local school districts will have its own set of English Language Arts standards. It is particularly important that reading teachers are aware of these standards by which their teaching will probably be judged. State standards are usually available online by going to the state's Department of Education website.

Political Environment

Probably because literacy skills are so important for an informed and productive population, the teaching of reading has come under intense pressure from outside the reading field. No other subject area labors under such intense scrutiny and control as the field of reading. While much of this outside pressure is ill-informed and rife with special interest agenda, nevertheless the reading teacher must somehow accommodate these political dictates in her classroom.

By far, the most important political influence on the contemporary reading classroom is the federal law, No Child Left Behind (NCLB), passed in 2001. This law is an effort to nationalize standards, especially concerning reading and mathematics. The law requires extensive testing, especially of literal reading skills, and puts in place extremely punitive consequences for schools that fail to make Adequate Yearly Progress. The literacy ideas put forth by the National Reading Panel (2000) became the basis in NCLB for Reading First, an initiative which stresses skills over the other components of a reading program. While the full report of the National Reading Panel advocated a fairly balanced approach to reading, the executive summary of this report did not fully represent the balanced approach found in the full report (Allington 2002; Garan, 2002). The ideas in the executive summary were, nonetheless, the ideas perpetuated by federal mandate. Subsequent legislation has continued the ideological and practical components of NCLB. Consequently, many reading teachers today struggle to maintain a balanced literacy classroom while complying with federal curriculum and assessment requirements.

Summing Up

While political and theoretical winds blow where they will, and change directions frequently, good teachers of reading have always found ways to effectively bring their students into literacy. Using a balanced approach that incorporates decoding skills, comprehension and reading volume in the right measures for individual children, recognizing that students use different cues to make sense of their reading, and keeping in mind that reading is a social skill designed for communication, these good reading teachers have consistently made readers out of non-readers. These teachers have also found ways to use children's literature to turn children who were merely literate into voracious and joyous readers. The next chapter explores some of the methods and materials these good reading teachers use to do that.

Chapter 2

Methods and Materials: How Do I Teach Reading?

Let's spend a few minutes in the classrooms of two very different first grade teachers. Both teachers plan to make their young students into real readers before sending them on to second grade. And both teachers fervently hope their students will do well on the mandated end-of-year achievement tests. But, as we will see, these teachers have very different methods for reaching these similar goals.

Top Down

Mrs. Emerson Teaches Reading

When we enter Mrs. Emerson's classroom, she has her students gathered together on the learning rug where they are engaged in a lively discussion about mice. Responding to Mrs. Emerson's questions, students are eagerly discussing where mice live, how big they are and what they like to eat. The discussion is enhanced by the happy coincidence that this classroom keeps two mice, Mick and Mack, as pets.

After discussing real mice for a while, Mrs. Emerson introduces today's story, *If You Give a Mouse a Coo*kie by Laura Joffe Numeroff (1985). The story is in the form of a big book and students will soon get small copies of the book for themselves. Mrs. Emerson asks questions about the information on the cover, such as title, author and illustrator. She asks students to compare their knowledge of real mice to the picture of the mouse on the book. Finally, she asks a leading question to help students focus on the story she is about to read. She reads the story out loud and pauses a few times to discuss a page or ask for a prediction. The students attend carefully and are delighted by the surprise ending that makes the story circular or never-ending. Mrs. Emerson makes sure the students have comprehended the story through additional questions of varying difficulty, especially focusing today on sequencing. Then she begins a shared writing activity in which the class will write its own never-ending story.

In subsequent days, Mrs. Emerson will use *If You Give a Mouse a Cookie* in a variety of ways to serve many of her curriculum goals. She will focus on the sound of M that is heard in Mouse, Mick, Mack and many other words in the book. She will teach a lesson on sequence using ordinal words like first, second and third. She will even grasp a teachable moment to discuss plurals when a child asks why Mick and Mack aren't called mouses. The book will be read several times by teacher and students for multiple purposes. And another Numeroff book, *If You Give a Moose a Muffin* (1991), will eventually join the mix.

Writing

Bottom Up

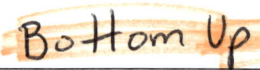

Miss Oakley Teaches Reading

When we enter Miss Oakley's classroom, we also join first graders fully engaged in their work. Miss Oakley is focusing today on the Common Core Standard that states beginning readers must know sound/symbol relationships. She has this standard posted on her classroom wall, and today she is focusing on the sound of /m/. First, Miss Oakley wants to make sure her students have phonemic awareness of this sound—in other words they can hear it in spoken words. She does this by singing a little song that goes something like, "M is for mom, M is for mom, mmm, mmm, mmm." Students join in almost immediately. Next, Miss Oakley says various words orally and asks if students can hear the /m/ sound. Thumbs-up for yes; thumbs down for no. Finally, Miss Oakley uses the classroom interactive whiteboard and has students come up individually to choose which pictures on the board begin with the /m/ sound.

Eventually Miss Oakley moves to the written symbol for M. Students practice writing capital and lower-case M's on their personal whiteboards. Now they are ready to start working with their new vocabulary words. Miss Oakley introduces the words, man, make and moon in context. The students sing a short little ditty about the Man in the Moon. Then they copy their new words onto their whiteboards three times and circle all the M's.

After this whole-class work, Miss Oakley will begin to call small groups back to the reading table. There the students will read a simple story in their basal reader that is leveled to early first grade and incorporates the new vocabulary words. Students who are not at the reading table will do several worksheets designed to give them practice on the new sound or the new words.

Methods and Materials for Literacy Instruction

Both of the teachers in these vignettes are engaged in good literacy instruction. They have planned for learning and their children are engaged and joyful. At the end of the year, nearly all of the students from both classrooms will have crossed over into Literacy Land. Yet in bringing this all-important skill of literacy to their students, these teachers obviously are following substantially different ideas about reading, and these philosophies are very noticeable in the methods and materials these teachers choose to use.

Mrs. Emerson is more of a top-down teacher. She starts with authentic literature, focuses on student background knowledge, highlights comprehension, and teaches decoding skills in an integrated way as they are necessary for understanding of the story. Both Collin and Whitney in our vignette from Chapter 1 would thrive in this classroom, though Whitney might appreciate a bit more focus on the small sub-skills like the sound of M.

Miss Oakley follows a bottom-up philosophy. She starts with the very earliest skill of phonemic awareness of one sound and then builds on that to teach the sound's graphic symbol and the way it is used in words. Miss Oakley's materials include board work, worksheets and basal readers that further understanding of the highlighted skill. Comprehension is not yet the focus of her instruction. Whitney, from our opening vignette will learn quickly from this lesson which stressed sounds and letters. Collin will solidify his understanding of the sound of M, but will want more emphasis on meaning to remain happy.

Keeping in mind that a balanced reading approach will use methods from both philosophical schools, let's look at the preferred methods and materials of each polar theory first.

Top- Down Methods and Materials

Teaching methods in the top-down classroom follow the tenets of whole language first popularized in the early 1970's by Goodman (1973). Whole language advocates do not oppose the teaching of skills, but they do oppose the teaching of reading skills in isolation. They feel that the language arts—listening, speaking, reading and writing—should be taught in an integrated, holistic way, and that the focus should be on comprehension of text rather than decoding. Two types of materials, authentic literature and the child's own language, are preferred in the whole language, top-down classroom.

Literature-based Instruction

Authentic literature refers to books written for children for their enjoyment and information rather than those written specifically to teach children to read. These books are sometimes called **trade books**. *If You Give a Mouse a Cookie*, which Mrs. Emerson used in the first vignette, is an example of a trade book. Reading instruction in classrooms using trade books is often called literature-based instruction.

Literature-based instruction can take several forms. One form is for all students to read the same core piece of literature and then do comprehension and decoding skill lessons that are designed around this common book. Published literature units which use picture books or novels for children abound to integrate language arts teaching through a good piece of children's literature. Additionally, teachers often design their own literature-based units. To do this, select a piece of good literature, brainstorm ideas using a web or other technique, then organize these ideas into curricular areas. A brainstorming web for a unit using *Ira Sleeps Over* by Bernard Waber (1972) is shown in Figure 2.1, and we will talk more about this technique in Chapter 11.

Recognize sound.
Phonemic Awareness - Focus on Sounds.
can do it w/ your eyes closed
-Rhyms Can students hear it?
Phonics - Connect sound w/symbol

Figure 2.1: Web of *Ira Sleeps Over*

Another way to use literature to teach reading is through a thematic unit. In this method, several books on a theme are chosen for the class to read. These books may represent several different reading levels so that all students in the class can successfully read books about a topic, but students at different reading levels would be working on different skills appropriate to their needs. A text set of possible books about World War II is in Figure 2.2. Again, we will discuss this more in Chapter 11.

Figure 2.2: Text Set for World War II

Picture Books	Chapter Books
Baseball Saved Us by K. Mochizuki	*Good Night, Mr. Tom* by M. Magorian
The Butterfly by P. Polacco	*Lilly's Crossing* by P. Reilly Giff
The Flag with Fifty-Six Stars by S. Goldman Rubin	*Sadako and the Thousand Paper Cranes* by E. Coerr
Nim and the War Effort by M. Lee	*Summer of My German Soldier* by B. Greene
One Candle by E. Bunting	*Under the Blood-Red Sun* by G. Salisbury

Literature based reading instruction is nothing new. Indeed, in the early days of the United States, the *Bible* was often used as the material for instruction largely because one of the main purposes of achieving literacy at that time was to be able to read the *Bible* (Smith, 2002), but also because this was often the only book available. While literature-based reading is long-standing and has shown years of success, however, it is not without its problems.

One problem with literature based reading instruction, especially for the youngest readers, is that trade books introduce multiple sounds, words and concepts all at once, which can sometimes overwhelm a beginning reader. Literature-based instruction also places enormous burdens on teachers to find appropriate books, discern what skills to draw out, design activities at different levels and assess student progress in a meaningful way. Finally, literature-based reading instruction assumes that teachers know a great deal about children's literature and are able to judge good quality. To help you with this, we will discuss quality markers in children's literature in Chapter 12.

Language Experience Approach

Using the language of the child is also a preferred material in top-down classrooms. The language experience approach (LEA) first discussed by Ashton-Warner (1963) and then popularized by Van Allen (Dorr, 2006) has remained a staple of meaning-centered classrooms. To paraphrase Van Allen, the Language Experience Approach theory says, "What I can think, I can write; and what I can write, I can read." In using this approach, teachers ask students to supply the words they most want to learn. Because these words are so important to the students, they are learned quickly and understood completely. Ashton-Warner (1963) terms these "one-look words" because children learn them so easily. A child can write or dictate a story about her/his experiences, and then this text is used by the teacher to teach reading skills. Experience charts may also be composed by the whole class about a mutual experience. The Language Experience Approach, since it is using the child's own oral language, has the advantage of easily meeting individual needs in reading. This is especially true for second language learners who may use a combination of first and second languages in their compositions. Figure 2.3 shows a sample language experience chart that was dictated to the teacher by a first grader. The teacher could now use this "story" to teach such skills as the sight word cat, the phonogram –at, and the sound of short a.

Sidebar 2.1: Key Terms

Authentic Literature: Books written specifically for children's enjoyment or information rather than for instruction in learning to read. Also called **trade books.**

Environmental Print: Common words seen in the world around children, such as *stop* or *exit*.

Experience Chart: A dictated account of a student or class experience which is then used as teaching material in the Language Experience Approach.

Literacy-Rich Classroom: A classroom that invites literacy by having lots of literacy materials and by including literacy throughout the daily schedule.

Teachable Moment: An unplanned teaching opportunity that is seized upon by the alert teacher.

Text Set: A group of trade books with something in common, such as theme, author, time-period, etc.

Figure 2.3: A Language Experience Chart

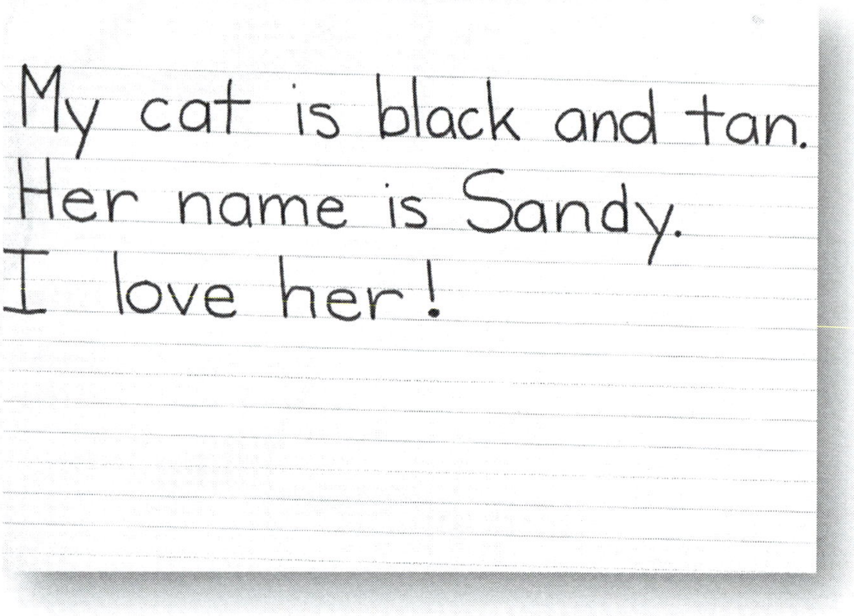

The materials and methods listed above all place the emphasis in learning to read on comprehension. Complete accuracy in decoding or vocabulary is not paramount, and small errors are glossed over in favor of extracting meaning from the text. An additional similarity in these methods and materials is that they are very enjoyable, and therefore, motivating to young readers.

Bottom-Up Methods and Materials

Miss Oakley, the teacher in the second vignette that began this chapter, is using a classic skills-based approach to the teaching of reading. Decoding skills take precedence over attention to comprehension, and the main materials used are those associated with basal or core readers.

Basal readers are the most common materials for the teaching of reading used in classrooms today, and have been for many years. Based upon the McGuffey Readers that were first introduced in 1881, basal readers are commercially manufactured materials especially written to teach children to read. Probably you learned to read using one of these systems as you followed the exploits of Dick and Jane, or Dot and Jim, or a host of other reading book characters. While basal readers have evolved over the years to be more colorful and to include more excerpts from children's literature, and while they are sometimes called core readers now, the basic attributes of these readers are largely unchanged.

Basal readers have several characteristics that set them apart from trade books. These include the following:

- A controlled vocabulary—only a few words are introduced and these are repeated often,
- Arrangement by grade level—preprimer, primer, first reader, second reader, and so forth,

- Clear attention to decoding skills especially phonics,
- A scope and sequence chart to organize skills development across grade levels,
- A teacher's manual with detailed instruction for teaching the student book,
- Practice materials like workbooks and worksheets,
- Supplementary materials like computer software or writing materials,
- Integrated assessment tools.

It is clear to see with so many pieces of a reading program arriving in one package why basal readers have remained popular for so long in so many schools. Busy teachers do not have to find their own literature and build their lessons from scratch. And they can be assured that all the necessary skills for reading are included somewhere in the program. Children can be tested and placed in reading materials at the appropriate level, and their progress through the materials can be thoroughly documented through ongoing assessment. Especially for the beginning teacher, this ready-made reading program can be very inviting and beneficial.

Basal readers have their difficulties and detractors, however. One main concern is the relatively superficial attention given to comprehension. While comprehension questions are provided, the often vacuous stories, especially at the earliest levels, mean that there is nothing much to comprehend. It is difficult to find deep meaning, after all, in a story whose real purpose is teaching the /-an/ phonogram (Jan can fan and tan). A further criticism of basal reading programs is the sheer volume of materials included. One basal reader, for example, had 70 pages of directions in the teacher's manual, and many more supplementary materials, for a 7 page story in the student edition. Teachers who try to do everything, or even most things, in the basal program will quickly find no room at all for anything else in their day.

The Everything—All the Time, Balanced Reading Classroom

Both top-down and bottom-up methods and materials have much to recommend them and also numerous drawbacks. As shown in the First Grade Studies (Bond and Dykstra, 1967/1997), and confirmed by other more recent findings (Arya, 2005), no particular method or material for teaching reading is clearly superior to any other method or material. This led Graves, Juel, Graves & Dewitz (2011) to say, "The most effective approach to instruction, the one most likely to lead the most children to a high level of literacy, is an eclectic, comprehensive, and balanced approach" (p. 46).

In other words, teachers should use the Everything—All-the-Time method of reading instruction which includes specific materials for skills instruction, trade books for comprehension and motivation, integration of all the language arts and individualization of instruction to provide just the right amount of challenge. Doesn't that sound wonderful? Yet, how is one small teacher supposed to be able to do all that? Let's look at a few ideas about organizing for instruction that may simplify matters a bit.

Classroom Environment

Before choosing any materials or formulating that first literacy lesson plan, it will be important for you to design your classroom environment to invite literacy. The **literacy-rich** classroom has several components. First, especially in the early grades, there will be significant student talking in this classroom. Keeping in mind that the literacy skills of reading and writing are built on the oral language skills of listening and speaking, purposeful student talking is a major component of a literacy-rich classroom.

Second, any classroom that hopes to invite students into Literacy Land must devote a great deal of space to literacy materials. This primarily means to have lots of books and magazines in the classroom. These should be at various levels, in various genres, and catering to wide interests. It also means to have electronic literacy programs and ample writing supplies, and the classroom walls should be filled with **environmental print**.

Third, the literacy-rich environment must have inviting places for children to read and discuss books Classrooms often have bean bag chairs, reading magic carpet squares, a reading loft, or the like, to provide comfortable places for children to lose themselves in books.

Finally, the literacy-rich classroom includes literacy activities all day long. Children read and write throughout the day for different purposes and in different genres. The focus is on literacy even while the secondary focus may be history, science or mathematics. We will discuss these content areas more in Chapter 11.

Scheduling

The next step in planning for student literacy is to organize your school day in such a way that reading and writing are the unrelenting focus of the day. Sometimes your literacy work will be with the whole class, sometimes with small groups, and sometimes with individuals. Whole class instruction is often used to introduce a new story or a new skill. Read-alouds, where the teacher reads from a big book, are done with the whole class, as are shared writing, language experience charts and content area extension activities.

Small groups are often used in order to teach necessary skills to the few children who need that skill and also to allow students to be placed in reading materials at an appropriate level. The main thing to remember about these groups is to keep them flexible. Students should be able to move in and out of groups easily depending on their needed instruction. Children's needs change frequently, and flexible groupings accommodate this. For small group instruction, basal readers and their accompanying skills activities are often the materials chosen since these readers are arranged by level and concentrate on individual skills development.

Besides whole class and small group instruction, students must spend a great deal of time working individually on becoming literate. Individual activities often include free-reading time, individual work at various reading centers, and writing activities that serve to apply the student's new reading skills.

Allowing student choice in the free-reading time will motivate students and naturally keep them at appropriate levels. You will need to monitor these activities, though, to make sure students are progressing in literacy development.

A sample schedule for a first grade classroom with a literacy focus is shown in Figure 2.4.

Figure 2.4: Sample Daily Schedule—First Grade

Time	Activity	Notes
8:30-8:45	Attendance/Calendar/Journals	Students write in journals on a designated topic
8:45-9:45	Small Reading Groups	Teacher meets with small skill groups by level. Other students do reading centers.
9:45-10:15	Whole Group Literacy Skills Lessons	Spelling, Phonics, Writing and other skills lessons.
10:15-10:30	Recess	
10:30-11:15	Literature Study	Study of book(s)—usually on a theme
11:15-11:45	Lunch	
11:45-12:00	Shared Reading	Teacher reads to the students
12:00-12:20	Whole Group Math Lessons	Mathematics skills lessons
12:20-12:45	Small Math Groups	Teacher meets with small skill groups. Other students have Sustained Silent Reading.
12:45-1:30	Nonfiction Reading work in Science or Social Studies	Science and Social Studies alternate weeks. Teach by theme using literature.
1:30-2:15	Planning Period	Students in Music or PE
2:15-2:30	Review of Day/Prepare to Leave	
2:30	Dismissal	

Lesson Planning

Building a literacy-rich environment and scheduling literacy throughout the day will go a long way toward inviting literacy in children, so now it is time to design that first reading lesson plan. All lesson plans, regardless of subject matter and regardless of the number of extra steps advocated by schools and districts, must essentially have three elements, which are the purpose, the procedure and the assessment. Think of your lesson plan as a trip to Chicago in order to understand how these three elements work together.

- PURPOSE: All lesson plans start out with a purpose. This can be called a goal, a learning objective, the core standard or the essential question. No matter what it is called, though, it establishes what we hope to achieve by this lesson. In this analogy, Chicago is my goal. I hope to arrive in Chicago, and for the rest of my lesson plan I will single-mindedly pursue this goal. Every action I take from now on will be designed to achieve my objective of arriving in Chicago. In a reading lesson plan, we might have as our purpose, teaching the sound of short /ĕ/, for example. Whatever we establish as our learning objective, we must now single-mindedly pursue. This is step one of any lesson plan, and here is the place to include any mandated standard.

- PROCEDURE: The second phase of any lesson plan is the procedure. It might be called the method or the description, but it essentially says how you will reach the purpose you established in step 1. In our analogy, this would be a map to Chicago. Just as a roadmap tells us when and where to turn in order to reach Chicago, so our lesson procedure gives us detailed instructions on how to reach our stated goal. The activities, the materials, and the methods of instruction that will be used to teach the sound of short /ĕ/, for example, should all be listed in this section in enough detail that we are sure to be able to follow them to the desired end. For the beginning teacher, this section is often quite lengthy and detailed. Later, once you have made the trip to Chicago numerous times, such procedural specificity may not be so necessary.

- ASSESSMENT: The final component of any lesson plan is assessment. In our analogy, we would ask ourselves, "Are we in Chicago?" For our hypothetical lesson on the sound of short /ĕ/, we would ask whether students now know this sound and can apply it in their reading. We might give students a written test or worksheet over this sound. Or we might ask students to apply this sound in their reading and observe whether they are able to do this. No matter how we choose to assess our learning objective, we must include this step in order to know how to proceed. If I had planned to reach Chicago and somehow I am now standing in Milwaukee, I must take some action to rectify the situation. As a teacher, if my students have achieved the desired objective, I am ready to move ahead in my teaching If, however, my students are standing in Milwaukee (do not know the sound of short /ĕ/), I must discern where my plan failed and re-teach this lesson in such a way that the desired objective is achieved.

The Trip to Chicago lesson plan, then, includes:

1. Purpose (goal, objective, standard, etc.)
2. Procedure (activities, materials, methods, etc.)
3. Assessment (testing, observation, application, etc.)

Any literacy lesson plan should contain these three basic components, and may also include additional components advocated by districts or individual schools. Obviously, using the Trip to Chicago format there are countless ways to plan a literacy lesson in the classroom. This can get overwhelming so let's concentrate on one all-purpose way of planning a reading lesson that can be used regardless of reading philosophy for literacy lessons in any genre and at any level. This all-purpose plan is variously called a Directed Reading Activity (DRA), a Directed Reading-Thinking Activity (DRTA), a Guided Reading Lesson (GRL), or a Directed Reading Lesson (DRL). While each of these plans has subtle differences, they all contain similar components. For simplicity's sake, we will use the DRL format designed by Cooper, Warncke, Shipman & Ramstad (1979). The DRL has three main parts: Pre-reading, Directed reading and Post-reading. Let's look at each phase individually as we consider this all-purpose reading lesson.

Sidebar 2.2: DRL for *Give a Mouse a Cookie*

Purpose:

a. Students will know and apply the sound of initial /m/.
b. Students will understand the concept of sequence using ordinals.
c. Students will understand the concept of a circular story.

Procedure:

a. PRE-READING:
Introduce vocabulary words (mustache, scissors, comfortable) in context of short sentences. Use a pocket chart and provide practice.
Introduce concepts of print (author, illustrator, title).
Activate schema by discussing mice
Set purpose question: The boy has a problem. What is it?
b. DIRECTED READING:
Sample Literal Question: What did the mouse want first? Second? Third?
Sample Inferential Question: What was the boy's problem? Proof?
Sample Critical Question: Was it wise for the boy to give the mouse a cookie? Why/why not?
Re-read the story in many different ways for different purposes: read to, echo read, partner read, etc.
c. POST READING:
Teach the sound/symbol relationship for M. Give words with initial /m/ to students (mouse, milk, mustache, make, etc.). Students bring words to pocket chart at appropriate time. Re-read story finding words with /m/.
Do extension activity of circular story. Write one as a class for practice.

Assessment:

a. Students complete an /m/ computer assessment with 80% accuracy.
b. Students are able to put story cards in correct sequence with ordinals.
c. Students write a circular story.

The DRL--An All-Purpose Reading Lesson

- *Pre-reading*: During pre-reading the teacher introduces the text to be read. She may concentrate on concepts about print, such as title, author and illustrator. She endeavors to connect student background knowledge (schema) with the text. She may conduct a picture walk of the story to encourage predictions. She will most certainly do something to motivate students to engage with the text, and she will ask at least one question which sets a purpose for reading this story. During this pre-reading portion of the lesson, the teacher may want to introduce a few vocabulary words necessary for success with the text. And she may want to focus at this time on a reading skill, such as a phonics sound.
- *Directed reading:* During this portion of the lesson, the teacher guides the students through the text using questions of differing difficulty levels. The focus is on comprehension here, and the purpose question set in pre-reading is often a good starting place. It is also appropriate during this phase to point out where any skills taught during pre-reading are being used in the text. The reading done during this phase can be shared, whole class, or small group. It can be oral or silent. Teachers usually find it helpful for students to do several re-readings of the text with varied circumstances and purposes.
- *Post-Reading:* During this final phase of the DRL, the teacher may teach or re-teach skills or vocabulary lessons. If these skills were not taught in pre-reading, they should certainly be included here. This section of the reading lesson is also where application and extension activities take place. It is especially important here to extend the reading activities associated with the text to writing activities where students apply their new knowledge. Finally, it is in post-reading that assessment takes place. Here the teacher must ask herself if her students are standing in Chicago with good understanding of the text, or are they off somewhere else, lost without the skills needed for adequate comprehension.

Both teachers in the vignettes at the beginning of this chapter used components of this all-purpose reading lesson, and they could easily have modified their teaching to follow this plan within their individual philosophies. Mrs. Emerson, for example, could have introduced some of the vocabulary words found in *If You Give a Mouse a Cookie*, and she could have focused more on the sound of initial /m/ putting students into flexible small groups depending on how much additional work they needed with this sound for mastery. Miss Oakley, who already uses small groups and emphasizes skills, could have added a literature component, such as *If You Give a Mouse a Cookie* to her pre-reading phase, using this book to enhance comprehension skills. She could also have added a writing assignment to the worksheets students did during post-reading in order to make sure students could apply their new vocabulary words and phonics skill. A full DRL lesson plan for *If You Give a Mouse a Cookie* is provided as an example in sidebar 2.2. This DRL uses the Trip to Chicago lesson plan format.

Summing up and Moving on

This chapter looked at some specific methods and materials to use when teaching reading. We considered both literature-based and skills-based classrooms, and we examined ways to encourage reading through a literacy-rich environment and a literacy-focused schedule. We discussed general lesson planning using the Trip to Chicago format, and an all-purpose literacy lesson plan called the Directed Reading Lesson.

As you are beginning to understand, there is quite a bit to this seemingly simple task of teaching a child to read. The previous two chapters have given you important background material with Chapter 1 focusing on philosophical underpinnings of reading instruction and Chapter 2 presenting a general look at the most common methods and materials used for teaching reading. These two chapters gave you a bird's-eye view of the field of reading, but they used lots of new terms and ideas that may have left you with many questions. So now let's begin at the beginning with our very earliest readers and slowly make sense of each stage. Now let's look at the very youngest children, those in the stage called emergent literacy, and consider the specific skills and abilities most necessary for a child to cross over the bridge from non-reader to reader and enter the exciting world of Literacy Land. Section Two of this book, *Early Readers: Cracking the Code*, deals with these aspiring readers.

Section Two

Early Readers:
Cracking the Code

Section Two consists of three chapters:

Chapter 3: Early Readers:

How do Students Move from Non-Reader to Reader?

And

Chapter 4: Cracking the Code:
Phonics and Other Word Attack Tools

And

Chapter 5: Beginning Meaning-Making:
Vocabulary and Sight Word Development

Chapter 3

Early Readers: How do Students Move from Non-Reader to Reader?

Mrs. Hargrove Welcomes Her Kindergarteners

It is September, and Mrs. Hargrove is welcoming her new batch of kindergarten students. She already knows a little about her new charges from reading the parent questionnaires included in each student's budding cumulative record. As she greets each child, she rehearses in her mind what she knows so far about each one.

Rosa: Rosa's parent questionnaire was completed in Spanish, so Rosa will be an English Language Learner. It remains to be seen how much English Rosa and her parents already know, but it is certain that Rosa's family's most comfortable language is Spanish. Rosa regards Mrs. Hargrove with inquisitive brown eyes and a grave manner when she is introduced. She chooses the Block Center in which to play this first morning.

Kerri, Jennifer and Douglas: These three children all arrive at the same time, and it is obvious that they know each other. Their mothers also know each other, becoming good friends during their children's two years at the same preschool. These three children enter the Kindergarten room confidently, say goodbye to their mothers without hesitation, and head for the Dress-up Center as if it is familiar territory. They are talkative, and Mrs. Hargrove hears illuminating snatches of language coming from the Dress-up Center, such as when Douglas says in a deepened voice, "I have arrived home from work, dear."

William: William's mother makes it clear on the parent questionnaire and again when she brings William into the room that William can already read—very well. This may be true because William heads directly to the Library Corner where he picks up a book correctly, and studies it carefully moving from front to back of the book. Even if William is not an adept reader yet, it is obvious that he has many concepts about print skills and will be ready to cross to Literacy Land very soon.

Derek: Derek does not have a parent questionnaire in his file, and no parent brings him into the classroom. The principal, who happens to find Derek sitting alone on the front steps of the school afraid to come in, brings Derek to the kindergarten room and introduces him with a sigh. Derek's parents are a mystery, and they might be illiterate themselves, which means Derek will not be able to be helped at home with school work. Derek appears to have very little expressive oral language, and no ability to choose one of the Centers in which to play. He sits where Mrs. Hargrove puts him and regards the room with puzzled, frightened eyes.

Other students arrive, and Mrs. Hargrove thinks about each one as she is able. The children in this group, naturally, have many unique characteristics and fall on a rather wide continuum of readiness for kindergarten. But though their needs are wide, the children do seem to divide into three major groups:

1. **Children who have had preschool or home experiences that encouraged oral language development and concepts about print.** These children already know a great deal about reading and writing though they are not really aware of that knowledge yet. They will probably be ready to become literate very soon. Mrs. Hargrove will work on phonological awareness by doing activities such as clapping syllables, and she will help her students with phonemic awareness by doing such activities as rhyming words. This group is also ready for lots of work with the alphabet.
2. **Those children for one reason or another who have not had experiences that encouraged oral language development and concepts about print.** These children will need to build missing oral language skills and will need a great many experiences with books and print before they will be ready to be successful at reading and writing. While the phonemic awareness and alphabet activities will also be appropriate for this group, they will need much oral language work and lots of shared reading experiences, too.
3. **Children whose first language is not English.** These children will not all have the same facility with English, but all of them will probably need some extra work on listening and speaking skills in English before they will be ready to move on to reading and writing skills. If possible, their oral language skills in their first language should also be strengthened, and literacy in that first language would also be a goal.

These three groupings are really too simplistic to explain the range of abilities and needs in Mrs. Hargrove's kindergarten, but they are at least a rough beginning for her today. Mrs. Hargrove doesn't care which group the children fall into. Her heart goes out to all of them. To Rosa and Mei Mei and Michael all chattering away in the Block Center in languages the others can't understand. To William with his white starched shirt poring intently over the dinosaur book in the Library Corner. And most of all to Derek with the scared, wild eyes who doesn't even know what Center to join. Somehow or another she hopes to make Kindergarten the best year of their young lives and send each of them on to first grade ready to succeed in school.

Emergent Literacy

Sometime in kindergarten or first grade, most children enter into the new land of literacy. However, in order to reach this new land, children have already been on the long journey toward it during all of their preschool years. Far from being a novel and isolated set of skills, becoming literate is a *process* which makes use of numerous developmental passages along the way. As you can easily see from Mrs. Hargrove's kindergarten, students will enter school at widely varying stages of development. To be effective, Mrs. Hargrove will need to use **Developmentally Appropriate Practices** gearing her teaching to the various developmental levels she finds in her students. In order to do this, she must first understand theories of child development, especially those related to cognitive and language skills.

A Short Course in the Cognitive Development of Children

Probably the most influential theorist in the cognitive development of children is Jean Piaget (1955). Piaget's astute observations of children led him to theorize that children go through four developmental stages as they progress in cognitive skill. These four stages are:

- Sensorimotor Stage (approximately 0-2 years). During this stage, children learn through movement and use of their senses. This is a very concrete and active stage.
- Preoperational Stage (approximately 2-7 years). During this stage, children still depend on their perceptions and do not display logical thought if it contradicts what their senses are telling them. Children gain symbolic thought during this stage which makes language learning possible. Their thinking is very egocentric which makes it hard for children in this stage to see another's point of view.
- Concrete Operations Stage (approximately 7-11 years). Children in this stage begin to use logic in concrete situations even if logic seems to contradict what their senses are observing. During this stage, children can use symbols and language to think, and conversation improves as egocentrism declines.
- Formal Operations Stage (approximately 12 years onward). During this stage, children are able to use logic even in abstract situations. Increasing facility with symbols and symbolic language make more complex thought possible.

These Piagetian stages are deeply relevant to the task of literacy. Very young children (sensorimotor stage) will be engaged in figuring out their world by physically acting upon it. But soon, by two years old or so when they enter the preoperational stage, the development of symbolic thought means that an explosion of oral language development can be expected. Preschoolers use language in their play, to communicate their needs, and to learn about the world around them. These early oral language skills are the base for later skills in reading and writing, and as indicated by the age range for the preoperational stage, much of this early language acquisition happens before children have any experience with formal schooling. Piaget believed that cognitive development led to language development, but that the ages for the four stages were fairly standardized. Figure 3.1 summarizes Piaget's stages.

Figure 3.1: Piagetian Stages

Stage	Ages	Developmental Tasks
Sensorimotor	0-2 years	Learns using senses and motor skills
Preoperational	2-7 years	Gains symbolic thought, Pre-logical, Egocentric, Language is concrete
Concrete Operations	7-11 years	Uses logic in concrete situations, Less egocentric so conversation improves
Formal Operations	11 years plus	Uses logic in abstract situations. Increased complexity in thought and language

Another developmental theorist whose work is so important to language acquisition is Lev Vygotsky (1986). Vygotsky, like Piaget, held a **constructivist** philosophy which asserts that children are active participants in their own learning as they construct meaning for themselves. Unlike Piaget, however, Vygotsky theorized that language development could actually affect the pace of cognitive development and that experiences the child has will make a difference in language acquisition. Vygotsky coined the phrase **Zone of Proximal Development** to explain this. (Please look back in Chapter 1, Figure 1.5 for a diagram of this). Vygotsky's research demonstrated that if a child in one zone of development was assisted by someone (teacher, parent or peer) from a slightly higher zone, the child could often do with assistance what she could not do alone. Eventually, with practice, the child was able to move to this higher zone permanently and do these same tasks unassisted. The theory of the zone of proximal development accentuates the importance of a challenging environment and a supportive helper if children are to acquire the rich oral language necessary to literacy.

A final theorist, Benjamin Bloom (1964), adds one more important idea to the concept of emerging literacy. Bloom synthesized numerous research studies of child development. His synthesis revealed that cognitive development can be quite accurately predicted by the time a child is eight years old. His research also showed that the effects of environment will be most pronounced during stages of greatest growth which for humans is during the early childhood years. Taken together, Bloom's findings mean that the environment of children before they come to school will produce enormous differences in children's' readiness to become literate. The ideas of Bloom, Vygotsky and Piaget are all borne out in the variety of developmental needs displayed by the children entering Mrs. Hargrove's classroom.

Oral Language and Becoming Literate

Think of the preschool child as one on a train bound for Literacy Land. One day the train will emerge from a tunnel and this bright new land of literacy will appear before the child. But the journey to this new land did not begin when the train emerged from the tunnel, but began years ago and encompassed many ups and downs and brave new vistas. The preschool child, the **emergent literate**, has been working diligently, perhaps since before birth, to prepare to enter Literacy Land.

One of the most important skills preschoolers will need to meet success with Literacy Land is a strong oral language base.If a child's early environment has encouraged oral language, so much the better. But if not, this is where the early childhood teacher of literacy must begin.

For most children, their success with the written word will depend largely upon their success with the spoken word. While teachers in the early grades would like to begin their reading instruction immediately, children without adequate oral language will not be as ready as their peers to focus on written language (National Institute for Literacy, 2010).

Language can be either coming in (receptive) or going out (expressive). And it can be receptive and expressive either orally or in writing. All work with written language will depend on a strong oral language base. And the base for all language work is the receptive, oral quadrant, or listening. Children who do not have a strong listening vocabulary will need additional work in this quadrant and in the oral expressive (speaking) quadrant before they will meet success in the reading and writing quadrants. Diagram 3.1 illustrates how oral and written language modes interact.

Diagram 3.1: Oral and Written Language Modes (The Blessing Chart)

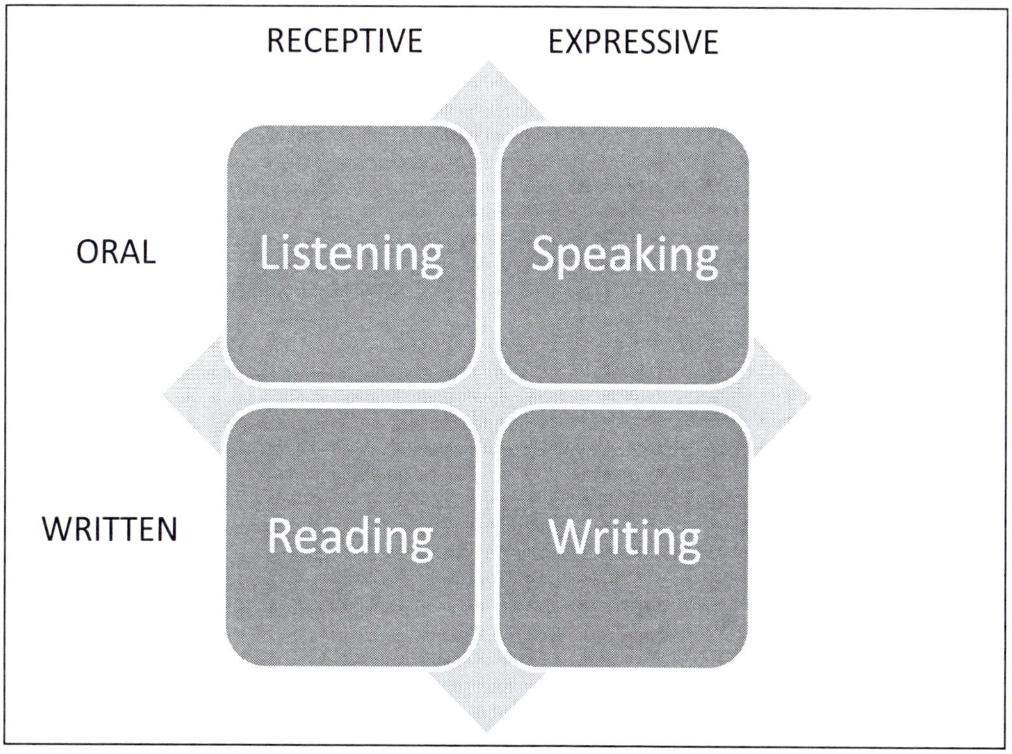

There are many reasons why children may come to school with inadequate oral language. For example, the child may have an undetected hearing or language impairment that, once corrected, can lead to rapid growth in oral language. Another common reason for inadequate oral language in preschoolers is lack of practice at home in oral language. The child who has not been spoken with very much by parents or caregivers, has not heard much vocabulary beyond simple commands, and has not been encouraged or allowed to engage in conversations cannot be expected to have developed a rich oral vocabulary out of thin air. Derek, in Mrs. Hargrove's classroom is likely one of these children. Whether he can speak at all has not been determined yet, but his unwillingness to communicate orally may certainly mask an inadequacy in oral language skills.

Finally, second language students may also struggle with oral language in English. It is clear from the chatter in the Block Center in Mrs. Hargrove's classroom that both Rosa and Mei Mei probably have well-developed oral language skills in their first languages. However, since the language of literacy instruction in this classroom is English, these students will suffer disconnection between their oral language base and their written language tasks. Diagram 3.1 reminds us that written language success depends largely on a strong oral base, and obviously, to support each other, the language used in each quadrant must be the same.

The importance of strong oral language to success in literacy cannot be over-emphasized. Luckily, many children will arrive at school with a fully-developed and rich listening and speaking vocabulary. For those who do not, or for those arriving with a rich oral base in a language other than English, the teacher must begin here. While activities designed to teach reading and writing do not necessarily need to be delayed, students who need support in oral language may not meet with the success their teacher hopes for until oral language skills are strengthened.

If you continue to think of the emergent literate as that student on the train bound for Literacy Land, it will be obvious that these students with oral language needs have not progressed as far as others along the track. In order to help them make progress, the teacher must move back along the track to the oral language skills that are often learned at home. To that end, the early childhood classroom should be a productively noisy place with children invited to listen and speak in a variety of ways. Imaginative and vocal play should be encouraged through the use of **learning centers**, such as a dress-up area or a housekeeping corner. The teacher must invite conversation by speaking often to individual students and small groups, and then listening attentively to the children's replies. And read-alouds of the best literature for children must be a daily (at least!) occurrence.

Oral language should develop naturally at home, but for those children without a strong oral language, the same natural, but enriched, environment that would have led to strong listening and speaking skills at home can be produced at school. This stage of the journey cannot just be skipped, however. Ignoring a weak oral language base in favor of pushing onward more quickly to written language skills is like trying to drive a train over a track with a missing piece.

Sidebar 3.1: Key Terms

Big Book: An over-sized book designed to be read aloud to a group.

Concepts about Print (CAP): A collective group of skills relating to how print works in words, sentences and books. Sometimes called **Concepts OF Print.**

Constructivism: The philosophical position that learners actively construct meaning from the information around them.

Developmentally Appropriate Practice (DAP): The technique of considering a child's developmental needs in order to provide appropriate instruction.

Emergent Literacy: The concept that learning to read is a process in which early oral language skills and concepts about print enable a child to become literate.

Learning Center: An area in a classroom devoted to a theme or to a particular type of learning. Common early learning centers would be Dress-Up, Housekeeping, Blocks and Library.

Phonemic Awareness (PA): The understanding that words are composed of individual sounds or phonemes. PA skills include segmentation, blending and rhyming.

Shared Reading: Another way to say reading aloud to children.

Emergent Literacy

An emphasis on oral language, which does not seem to relate directly to reading and writing, illuminates the concept of emergent literacy. As opposed to the idea of reading readiness that viewed reading as a point at which instruction in reading should be begun, the concept of emergent literacy views reading as a continuing *process* that begins at birth and continues throughout life. In this process of becoming a reader and writer, listening and speaking skills are important stages along the way to beginning literacy. The act of reading is both process and point, and as children emerge as readers, there are many other early skills along the way that can be taught to them and that will mean the success or failure of their development as readers.

The term, **Emergent Literacy**, refers to those learnings that precede conventional reading and writing but are, nonetheless, crucial to becoming literate. Oral language is one of these skills. Other skills necessary during the emergent literacy stage are **concepts about print**, **phonemic awareness**, and **alphabet recognition**. In addition to a good oral language base, these three constellations of skills will be necessary before children will emerge into Literacy Land. Let's look at each group of skills separately.

Concepts about Print

According to Marie Clay (1991), a New Zealand researcher of emergent literacy, for children to make the move from oral to written language they must develop certain concepts of how the printed word works. She terms this collective grouping of pre-reading skills, Concepts about Print. One of the earliest concepts about print is the realization that print carries meaning, and that it does this in an orderly and predictable way.

Children developing concepts about print, then, will begin to understand how a book "works," that it opens a certain way, and that pages are turned in one direction. They will learn book language, such as title, author, illustrator and cover page. In working with print, these emergent readers will discover that reading in English proceeds from left to right and from top to bottom. They will notice breaks along the page and begin to develop the concepts of a word and a sentence. Individual letters will begin to be recognized, and the idea that these letters carry particular sounds will begin to dawn.

Many of these Concepts about Print develop naturally for children during the preschool years if children are in a literacy-rich environment. If they have had many experiences at home with books and other print, especially with the support of a parent or other reader, then children coming to kindergarten will have developed significant concepts about print already. Collin, in the vignette for Chapter 1 was one of these children. For those children coming from environments not so conducive to emergent literacy, though, the teacher can, and must, develop these concepts at school.

The most efficient way to develop Concepts about Print for children is to immerse them in a print-rich environment. This means that the printed word must be everywhere in the classroom. Environmental Print must litter the walls and surfaces of the classroom with objects labeled, important words placed on walls, and classroom directions posted. Books of all sorts, magazines and children's newspapers must be in abundance. And children's names, an important bridge to literacy, must be here and there where children can see them.

Beyond immersing children in this print-rich environment, teachers should use books and other printed materials regularly in the classroom. Regular **shared reading** or read-aloud times help children who have not had regular exposure to books begin to realize how books "work". An over-sized book, called a **Big Book,** is useful for this when reading with the whole class. When a teacher introduces a book, she should be intentional in bringing in specific Concepts about Print. She can discuss the title and author for example, or run her finger along a line as she reads to demonstrate directionality.

Phonemic Awareness

A second set of skills important for emergent literates to develop is **Phonemic Awareness**. Just as in Concepts about Print children develop understandings about printed language, so children must also develop concepts about what they are hearing. When we hear language spoken, it often sounds like a continuous run-together string of sounds. Try listening to someone speak in a language foreign to you, and you will realize how true this is. Native speakers of any language speak quickly and without pause between words and letters. Children, as they are acquiring oral language, speak in this same run-together style, often without realizing that each word and each sound is important. Ramona Quimby, in Beverly Cleary's *Ramona the Pest* (1968, p. 21), illustrates this error clearly when she puzzles over the "dawnzerly light" she hears sung about in the national anthem.

For the emergent reader to begin to hear separate words and then separate sounds she must develop Phonemic Awareness. While phonemic awareness is a precursor to phonics (connecting sounds to letters), emergent readers are not yet ready for phonics. First these young readers must simply HEAR the different sounds in words. Skills such as phoneme segmentation (pulling sounds apart), phoneme blending (putting sounds together) and phoneme comparison (rhyming, alliteration) are important precursors to phonics instruction.

The importance of phonemic awareness to success in early reading has been widely studied and almost universally endorsed (Juel, 1994; National Reading Panel, 2000; Adams, 1998; Yopp, 1988). Yet children entering kindergarten, even those with a well-developed oral language, may not have developed phonemic awareness. Many young children do not yet have the sense that the sentences and words they so confidently speak are made up of individual, discernible sounds. Since phonemic awareness is so important to later reading success, early childhood teachers should include lessons in phonemic awareness in their classrooms. Luckily this is very easy to do and often just looks like word play to the children. Here are some examples of activities that focus on phonemic awareness:

1. **Segmenting**—Ask children to say the sounds they hear in a word. Their names are a good place to start. For example, Anne would say she could hear /ă/ and /n/ in her name.
2. **Blending**—Say to children, "I took my /d/, /ŏ/, /g/ for a walk. What did I take?" Children should be able to blend the distinct phonemes into the word dog. Notice that you are saying the sound not the letter name.
3. **Comparing**—Read stories that have lots of words that begin with the same sound (alliteration) or end with the same sound (rhyming). Emphasize these words, have children identify the like sounds they hear, and then make new words that fit into the pattern. Singing and reciting nursery rhymes are also very useful activities for comparing sounds in words.

Alphabet Recognition

In order to become readers, children must not only recognize that oral language is made up of distinct individual sounds (phonemes), but that written language is also made up of distinct letters (graphemes). In phonemic awareness, children were challenged to hear the different sounds in a word. In **Alphabet Recognition** children are challenged to see the different written symbols in a word. Just as phonemic awareness is a precursor to instruction in phonics but is not phonics, so work in recognizing the letters of the alphabet is also a precursor to phonics, but not yet phonics. Before children can connect letters and sounds (phonics) they must know the shapes of the letters in the alphabet.

The National Early Literacy Panel (2008), among many others, found that knowledge of the alphabet was an important predictor of early reading success. Students who could recognize and name letters of the alphabet were more likely to meet success in learning to read. Happily, work with the alphabet is one of the most common teaching-type activities parents engage in at home, so many children came to school having sung the alphabet song and practiced writing at least some of the letters. For those children without experience with the alphabet, though, it will again be important to provide experiences in this area.

Early childhood teachers can, and do, provide lots of experiences with the alphabet for their emergent literates. Posting the alphabet above the chalkboard is a time-honored tradition, and smaller displays of the alphabet should also be posted at each desk. Teachers can use books or environmental print to do letter searches (find all the r's). And they can play lots of games, such as alphabet match or alphabet bingo to practice skills. Finally, writing should be incorporated into alphabet work, with each child practicing writing various letters. Again, the letters in a child's name are a good place to start.

Figure 3.2 summarizes the skills of emergent reading that you should develop in your young students.

Figure 3.2: Important Skills in Emergent Literacy

Skill	Ways to Encourage
Oral Language	Lots of speaking and listening; Much conversation in play; Shared reading
Concepts About Print	Use of Big Books to illustrate book terms (author, title, etc.); Moving finger along print to show directionality; Lots of books available to explore
Phonemic Awareness	Lots of word play and nursery rhymes; Work with rhyming, beginning sounds, segmenting and blending of sounds
Alphabet Recognition	Lots of books and environmental print to show letters; Focusing on the letters in child's name; Practice with magnet, foam or other letters

Emergent Writing

In Diagram 3.1, four types of language are listed. These are listening, speaking, reading and writing. Recall that oral language modes (listening and speaking) were the base for written language modes (reading and writing), and that all of the four modes of language influence and support the others. Up to now, we have focused on oral language and on reading, but writing develops alongside reading for the emergent literate. And especially as the letters of the alphabet are being taught, it is natural that writing is nourished as well as reading.

In considering Diagram 3.1, it is obvious that written expressive language will be the most advanced language skill to be developed, but this does not mean that teachers should allow writing to lie fallow until reading skills are firmly in place. Indeed, increased writing skills will aid reading skills and vice-versa. So the early childhood teacher must also include emergent writing skills in her classroom.

If you think of how a baby developed expressive oral language (speaking), you will remember that this was a long-term developmental project with multiple stages. First the baby listened for a long time and then experimented with random sounds, cooing and babbling, until finally something resembling a recognizable word came out. No one expects a baby's first utterances to be perfectly articulated with correct grammar. Instead, a baby starts with very ragged approximations of language, but then progresses quickly so that by the time this child enters school he is nearly a perfectly conventional speaker of his native tongue.

The development of written expressive language (writing) happens in much the same way, involving a time of active observation of written language and then ragged tries to communicate in writing with more and more conventions of language observed as development progresses. No one would think to tell a baby to be still until she can speak correctly, and we should not silence children's attempts at written communication because of early errors either.

Gentry (1982) delineated several particular developmental stages that children go through as they learn to write. These stages will be discussed in detail in Chapter 8, but briefly here are Gentry's five stages:

Pre-phonetic-------------- No relation of letters to sounds

Semi-phonetic------------ Some relationship between letters and sounds

Phonetic--------------------All sounds are represented though some words are misspelled

Transitional--------------- All sounds are represented, and some correct conventions of the language are used

Conventional--------------Correct spelling, grammar and usage

Wherever children are on this developmental continuum, they must be encouraged to write often just as they are encouraged to read often. Remember that each language mode influences all the others, so as children become better writers they also become better readers. Of course, conventional writing with correct grammar, spelling, punctuation, etc. is the ultimate goal, but as children emerge as writers, incorrect spelling and other assaults on conventional English should be tolerated as a developmental stage. There are numerous ways that early childhood teachers can encourage budding writers. Here is a partial list:

1. Individual journal writing each day.
2. Shared writing activities in which the class dictates and assists the teacher in the writing of a story.
3. Dictations or partial writing of an individual story as in the Language Experience Approach.
4. Functional writing, such as writing a note to a friend or writing out directions.

5. Communication with the teacher in writing.
6. Response to literature activities in which children write about a book that was just read.

The Journey Continues

The early childhood years are a time of intense cognitive and language development for children. This early development has put them on the track toward becoming literate, though due to early environment, some children will be farther along in the literacy journey than others when they show up that first day of school. In Mrs. Hargrove's classroom, it appears that William has already crossed into Literacy Land, that Kerri, Jennifer and Douglas have had preschool and other experiences that helped them be ready for literacy instruction, that Derek may have so little oral language background that literacy instruction must begin with listening and speaking skills, and that Rosa and Mei Mei will need special attention in order to cross from an oral language base in another language to being able to read and write in English.

Mrs. Hargrove will need to concentrate on oral language skills at the same time that she teaches Concepts about Print. She will need to help her students with both Phonemic Awareness and Alphabet Recognition. And she will need to incorporate writing and read-alouds into her daily schedule. Though her students are entering kindergarten at radically different places in the emergent reading journey, with good teaching, all of these students can be brought along the track ready to emerge into Literacy Land soon.

Summing Up

Chapter 3 focused on our youngest aspiring readers, those that have not yet become literate. Oral language development in both listening and speaking modes will be important before written language can progress well. The skills of Concepts about Print, Phonemic Awareness and Alphabet Recognition were all explained in this chapter as well as stages for beginning writing. For emergent literates, the next step is to put all those sounds and letters together. In Chapter 4 we will address that as we focus on phonics.

Chapter 4

Cracking the Code: Phonics and Other Word-Attack Tools

Mrs. Williams is a first grade teacher who follows a balanced reading approach in her classroom. She believes that word attack skills are vitally important for emergent literates, but that these skills must not be considered the complete package of what it means to read. She teaches these skills in an embedded fashion during other work in the language arts. She is particularly careful to help her children learn the skills of phonics. Let's join her as she teaches an *embedded phonics* lesson on the sound of W.

Mrs. Williams Teaches the Sound of W

When we enter her classroom, all of Mrs. Williams' students are on the "Working Rug" preparing to do a shared reading activity. In order to prepare, each child sits crisscross-applesauce (cross-legged) on an alphabet letter on the rug. Everyone wiggles their fingers, hands, arms then shoulders until their hands drop quietly into their laps. An expectant stillness descends, and Mrs. Williams uses a Big Book to begin the shared reading of *Whistle for Willie* by Ezra Jack Keats (1964). Before she begins her read-aloud, she asks questions about the title and author of the book. She runs her finger from left to right as she reads the words on the cover. She teases the children by opening the book from the back and is quickly corrected by a chorus of "NOOO, that's wrong!" All of these Concepts About Print skills are seamlessly integrated into beginning the story.

Next, Mrs. Williams points out the W's in the title. She discusses with the class the name of this letter and what it looks like. The children trace the letter in the air and then on their neighbor's back. Mrs. Williams points out how /w/ sounds by asking students to blow on their index fingers to feel the wind made by /w/. The students try this using "whistle" and "Willie" and several other words Mrs. Williams supplies. She then reads the story through one time for enjoyment and then a second time asking comprehension questions as she goes along. Finally, Mrs. Williams brings the children's attention back to /w/ and on the third read of the story she asks the children to blow on their index fingers every time they hear the sound of /w/.

After this final read of the story, Mrs. Williams and the children start a list of W words. They name several from the story, add extras from their experiences, and are especially delighted to discover that Mrs. Williams' name belongs on this list. Several of these new W words are chosen to go onto the class word wall. Mrs. Williams makes sure that the early sight words "with" and "was" also make it to the word wall. Then each child chooses three or four of the W words to add to her personal word bank. Everyone practices wiggling and whistling together for a few minutes, then they go back to their seats to work with their new words.

Back at their seats, children will write their new words several times on white boards, add these words to their personal word banks, and read a personal copy of *Whistle for Willie* putting little sticky dots under each W. Finally, children will write in their journals using at least three words from the W list on the word wall. Early finishers can play sight word matching or have extra free-reading time. When Mrs. Williams assesses each child on phonics skills next week, she will find that nearly all of them remember the sound of W. Some have even learned to whistle now!

Using Phonics to Crack the Code

English is a code-based language which means that its written symbols more or less stand for oral sounds, and these symbols combine to make recognizable words, sentences and thoughts. The children in Mrs. Williams' class, as well as all the children in every chapter vignette so far, are engaged in trying to crack this code. Their work is impeded by the fact that so much of English is irregular and does not follow its own code well. But their work can be helped a great deal by someone (a teacher, parent or older child) who understands the code and is willing to point out some of its features.

Let's examine how this works. Please read this sentence:

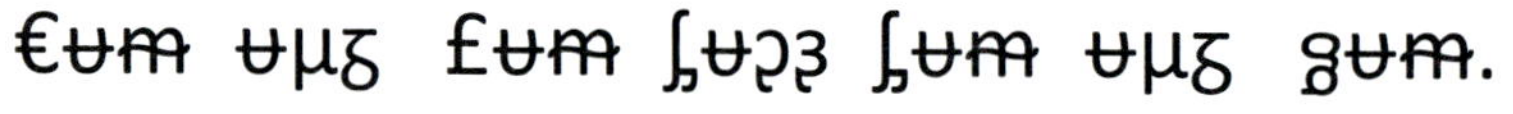

Even though you are a fully literate person, probably you had some difficulty with this. This sentence is written in Sherylbet, an idiosyncratic alphabet known only to the author (Sheryl) and a select group of insiders (her students). For you, though the sentence was very short and contained many similar shapes, it probably looked like nonsense. You probably gave up trying to read it almost immediately, labeling the task as clearly impossible. Yet this is exactly the task presented to nonreaders. And usually the examples they see are much longer, often involving numerous sentences with symbols covering entire pages of print. Clearly cracking a code is not that easy.

Now let me try to provide a little help for you in cracking the code of the sentence above.

- First, some context: This is a sentence about two friends, Pam and Sam, who get together for lunch.
- Next let me point out that 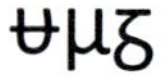 is the sight word **and.** Do you see both places where it appears?
- Finally, let me introduce two phonics skills: the letter  which sounds like/ă/, and the word family which sounds like /-ăm/.

Now try to read the sentence. Much easier this time, right? Just a little help from someone familiar with the code changed a clearly impossible task to one not so difficult at all. (By the way, this sentence in English says, Pam and Sam have ham and jam.)

When children become literate, what they are doing is translating the written squiggles they see on a page into the sounds, words and thoughts they already recognize in their oral language. This is why a rich oral language is so important to literacy development as pointed out in Chapter 3. Yet, a rich oral language will usually not be enough in itself to assure success in reading. Just as you had difficulty cracking the code of the sentence above without help, most children will need some sort of guidance in order to finally make sense of the squiggles they see on the page. As in the help given above, context and sight words will be important, but a major tool in cracking the code is figuring out common sound/symbol relationships. This skill is called **phonics.**

Phonics, or the sound/symbol relationships of a language, is the most common and the most useful word attack skill we can teach emergent literates. Indeed, in the three-legged stool of balanced reading, the skills leg for early readers consists almost exclusively of phonics skills. Unfortunately for early readers, phonics is the part of reading that most often becomes a political football with some teachers de-emphasizing it almost to the point of extinction and other teachers so committed to phonics that they teach phonics "rules" that apply less than 5% of the time.

Let's be clear about the place of phonics in a balanced reading program. Phonics is not the point of reading. The point of reading is to gain meaning from the printed page. Phonics, then is not the point of reading, but is a means to an end. Further, it is a <u>powerful</u> means to an end, and children should not be deprived of this tool. Phonics, though, suffers from an excess of specialized jargon and a surplus of obscure rules. Let's try to de-mythologize phonics a little by first looking at some of this jargon and then examining some phonics rules.

<u>**Sidebar 4.1: Key Decoding Terms**</u>

Phoneme: The smallest unit of sound—a sound

Grapheme: The smallest written unit—a letter

Morpheme: The smallest unit of meaning

Phonological Awareness: The awareness of sound patterns such as syllables

Phonemic Awareness: The understanding that speech consists of individual sounds

Phonics: The ability to connect sounds to letters (phonemes to graphemes). Also called the Alphabetic Principle

Onset: All of the letters in a word that come before the vowel

Phonogram: all the letters in a word from the vowel onward. Also called a rime

Rime: All of the letters in a word from the vowel onward. Also called a phonogram

Phonemes and Graphemes and Morphemes, Oh My!

It's easy for a teacher (or a child) to get lost in the Phearful Phorest of Phonics. One of the things that makes this Phorest so Phearful is that there are so many new words here. These terms are not common in our listening vocabulary, and many of them seem to have such similar meanings. Take the terms **phonological awareness, phonemic awareness** and **phonics**, for example. We can tell by the common stem of phon- that these words all have something to do with sound, but there are subtle differences in their meanings. Please look at sidebar 4.1 now to familiarize yourself with a few of the basic terms in phonics. I'll wait for you to get back before we discuss these.

Well, now you know from Sidebar 4.1 the subtle differences between phonological awareness, phonemic awareness and phonics, and you probably remember seeing teachers practice phonological awareness with their students by clapping syllables, and working on phonemic awareness by playing with rhyming words. These teachers move their young students toward literacy by doing lots of work with the alphabet, and daily shared reading to help children develop necessary Concepts About Print. With luck, if Mrs. Hargrove in Chapter 3 has done these things, her students who are now Mrs. Williams' first graders are ready to connect written symbols (**graphemes**) to spoken sounds (**phonemes)** in what is known as the **alphabetic principle**. In short they are ready for **phonics**. Figure 4.1 shows how connecting sounds and letters can lead to the act to reading.

Figure 4.1: Connecting Sounds and Letters

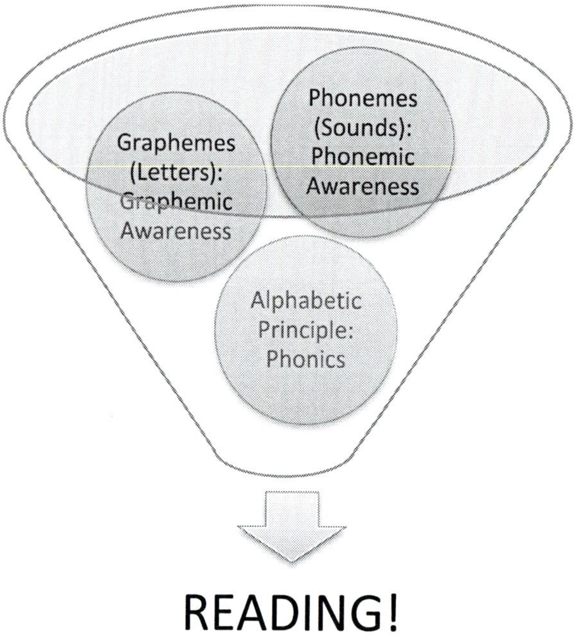

Sidebar 4.1 starts with three terms—**grapheme, phoneme and morpheme**—which all end in the –eme suffix. Let's look at these three a bit more closely while we decode the word "fish".

- Fish has 4 graphemes or letters—f i s h.
- Fish has only 3 phonemes or sounds—/f/ /ɪ/ /sh/.
- Fish has only 1 morpheme or unit of meaning—fish—the animal that swims in the water, or the act of catching that animal.

Now what if we made the word into "fished"? Here is how it would be:

- Graphemes—6—f i s h e d.
- Phonemes—4—/f/ /ɪ/ /sh/ /t/
- Morphemes—2—fish ed

  —fish is a *free morpheme* which means to try to catch the animal that swims in the water; and —ed is a *bound morpheme* which shows that this action took place sometime in the past. Fish could stand alone making it free, but –ed could not stand alone making it bound.

We will look at morphemes more carefully when we discuss structural analysis, but in the teaching of phonics, graphemes and phonemes are paramount. Unfortunately, phonics often turns out to be quite difficult for some children because of the irregularity of its sound/symbol combinations. While English is not random in its sound/symbol relationships, neither is it particularly dependable. We certainly cannot depend on one sound relating to one symbol, and numerous sounds have multiple ways of being spelled.

Here is a popular riddle: What does "ghoti" spell? The answer is "fish". If we took the /f/ as spelled in tough, the /ĭ/ as spelled in women, and the /sh/ as spelled in portion, fish would be spelled ghoti. No wonder young readers are confused! This irregularity of English will frustrate early readers and teachers alike but there are some sounds and patterns worth knowing even in our unpredictable language. Here is a short course of those sounds:

Vowels and Consonants—The Basic Building Blocks

English is made up of only **vowels** and **consonants**. The vowels are a,e,i,o, u and sometimes y. These are quite irregular. They each carry a long sound which is represented by their name, and a short sound as represented by the vowels in fan, fed, fit, fox, and fun. In addition, they can be combined into **diphthongs** (2 vowels glided together) like the vowels in boil. This is really only the tip of the vowel iceberg, however, because besides being long, short, or diphthongs, vowels can behave in all sorts of unpredictable ways that defy all the rules. Still, if children can master these main vowel sound/symbol relations, they will be able to decode a great many words that do behave more or less regularly.

If a letter in English is not a vowel, it is a consonant (the letter y can behave as either a consonant or a vowel). There are many more consonants than vowels, but the consonants are much more dependable. The letter b, for example, can generally be counted on to make the /b/ sound that you hear in big. Consonants, too, though, can combine to make new sounds. Sometimes they combine into **consonant digraphs** (2 consonants/one sound) like the sound made by sh in the word "fish". Or they can combine into **consonant blends** (2 or 3 consonants that glide together) like the sound made by tr in "train" or spl in "splash."

As if the various sounds of vowels and consonants weren't enough trouble by themselves, vowels and consonants often combine with each other to get into more mischief. This usually occurs when a vowel is followed by an r. In these cases, the vowels will not be either long or short, but will have a new sound, such as the sound made by a in far. In these cases, the vowel is said to be **r-controlled**. Chart A, on the next page, can serve as a very quick summary of the most common ways in which letters behave in English. Please take a moment to study it now.

Chart A: Just the Bones of Phonics

VOWELS

The Letters: A,E,I,O, U and sometimes Y
Main Sounds: Long, Short, R-Controlled and Diphthongs
Main Diphthongs: OO (cook, moon); OI (boil); OY (boy); OU (loud); OW (cow); AU (haunt); AW (lawn)

Examples of vowel sounds:

Vowel	**Short**	**Long**	**R-Controlled**
A	Făn	Tāme	Arm
E	Fĕd	Tēam	Her
I	Fĭt	Tīme	First
O	Fŏx	Tōe	More
U	Fŭn	Tūne	Turn

CONSONANTS

The letters: Every letter that is not a vowel. Y can be either a consonant or a vowel.
Main Blends: S (such as st, sp, str), L (such as fl, bl, pl), and R (such as tr, fr, dr)
Main Digraphs: SH, TH, CH, PH

IMPORTANT RULES

Vowel is often short: V̆C combination (such as ran, fun),
V̆CC combination (such as fast, pump)

Vowel is often long: V̄VC combination (such as boat, team)
V̄Ce combination (such as rake, tune)
CV̄ combinations (such as go, me)

Are You Sure That's How You Spell Rime?

As you studied Sidebar 4.1 at the beginning of this chapter, you probably noticed three terms we have not yet discussed. These three terms—**onset, rime, and phonogram**—are all related. Let's examine them by looking at the word "sat". Remember that the onset is all the letters in a word before the vowel, and a rime (yes, this kind of rime is spelled like that!) is all the letters from the vowel onward. In the word "sat", S is the onset, and -AT is the rime. If the word were "spat", the onset would be SP and the rime would still be -AT. Change the word to "splat" and the onset becomes SPL but the rime does not change. Another name for rime is phonogram. In all of these words -AT is the phonogram.

By using words that end in the same rime or phonogram, we can collect similar words into word families and teach a great many words by only changing the onset. For example, if you had known the rime

/-am/ and had worked with this phonogram to make the words jam, ham, Sam, and Pam, you would not have had such a hard time reading the Sherylbet sentence earlier. Working with word families in this way is an efficient way for children to increase their reading vocabularies very quickly.

The 6000 or so Most Important Phonics Rules

As stated earlier in this chapter, the study of phonics is made more difficult for teachers (and students!) by the excess of both jargon and rules in the field. Hopefully, you now feel somewhat more at ease with the terms of phonics and are ready to turn your attention to the rules. The bad news is that there are so many rules in phonics that no one has ever been able to establish an accurate count of just how many there are. The good news is that only a very few of these many rules work often enough to be worth teaching to children. We will concentrate on these few.

The few phonics rules we will teach to children mostly involve encoded directions for how to pronounce the vowels in a word. As noted earlier, the consonants behave much more consistently than the vowels. Yes, there are a few consonants that get tricky, such as c, g, and y, but mostly it is the vowels that need rules in order for us to decide on their pronunciation. Teaching children a few basic vowel/consonant patterns, and the rules that govern these patterns, will usually be enough to help them crack the code of reading. The five patterns you should teach are below. In each example, the V stands for vowel and the C stands for consonant.

SHORT VOWELS:

Pattern	Example	Sample Words
• **-V̆C**	–ăt	mat, rat, sat
• **-V̆CC**	–ăsh	mash, rash, trash

LONG VOWELS:

Pattern	Example	Sample Words
• **-CV̄**	–ō	go, so, no
• **-V̄VC**	–ōat	boat, float, coat
• **-V̄Ce**	–āte	rate, late, slate

These five patterns often, though not always, function consistently to tell us whether a vowel is long or short. Teachers have devised memorable ways to teach these patterns, such as the well-known saying, "When two vowels go walking the first one does the talking" to explain the–V̄VC pattern, or calling the e in the –V̄Ce pattern the magic e because it changes the vowel before it from short to long While the –V̄VC pattern only works 45% of the time, and the –V̄Ce rule only works 63% of the time (Clymer, 1996), these are still two of the most useful rules and should be taught to children.

Obviously, if the best English rules only work about half of the time, there are many exceptions which will baffle children. Most exceptions must be taught as exceptions, but there are two vowel rules that account for many of these deviations, and these should also be taught to children.

The first of these relates to consonant-controlled vowels. Vowels followed by an -r will often have a sound that is neither long nor short. Children can be taught to look for this consonant in words and try giving the vowel the r-controlled (far) sound rather than the sound the –V̆C or –V̆CC patterns would otherwise indicate. For more examples of r-controlled vowels see Chart A.

In the same way, children should be taught to look for the common diphthongs(oo,oi,oy,ou,ow,au,aw), and remember that these vowel combinations often have special sounds rather than the long vowel sound a –V̄VC pattern would usually signal. The following words can be used as examples for the sounds commonly made by these diphthongs:

Diphthong	Sample Word	Diphthong	Sample Word
oo	cŏŏk or mōōn	oi	boil
au	haunt	oy	boy
aw	lawn	ou	loud
		ow	cow

Let's Talk Teaching

Though this chapter is replete with the specialized terms and rules that make up the tool of phonics, hopefully you have begun to find it less Phearful. In actuality, English is made up of a finite set of letters (26), a relatively limited number of sounds those letters can signify, and only a few rules that regulate these sounds with enough consistency to be useful to children. These are the facts you must now teach to your emerging and beginning readers. Throughout the years, people have advocated several basic ways of teaching phonics skills to children. Let's look at these now.

Synthetic Method

The synthetic method sometimes is called the spit-and-sputter method, but despite this rather derogatory label, it is probably the most widely used method of phonics instruction. As its name implies, the children learn the sounds of each letter and then put these sounds together to pronounce the word in question. For example, in the word "top", children would learn the sound of /t/, the sound of short /ŏ/, and the sound of /p/. they would then try to blend these three sounds into a word they recognize in their oral vocabulary by saying:

tttttt oooooo pppppp

tt oo pp

t o p

top

This method is what teachers mean when they advise a student to "sound it out". It has the advantage, as a method, of letting the teacher break the learning down into small discrete skills, so that this can be /t/ week, for example, and lots of learning activities can focus on this one sound. It has the disadvantage, though, of often just not working well to move children from practicing discrete skills to actual reading. Often, no matter how quickly and correctly children repeat the individual sounds in a word, the word itself remains unknown. In the example above, for instance, Whitney the efficient phonics student from Chapter 1, could say every sound correctly but remain at the ta—ah—pa stage never recognizing that those sounds added up to the word top.

Analytic Method

The analytic method sometimes is explained as the mirror image of the synthetic method. Instead of learning discrete sounds and putting them together to form words, the analytic method of teaching phonics teaches words first and then uses these words to teach the sounds. In this method, the teacher focuses on teaching some simple sight words, such as big, bat, boy and bark. She then uses this list of words to teach /b/, and then asks children to apply this new knowledge to other words. The advantage of this method is that sounds are never taught in isolation so the connection between the phonics skill and actual reading is easier to make. The disadvantage, though, is that children must have a reasonably good set of sight words in order to have enough words of a certain type to analyze. Collin, the holistic reader you met in Chapter 1, used this method to deduce the sounds of individual letters once he knew enough sight words to begin seeing patterns.

Analogic Method

The analogic method makes use of word families (phonograms or rimes) to allow children to use phonetic knowledge they already have to learn new words In this method, the teacher teaches a particular rime, such as –ŏp. The children learn this as a word chunk instead of the sounds of the isolated letters. After the children have mastered this rime, they add quickly to the words they can recognize by merely changing the onset, or initial consonant. In this case, they might quickly learn the words top, mop, pop, hop, drop and shop, using their knowledge of the –op phonogram. The advantages of this method are that children learn numerous words all at once, and many of the sounds are learned in chunks rather than in isolation. A disadvantage is that children must have a significant amount of phonics knowledge already in order to employ the word families. In the example given above, children would already need to know the sounds of the consonants t,m,p and h, the blend dr, the digraph sh, AND the rime –op in order to be successful.

While there are many other ways to teach phonics, these three methods are the most widely used. As you can see from the advantages and disadvantages listed for each method, no one method is going to be adequate for teaching phonics. As Patricia Cunningham (2013) unambiguously states, "There is no research-proven best way to teach phonics..." (p. 250). Therefore, most teachers will use all three methods in conjunction and combination with each other. This is often done by embedding phonics instruction into other instruction in reading. This is sometimes called the embedded method of phonics instruction.

Embedded Method

The embedded method is not so much a method as a philosophy. Teachers who teach phonics in an embedded way may use all three of the other methods of phonics instruction as these suit their purposes. The main distinction for embedded phonics is that whatever phonics instruction is done is woven into other reading instruction using authentic materials for the real purpose of understanding a text.

This method is illustrated by the phonics lesson described at the beginning of this chapter. Mrs. Williams' main purpose in this lesson was to give children enough reading skill to be able to comprehend and enjoy the book, *Whistle for Willie* (Keats, 1964). She did many activities aimed at making this book accessible to her students. She did a picture walk with them, discussed various concepts about print, asked comprehension questions at different levels, and read the book several times for different purposes. Among all of these activities, she also wove in a phonics lesson. She focused on the initial sound of /w/ because this sound occurred so frequently in the book. She used both a synthetic method (blowing on finger) and an analytic method (looking at a variety of words in the book that began with w). She expected children to recognize and then apply the sound of /w/ in words they encountered in the story. But her main goal remained the comprehension of the story, and phonics was treated as one tool among many for helping students achieve that goal.

This method has many advantages. It keeps the main goal of reading in the fore; it allows literature to be

Sidebar 4.2: Key Morphology Terms

Morpheme: The smallest unit of meaning. Morphemes can be free or bound. In the word "fished", fish is a free morpheme because it can stand alone and –ed is a bound morpheme because it must attach to a root for meaning.

Morphology: The ability to use morphemes to decode a word. Also called structural analysis

Structural Analysis: Using meaning units to decode a word. Also called morphology

Root: The part of a word containing the main meaning. Also called the base word

Prefix: Affixes added to the front of a root word

Suffix: Affixes added to the end of a root word. Suffixes can be inflectional or derivational

Contraction: Words formed by truncating two words and putting an apostrophe in place of the deleted letters

Compound: Words formed when two or more free morphemes combine to make a new word enjoyed and understood as more than just a backdrop for skill practice; and it means that the abstract skills of phonics are taught concretely in the context of an authentic reading task. Additionally, the bridge between phonics and actual reading is easy to make when phonics instruction is embedded.

A disadvantage of this method, though, can be seen if the teacher does not plan carefully for the full scope of her phonics instruction. The National Reading Panel (2000) recommends an explicit, systematic phonics program. The teacher who is embedding phonics instruction into literature must think carefully about the scope and sequence of her teaching so that phonics instruction does not turn out to be haphazard.

Morphology—Looking Beyond the Sounds of Letters

Up to now in this chapter on decoding skills we have concentrated on the connection between letters (graphemes) and sounds (phonemes) that is called phonics. Phonics is a very powerful decoding skill and should be taught well to beginning readers. However, phonics is only concerned with being able to pronounce a new word. Once this new word is sounded out, we assume that the word is in the child's oral vocabulary, and so the meaning is now known. If the word is not in the child's oral vocabulary, however, then all of that sounding-out effort will be of little use. Phonics is only concerned with what the word sounds like, not what it means. In order to go beyond this very rudimentary word attack skill, teachers should also teach the decoding skill of structural analysis or morphology that makes use of morphemes.

Remember at the beginning of this chapter we looked at three "*-eme*" words. Phonemes were sounds, graphemes were letters, and morphemes were meaning units. Go back and review the "fish" exercise about morphemes at the beginning of this chapter now. Morphemic analysis, or **morphology**, does not ask children to look at individual letters and sounds or even at chunks of letters and sounds like rimes. Instead morphemic analysis asks children to look at meaning units within a word. As such, morphology is not primarily concerned with how the word sounds, but with how it is meaningfully structured.

Morphology (or structural analysis as it is sometimes called) is a word attack skill that can be used with readers of all ages. For example, if you and I met the long word *indefensible*, we would probably automatically break it into the meaning units of *in- defense- and –ible* to try to discern its meaning. So structural analysis is a decoding skill that readers can use for the rest of their lives. For beginning readers, though, morphemic analysis usually concentrates on four areas: **roots, affixes, compounds** and **contractions.** Let's look at all four of these now.

Roots

Roots are sometimes called root words or base words. This is the part of the word that carries the main meaning. For example, in the word *helpful*, *help* would be the root which means *assist*. With mature readers, a study of the meanings of common Greek and Latin roots found in English may be helpful. For beginning readers, though, identifying which part of a word is the root is usually enough to assist with the meaning of common early words.

Affixes

Affixs are meaning units that are added (or affixed) to root words. These units can be added either before or after the root.

Prefixes are added before the root as in *unhappy*. The most common prefixes are:

Prefix	Meaning	Examples
Un	not	unhappy, unfriendly, unlucky
Re	again	rewrite, rename, revisit
In	not	inexpensive, inactive
Dis	not	disagree, disconnect

Suffixes are meaning units added to the end of the root. Suffixes can come in two varieties—inflectional or derivational. *Inflectional* suffixes change the number, degree or tense of the root but do not change its base meaning. These endings are mostly used for grammatical purposes. For example, changing the word *stop* to stops, stopped, or stopping, does not change the meaning of stop, but does indicate when the stopping is done. The main inflectional suffixes children may encounter are:

Suffix	Use	Examples
s/es	change to plural	cats/dishes
ed	change to past tense	fished
er/est	change of degree	tall/taller/tallest
ing	change part of speech	helping
ly	change part of speech	friendly

Besides inflectional endings, suffixes can also be *derivational.* These endings do change the meaning of the root as seen in the difference between thoughtful and thoughtless. The suffixes in these two words make the root *thought* into two very different meanings. The main derivational endings are:

Suffix	Meaning	Examples
-ful	full of	thoughtful
-less	without	thoughtless
-able	capable of	movable
-er	one who	teacher
-tion	state of	imagination
-ment	state of	encouragement

Compound Words

Compounds are words made up of two or more free morphemes, such as *bluebird* or *bookshop.* Think again about the morpheme example of "fished" given at the beginning of this chapter. Fish was termed a free morpheme because it carried meaning when standing alone. The *–ed* suffix in fished was termed a bound morpheme. It carried meaning only when attached to a free morpheme. In the word bookshop, for example, both *book* and *shop* carry meaning alone and then contribute to the meaning of the new word, *bookshop*. Beginning readers with growing sight word vocabularies can easily add to these vocabularies by recognizing sight words they already know in a new compound word made of the smaller ones. The following words are examples of common compound words: afternoon, bedroom, bookcase, bluebird, cupcake, football, grandmother, homework, keyboard, mailbox, pancake, raincoat, someday and website.

Contractions

Contractions are two words that have been squeezed together and made smaller by omitting some of the letters in the words. The main contractions involve shortening the word *not* when it is joined to a verb, such as can't, doesn't, don't, wouldn't and shouldn't. Contractions can be made in other ways, though, such as the joining of it and is to form it's, or the joining of you and are to form you're. The apostrophe often signals to children that they are dealing with a contraction, and since the words used in a contraction are familiar sight words and most likely are in the child's speaking vocabulary, contractions are often an easy way for children to add new reading vocabulary. The following words are examples of common contractions: aren't, can't, couldn't, didn't, doesn't, don't, wasn't, won't, it's, let's, there's, she's, I'll, I'm, there's, and we're.

Let's Talk Teaching—Again

The most important thing to keep in mind when working with structural analysis is to let the joy you feel about words come through to your students. Much work with the structure of words can come across as just playing with words. Noticing the components of a new word and commenting with delight about how this word is composed and how it is related to similar words should happen frequently throughout every school day. Students will then get into the habit of looking at words more carefully as meaning units, and move away from overdependence on sound/symbol relationships as their only decoding tool.

Beyond this delight in words that leads naturally to the use of teachable moments to discuss word structure, teachers of young readers can increase their students' reading vocabularies significantly by including mini-lessons on the most common prefixes and suffixes, compounds and contractions. Cunningham and Allington (2011) have estimated that knowing only the prefixes un-, re-, in-, and dis-, can help students begin to decode over 1500 words, for example. To teach mini-lessons on these morphemic units, the following is a good general plan:

- Choose a morphemic unit on which to focus—for example the prefix un-.
- Have a good list of examples ready to begin the discussion. Point out the feature and discuss what it means in conjunction with the roots in the examples.
- Read a story, or other bit of text, which includes this new feature in a noticeable way.
- Find additional examples of the feature's use in other text or environmental print.
- Add a few words which use this feature to your word wall or to students' word banks. You could also begin a special list of these words alone.
- Ask students to use this new feature in their own writing.

We will visit morphology again in Chapter 11 when we discuss ways to teach reading in the content areas.

Summing Up

In this chapter we have discussed some of the basic building blocks children need in order to crack the code of reading. The two main skills we discussed were phonics and structural analysis. Phonics examines the relationships between letters and sounds and helps children to pronounce words. Structural analysis looks at meaning units of words and helps students to understand the words they read. Both of these skills are very important for new readers to learn. However, not all words lend themselves to either phonological or structural analysis. Some words must be learned in complete gulps as sight words, and nearly all words must become sight words eventually if a child is to become a fluent reader. In the next chapter, we will focus on the area of vocabulary as another skill vitally important to the beginning reader.

Chapter 5

Beginning Meaning-Making: Vocabulary and Sight Word Development

Mr. Green Teaches a Vocabulary Lesson

It is early fall, and Mr. Green's first graders are happily eating apples. Well, actually they are doing much more than just eating apples. When Mr. Green handed each pair of students an apple he had cut in half, his directions had been to really observe this apple and to talk with your partner about as many apple words as you can think of. The first question from the children, of course, was "Can we eat them?" To this Mr. Green answered, "Eat them, smell them, look at them, see what they feel like, just come up with lots of ways to describe this apple." So now the students are happily munching and talking and mostly staying on task.

Soon Mr. Green will help his students to make a brainstorm cluster of the word *apple.* It might end up looking something like this:

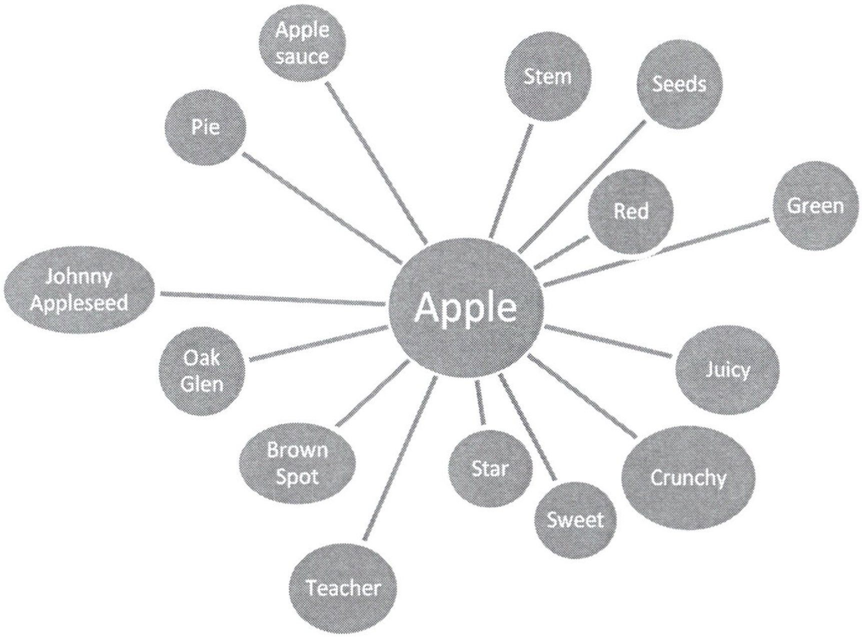

After Mr. Green's students have generated as many apple words as they can, and they have talked about a few of the words, he will give them individual little books he has made in the shape of an apple. The books contain sentence stems that read: An apple is ____________________. Mr. Green is focusing today on the sight words "*an*" and "*is*". He will introduce these two words in the context of this sentence stem, having the children write these words several times on personal white boards while saying the letters out loud. Then the class will do a couple of examples filling in the sentence stem together before Mr. Green turns them loose with their own books. Later today the words "*an*" and "*is*" and "*apple*" will be added to the class word wall and to each child's individual word bank. Two additional new apple words will also be chosen by each child for their word banks. Eventually, Mr. Green will read the book, *Ten Red Apples* by Pat Hutchins (2000) to his class pointing out "*an*" and "*is*" occasionally as they appear in this predictable book.

Sight Words and Phonics: Are They Really Natural Enemies?

In 1955, Rudolph Flesch published *Why Johnny Can't Read.* This popular book was a blistering attack on the look-say method of reading instruction and an appeal to return to the teaching of phonics. Thus began the decade's old reading wars that pit phonics and sight word advocates against each other. In actuality, though, this is an unnecessary war. As important as phonics skills are to beginning readers for decoding words, some words should, and must, be taught as whole units. As Graves, et al. (2011) state, "Skillful readers recognize most of the words they read at sight" (p. 195). So, as important as phonics is as an early decoding skill, the goal of reading teachers is to move students to a place where phonics is largely unnecessary and nearly all words they encounter are classified as **sight words**.

Sight words are words the reader has in his written vocabulary and can recognize instantly. The meaning of these words is also in the reader's oral vocabulary, and since the written symbols for these words are recognized on sight, no further action is needed by the reader in order to comprehend a passage. For example, probably all of the words in the paragraph you are now reading are sight words to you. You can read through the whole paragraph smoothly and quickly with good understanding. If a word is in a child's oral and written vocabulary, no further action will usually need to be taken by the child in order to comprehend it. This is the goal. We want all children to know by sight nearly all of the words they encounter.

Readers will use other methods to recognize a word only if that word is not in their sight vocabulary. For example, readers may use a decoding skill like phonics or morphology to decode an unknown word. Or readers might try to think of other words that are similar to the unknown word. Or readers may use context clues to figure out the word. These techniques only come into use, though, when the word is not in the reader's sight vocabulary. To repeat, to be a fluent reader, nearly every word a student encounters must be in that sight vocabulary.

Let's say, for example, that I threw the word *obstreperous* in right now. This is a little-known word, probably not in your sight vocabulary or even in your oral vocabulary. You probably stopped briefly to sound it out using your knowledge of both letter/sound relationships and your knowledge of syllables and morphemes. You probably were able to come up with a credible pronunciation, but since you had no similar words given and I provided no context, this was probably of limited use to you. And it slowed you down a great deal, distracting your mind from comprehension of the paragraph as a whole to recognition of one problematic word. With only one unknown word in a paragraph distracting you and slowing you down, you can see how important it is that children recognize at sight nearly every single word they read. (Obstreperous, by the way, means noisy and unruly. On Halloween, Mrs. Smith's class was obstreperous!)

Why Teach Sight Words?

The *obstreperous* example illustrates two important points about sight vocabulary. First, it illustrates the extreme importance of a reader's oral vocabulary. Figure 3.1 in Chapter 3 (The Blessing Chart) has been reproduced below as Figure 5.1 to remind your of how the four vocabularies—listening, speaking, reading and writing—all work together for comprehension. Having a word in a sight reading vocabulary or being able to decode the word beautifully will be of little practical use if the meaning of the word is not already in the child's oral word bank.

Figure 5.1: Oral and Written Language Modes (The Blessing Chart)

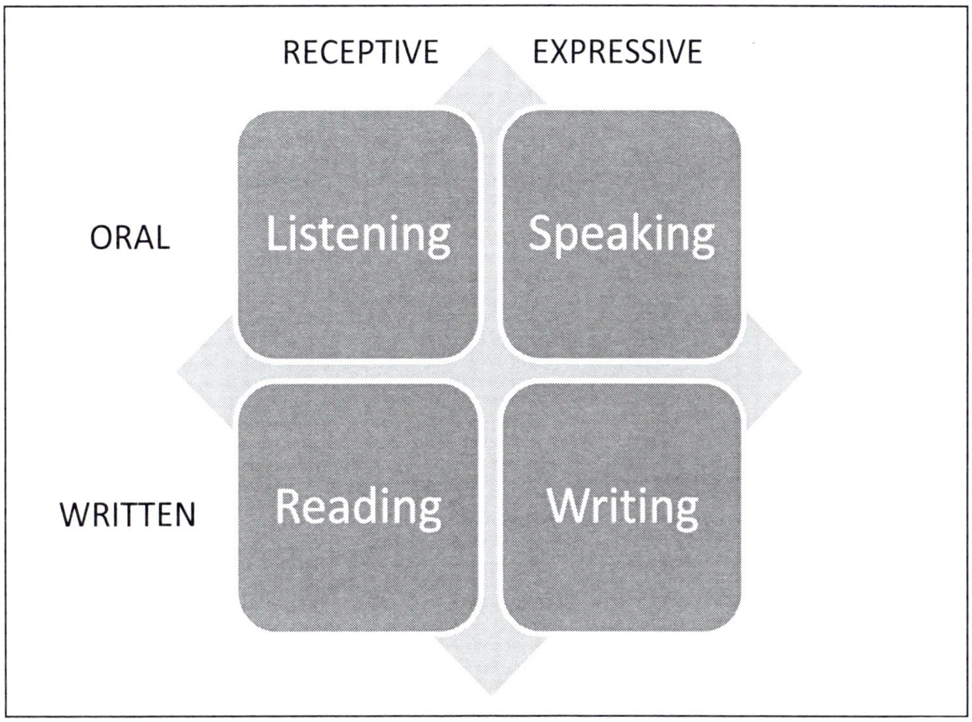

Second, the *obstreperous* example also illustrates why it is so important for nearly all words to be in a reader's sight reading vocabulary. When a child must stop to take some action on an unknown word, fluency suffers. When fluency suffers, comprehension is also reduced. Since the goal of reading is comprehension of the text, we cannot afford to let children labor over very many words as they read. Decoding and other word attack skill must quite quickly be reserved for a very few instances of unknown words. In fact, it is estimated that a child must recognize about 99% of the words in a passage on sight if she is to be considered an independent reader of that passage. Recognizing only 90% of the words in a passage puts her at her frustration level. So it is clear that nearly all words must be sight words for a child to read anything independently.

There is another good reason for teaching some words as sight words immediately. This is because so many words are phonetically irregular in English. Consider the very frequently seen words of *the, of, you* and *to*, for example. Students who have successfully mastered the sounds and rules of phonics will only be frustrated when they try to sound out these words and many others like them. English is replete with words that cannot be sounded out well, and these words will resist decoding and need to be taught as sight words from the beginning.

Which Words Should Be Taught as Sight Words?

There are four general categories of words that should be taught as sight words early in a reader's career. These four categories are:

- High-frequency words
- Phonetically irregular words
- Words of importance to the child
- Words needed to comprehend a specific text

These categories are not mutually exclusive, but let's look now at each category more closely.

High-frequency Words

Just as it sounds, a **high-frequency word** is one which occurs very often in the print children read. Periodically researchers endeavor to count and analyze the words that appear most frequently in English in the reading material of children. The two best known lists were done by Dolch (1936), and Fry (2004). Both Dolch and Fry arranged a relatively short list of English words by the frequency with which they appear in print. You may find the Dolch word lists atwww.k12reader.com/dolch-word-list and the Fry lists at www.k12reader.com/subject/sight-words/fry-wordsThe lists turn out to be quite similar so let's use Fry's *Instant Words* list as an example.

Fry estimated that the first 100 words on his list make up about 50% of all reading material. Even more impressive, the first ten words on his list make up almost a quarter of all reading material. These ten words are: *the, of, and, a, to, in, is, you, that, it.* Obviously, teaching these high-frequency words early as sight words can have an enormous impact on how much of a text a reader can read quickly.

Sidebar 5.1: Key Terms

Sight Words: Words that are recognized instantly by a reader

High Frequency Words: Words that appear very often in written text

Function Words: Words that carry little meaning but are grammatically necessary

Content Words: Words that carry the meaning of the text

Phonetically Irregular Words: Words that do not follow phonics rules well and can, therefore not be decoded by readers

These high-frequency words are vital to a reader's success, but unfortunately they are not the easiest words to teach. For one thing, you probably noticed that phonics often will not work for the words in that short list of ten. The first 100 words are no better. Some of the words are phonetically regular, but many are not. These will just need to be memorized by sight.

Another reason these words are difficult to teach is that so many of them are **function words** rather than **content words**. Content words carry the meaning of the text. It is relatively easy, for example, to explain the meaning of the word *elephant*. But try giving meaning to the words *the* or *of*. These function words are necessary for the grammar of a sentence, but they carry very little meaning themselves making them hard to remember.

Finally these high-frequency words are hard to teach because so many of them look so much alike. Again, the example word of *elephant* has special visual features that make it easy to remember. But high-frequency words *the, that, they, this* and *there* are all too similar for young readers to keep straight. Later in this chapter we will discuss ways to teach these difficult, but important words.

Phonetically Irregular Words

It isn't just the high-frequency words that contain so many **phonetically irregular words**. Lots and lots of other English words defy a child's best attempts to sound them out using the sounds and rules they have so conscientiously memorized. This can be quite frustrating to beginning readers. Developmentally, young children tend to be quite rule-bound. Once the teacher gives them a phonics rule, they expect the world to live by it. Unfortunately, the English language has a mind of its own, and students will repeatedly come up against words like *mustache, scissors, through* and *women* which will resist a child's best decoding efforts. Again, these words will just need to be taught as sight words, and acknowledging that they do not follow the rules is often of some comfort to children.

Words Important to the Child

Many children will come to school already being able to recognize a few words they consider to be very important. Remember the emergent readers, Collin and Whitney, described in Chapter 1 who learned to recognize such important words as "*McDonald's*" and "*Toys R Us*" almost before they could talk? The words important to a child are learned nearly effortlessly. Sylvia Ashton-Warner (1963), in working with Maori children in New Zealand, developed her entire Organic Reading Method out of using these important words. Working with children others had labeled as uneducable, Ashton-Warner found that if she asked the child what word he or she wanted, and then wrote that word on a sturdy card to take home, the children nearly always remembered their words. She termed these "one-look words" because they were so effortlessly recognized and retained.

A word that is very important to a child is his or her name, and names would be a very good place for any teacher of beginning readers to begin sight word instruction. Beyond names, teachers should follow the lead of Ashton-Warner in allowing at least some of the sight words taught in the classroom to be self-selected by students. Unlike the high-frequency words and the phonetically irregular words, the words of personal importance to children will be quickly learned and used.

Words Needed to Comprehend a Specific Text

A final category of sight words that should be taught consists of those specific words needed to meet success with a specific text. Basal readers provide lists of new vocabulary words that should be taught for each story. Some of these words may be phonetically regular enough to sound out, but others will probably need to be taught as sight words. It will be important for teachers to not only teach students to recognize these words, but to also make sure children understand the meanings of the words as not all of the new vocabulary words may be in a child's oral vocabulary. Teachers who are not using a basal series with stipulated vocabulary words will need to judiciously select new vocabulary words from the reading material they are using. Think back to the words Mrs. Emerson used in the opening vignette of Chapter 2 when she introduced the book, *If you Give a Mouse a Cookie*. This will give you an idea how to choose appropriate words.

Figure 5.2 summarizes these four types of words that should be taught as sight words.

Figure 5.2: Types of Words to Teach as Sight Words

Type	Definition	Examples
High-Frequency Words	Words that occur very often in a child's reading	a, and, the, of, if, then
Phonetically-Irregular Words	Words that cannot be sounded out by the child	there, you, scissors, women
Words Important to the Child	Words that will be learned very quickly because they are so necessary to the child	the child's name, relatives' and friends' names, home, stop, bathroom
Words Needed to Comprehend a Text	Special words occurring in a particular story	In *If you Give a Mouse a Cookie*, mustache, scissors, comfortable

Principles for Teaching Sight Words

Now that you are aware of the importance of teaching some words by sight and have an idea of the many words that may need to be taught in this way, the next question is always how to go about this instruction. Let's begin by looking at a few general principles that will apply to the teaching of any sight words.

- *Principle One: Always teach new sight words in context.* The brain works by making connections between new learning and what it already knows. The more you can help children to make these connections, the more successful they will be in adding new sight words to their reading vocabularies. Introducing the word *is* in isolation, for example, will not lead to much comprehension of this function word and will make it harder for students to remember it quickly. Introducing this word in the context of several sentences—An apple *is* red; an apple *is* juicy; an apple *is* sweet—as Mr. Green did in our opening vignette, will connect the new word to old information about apples in the child's brain, making it easier to remember. Therefore, all new sight words should be shown in the context of a phrase or sentence and as necessary in a real reading task. It is especially important to put function words into context because these words carry so little meaning on their own.

- *Principle Two: Always introduce new sight words in the most active, concrete way you can.* Mr. Green, in our opening vignette, does a beautiful job of focusing on the very abstract function words of "an"and "is" through an active lesson that connects these two words to the concrete apple the children are eating. It is much more likely that children actively engaged in constructing meaning in this way will remember these two words and begin to use them in their own writing than if these words had been part of a list of 10 new spelling words they needed to copy and remember by rote.
- *Principle Three: For now, de-emphasize phonics and other decoding skills.* This may seem to go against all of the advice in Chapter Four that encouraged you to teach phonics actively and systematically, but it really does not. Of course, phonics and other word attack skills are important, but it is also important to remember that your goal in creating an independent reader is to make these skills largely unnecessary and only used in rare circumstances. Early readers are often so drenched in the phonics bath that they want to conscientiously sound out every single word. A reader stuck at this stage will never become fluent or develop good comprehension. So while you continue with early readers to help them with decoding skills, during sight word instruction these skills must take a back seat to rapid, automatic recognition of whole words. Even though some of the high frequency words are phonetically regular (like *an* and *is*), needing to sound these words out each time they are encountered will be increasingly cumbersome to the reader. In sight word instruction, de-emphasize decoding in favor of automaticity and fluency.
- *Principle Four: Keep in mind the four vocabularies children have, and the differences in teaching that these different vocabularies demand.* For a moment, go back to Chapter 3 to the Blessing Chart which shows the four vocabularies we all have. Two of these vocabularies are oral (listening and speaking), and two of them are written (reading and writing). When you are introducing new sight words (reading and writing vocabularies), it will make a great deal of difference in your teaching whether or not children have the new word already in their oral vocabularies. The word *apple*, for example, was probably in the listening and speaking vocabularies of Mr. Green's first graders. He did not have to teach his students the meaning of the word, only what the word looked like in writing. If he had been teaching the word *oil*, though, which is also on Fry's 100 (2004) most frequently encountered words list, Mr. Green's task would probably have been quite different. In addition to helping his students recognize this word in print, Mr. Green would have probably needed to clarify the meaning of this word that his students may hold in their oral vocabularies in only the most superficial or hazy way. Recognizing which vocabulary is the focus of teaching will be especially important for English language learners who will have a large difference in oral vocabularies between their first and second languages. Figure 5.3 summarizes these four principles using as an example the book, *If You Give a Mouse a Cookie*(Numeroff, 1985).

Figure 5.3: Principles of Good Teaching of Sight Words

Principle	Do This...	Instead of This...
Introduce words in context	"The mouse had a milk *mustache*."	"Mustache" (word alone or in a list of vocabulary words)
Be concrete and active	Drink milk and observe mustache	"Mustache"—look up in the dictionary and use in a sentence
De-Emphasize decoding skills	"This word is *mustache*."	Sound this word out letter by letter
Consider the vocabularies in the Blessing Chart	Since we know what a mustache is now, let's remember what the word looks like.	Don't worry if you don't really understand this word; just memorize it so that you can read it out loud.

Let's Talk Teaching

There are two basic ways in which teaching happens, implicitly and explicitly, and these two ways are especially noticeable when it comes to vocabulary development. Let's look at each one.

Implicit Teaching

Implicit teaching is the indirect teaching that happens naturally in the normal course of living. Nearly all of the vocabulary development children have undertaken before they come to school has been done through implicit teaching. When you think about how a toddler learns oral language, you will understand how implicit learning happens. It is the rare parent who sits a toddler down to focus on verbs! Mostly parents don't even define or explain for their children the meaning of the words they use. Nevertheless, children come to school with surprisingly vast listening and speaking vocabularies that they have somehow "picked up" from the conversation and experiences of their preschool years. The world has been implicitly teaching these children oral vocabulary by immersing them in daily language used in authentic and interesting ways.

This indirect teaching that works so well in forming the oral language of preschoolers can be just as effective in forming the written vocabularies of school-aged children. For example, Krashen (1993) found that daily independent reading of only 10 or 20 minutes per day will greatly enhance a student's reading and writing vocabularies. Just the natural, regular immersion in print that schools should provide will rather effortlessly build strong written vocabularies for students in much the same way as the natural, regular conversations of adults built rich oral vocabularies for these same students when they were toddlers.

Recognizing that implicit, indirect teaching can have such a strong impact on students' written vocabularies, here are some easy ways to make your classroom print-rich:

- *Environmental Print.* Please look for this term in the Chapter 2 sidebar. Environmental print is the print students see around them all the time in their environment. Some will happen naturally (*stop, exit, restroom*), but you can add lots of environmental print by labeling many of the things in your classroom. Most of your students will already know the meaning of *table, chair* and *door*, and all you are doing is helping them connect the concept to the written symbol. For your second language learners, though, your labeling will also be helping them learn the meaning of English terms for common objects. Periodically focus on some of your labels and talk about them so that students continue to notice them and learn from these labels.

- *Shared Reading.* Teachers should read aloud to their students every single day from fine children's literature. There are many good reasons to do this, and one of these is for vocabulary development. Cunningham and Stanovich (1998) found that children's books aimed at elementary-aged students had 30.9 uncommon words per thousand words. This was more than adult speech (17.3) and prime time television (22.7). If children are to learn to read new vocabulary words, they will first need to have them in their oral vocabulary, and a very efficient way to hear uncommon words is through children's literature. Since beginning readers will be limited in the texts they can read themselves, it is especially important that an expert reader (you!) reads this fine literature out loud to them.

- *Sustained Silent Reading.* In 1986, Keith Stanovich coined his now famous **Matthew Effect.** Taken from the Gospel story in Matthew in which the rich get richer, Stanovich found that the same effect happens for readers. Good readers read more thereby becoming better readers, and consequently reading more. The Matthew Effect is a positive spiral of success leading to increased practice leading to increased success and so on. Unfortunately, the negative spiral can also occur. Poor readers tend to read less, thereby becoming ever more handicapped readers.

  Common sense tells us that anything we learn must be practiced to be improved, and reading is no

Sidebar 5.2: Teaching Terms

Implicit Teaching: Indirect teaching that happens naturally in the course of living

Explicit Teaching: Teaching that is planned and focused on specific learning

The Matthew Effect: The cumulative effect that comes about when a reader reads more, becoming a better reader, reading more, etc.

Sustained Silent Reading: A time set apart each day for students to do self-selected, free reading

Word Wall: Vocabulary words placed on the walls of the classroom, usually alphabetically or by themes

Word Bank: An individual word wall kept in the form of word cards or a personal dictionary different. Instituting in your classroom a time of 10-30 minutes each day in which students must read self-selected materials will increase their reading and writing vocabularies rather effortlessly. This is often called Sustained Silent Reading. What students read is less important than the fact that they are engaging in sustained, pleasurable reading. The study cited above concerning uncommon words (Cunningham & Stanovich, 1998) also found that comic books have 53.5 of these words per thousand and popular magazines have 66.7. This lends credence to the idea that nearly any kind of reading will increase a child's vocabulary and reading skills if engaged in often enough.

Explicit Teaching

Immersing students in a print-rich environment in which speaking, listening, reading and writing are routinely practiced in the classroom will go a long way toward indirectly increasing students' vocabularies. However, the teacher will also want to do regular, focused, explicit vocabulary teaching, too. Indeed, the National Reading Panel (2000) recommended explicit vocabulary instruction as wise classroom practice. Here are three ways for explicitly teaching vocabulary:

- *Teach/Practice/Apply.* TPA is really an undergirding technique for doing any explicit teaching lesson. It can be used for phonics, comprehension or content area reading. In using this acronym for teaching vocabulary, the lesson might look like this:

  Teach: Introduce 2-4 new words in context. Do this visually using a whiteboard or other visual method. Point out the features of the words. Discuss the meanings and the pronunciations. Read the words out loud and have students read them, echo read them, and spell them out loud. Chant the words and clap the letters. Have students write the words—in the air, on their neighbor's back, on a personal whiteboard, etc.
  Practice: Have students write the words repeatedly and check their spellings. Practice recognizing the words using games and other activities. Include new words on class word walls and personal word banks.
  Apply: Have students read a story which contains the new words. Finally, have students use the new words in their own writing, such as in their journals.

- *Language Experience Approach.* As discussed earlier in Chapter 1, this approach uses the child's own language to teach reading, but that does not mean explicit vocabulary teaching cannot also be part of this approach. For example, after Mr. Green and his class made the apple cluster together, and made their individual apple books, they did a shared writing activity which produced the following account of their class field trip to an apple orchard:

  •

  Once this group story was recorded on chart paper, Mr. Green used it to reinforce the word *apple* and then to extend his focus to the color words of *red, green* and *brown*. He used the TPA method, above, to teach these three new words.

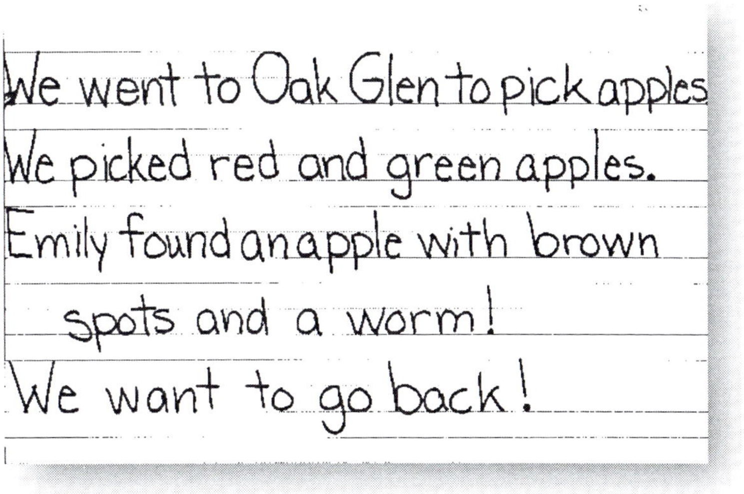
We went to Oak Glen to pick apples
We picked red and green apples.
Emily found an apple with brown
spots and a worm!
We want to go back!

- *Word Walls and Word Banks.* Mr. Green also used these two corollary methods in his lesson in the opening vignette. **Word walls** are just what they sound like—the words papering the walls of many classrooms. Usually these are arranged alphabetically and contain common words that students should be able to read and write correctly. The **word bank** is a sort of personal word wall, usually contained in an index card box or in a personal dictionary. It will usually contain many of the same useful words as on the word wall, but will also contain additional words useful to the individual child. Below is an example of part of a primary word wall.

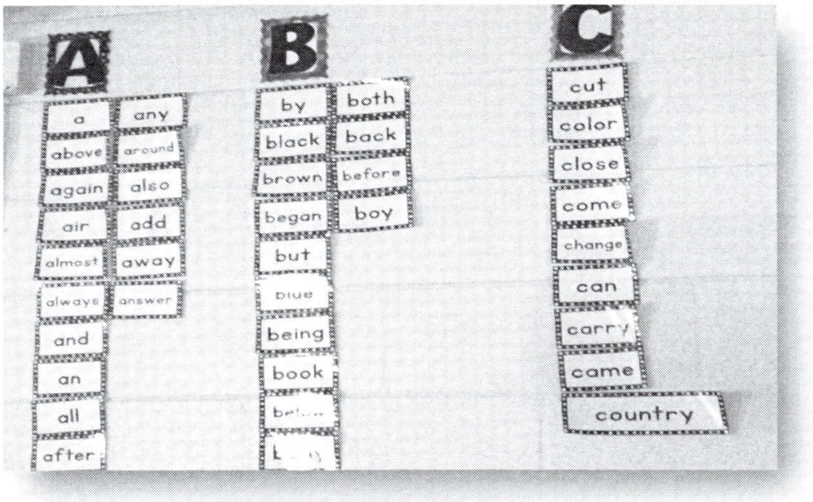

Patricia Cunningham points out in her book, *Phonics They Use* (2013)that it is not enough to *have* a word wall, though, you must also *do* the word wall, and this involves explicit vocabulary teaching. Cunningham recommends that teachers limit the number of words they include on their word wall to a manageable level. Then teachers should use these words in a variety of ways that allow students to practice the words and use them in their own writing. For example, words on the word wall or in the word banks could be sorted by initial sound or by theme. They could be alphabetized or considered by a feature, such as a suffix. Initial consonants, rhyming and syllabication could all be taught using these words.

And, of course, students should be expected to use these words, spelled correctly, in their journals or other writing.

You may recall that Mr. Green put the words *as, is* and *apple* on the class word wall after the students made the apple cluster. He also asked students to add these words to their personal word banks. The final journal activity of the apple lesson in his classroom showed lots of journal entries in which the words *an, is,* and *apple,* as well as the words *red, green* and *Oak Glen,* were used and spelled correctly. Vocabulary success!

Summing Up and Moving On

In this chapter we learned that the "Everything—All the Time" balanced approach to teaching reading means that both word attack skills, like phonics, and sight words must be taught. Most of the words students read must eventually become sight words, and it is prudent to teach the high-frequency words, phonetically irregular words and important words to children by sight. Vocabulary words must be taught in context in as concrete a way as possible, and some of this teaching must be explicit using a Teach/Practice/Apply approach. A great deal of this vocabulary teaching can be done implicitly, though, through the use of environmental print and free reading.

In Section Two of this book, we have concentrated on those youngest children who were just approaching the wondrous world of Literacy Land. These emergent readers have used their early experiences with oral language to move into reading and writing. They have found tools, like phonics and sight words, to help them live in Literacy Land. It is time now for them to become true citizens of Literacy Land by increasing their skills and becoming better readers and writers focused on comprehension. In Section 3 of the book, we will meet children who are doing just that.

Section Three

Developing Readers:
Becoming Literate

Section Three consists of three chapters:

Chapter 6: Developing Readers:

Focusing on Fluency

And

Chapter 7: Comprehension:
The Point of it All

And

Chapter 8: Writing:
What Does it Have to do with Reading?

Chapter 6

Developing Readers: Focusing on Fluency

It was mid-November, and Mrs. Leffler was startled one day to see Miss Aylsworth standing rather shyly at her classroom door. Miss Aylsworth was a "downstairs" teacher meaning she taught the primary grades, and Mrs. Leffler was an "upstairs" teacher because she taught the intermediate grades. Upstairs and downstairs teachers did not mix. It wasn't that they really had anything against each other, but since they did not share recess or planning times, there was very little opportunity or reason to mix. Still, here was Miss Aylsworth, upstairs!

"Would your kids like to read with my kids on Friday afternoons?" Miss Aylsworth began without prelude. "I was thinking it would help my first graders to have someone to read to, and maybe your fifth graders would benefit, too," she explained. And so began the Westfield Elementary School Reading Pals Program.

Miss Aylsworth decided the best path for her first graders, some of whom were only barely beginning readers, was to practice reading a "little book" from the reading series. Since she had three levels of reading groups in her room, each student got a little book at the appropriate reading level. During reading group each day, some time was spent reading, discussing, and practicing these little books, with Miss Aylsworth modeling good reading of each book occasionally. Later, the first graders practiced reading these books both silently and out loud during free reading time using such techniques as choral, echo and partner reading. By Friday of each week, the first graders could proudly carry a book they could read up the 14 steps to the upstairs classroom of their fifth grade Reading Pal.

Mrs. Leffler was able to allow her fifth graders more freedom since even her most challenged readers were beyond the beginning reader stage. The process she followed, though, was much the same as Miss Alysworth's. On Monday, every fifth grader chose a picture book they thought their Reading Pal would like. Throughout the week, time was set aside each day to practice reading this book. Mrs. Leffler focused on helping her students read their books smoothly and with expression. She sometimes did mini-lessons on paying attention to punctuation marks, reading rate, and the like to help her students become better oral readers. Sometimes she chose one of their picture books to read aloud herself so that her students could hear good reading.

By Friday of each week, the fifth graders, just like the first graders, were fully prepared and excited about Reading Pal time. And, every Friday afternoon a babble of happy voices could be heard on the upstairs hall as little kids and big kids proudly entertained each other with good books read well. By year two, more upstairs and downstairs teachers had joined forces and the Westfield Elementary School Reading Pals Program was off and running.

Focusing on Fluency

As students move from the beginning reader stage to the developing reader stage, the focus of instruction also shifts somewhat. The very earliest readers are likely to be concentrating so hard on word attack skills and on reading each word correctly that they have little attention left over for anything else. Most young readers will go through a stage of reading everything word-by-word, and sometimes letter-by-letter if the words are unknown. This very halting, mechanical type of reading will be necessary for a short while as students focus on sounds, letters, rules and other skills needed for cracking the reading code. However, quite quickly, developing readers must move beyond this stage to become smoother readers more focused on the big picture. In short, they must become more fluent.

What Makes a Fluent Reader?

Graves, et al. (2011) define reading **fluency** as, "the ability to read rapidly, smoothly, without many errors and with appropriate expression." (p. 224). And Padak and Rasinski (2008) say fluency is "the ability to read expressively and meaningfully, as well as accurately and with appropriate speed." (p 3). Both of these definitions encapsulate the most common components of reading fluency. Let's look at several of these components more closely.

Rate and Accuracy

Two fluency components, rate and accuracy, go together because neither a very rapid reader who makes many mistakes nor a completely accurate reader who reads extremely slowly would be considered fluent. There is interplay between these two components because they both relate to the concept of **automaticity.**

The term automaticity comes from the ground-breaking work of LaBerge and Samuels (1974) who hypothesized that the human brain has a very limited capacity to multitask. What we think of as multitasking is really the brain shifting its attention quickly from one task to another. This is only possible if the tasks involved are all automatic (Ormond, 2011). But if one task the brain needs to attend to is very difficult and compelling, then the brain will have little resources left over to attend to anything else.

Applied to early reading, this means that children who are concentrating very hard on decoding skills will not be able to focus much attention on comprehending what they are reading. In order for comprehension to become primary, the early decoding skills must become automatic. When students have some level of automaticity in their word attack skills, then they will be able to read more rapidly (rate) and more accurately. Until this automaticity is developed, however, readers will read slowly and haltingly with numerous errors, and comprehension, which is the obvious goal of reading, will suffer.

Sidebar 6.1: Key Terms

Fluency: Smooth, correct reading that has appropriate rate and expression

Automaticity: The ability to do something quickly and without apparent thought

Prosody: Reading with expression. Includes such factors as smoothness, intonation and phrasing

Volume: In this case, volume means amount of reading not how loudly someone reads.

Round Robin Reading: Students reading a cold reading (one they have not practiced) in turn one after the other around the room

No one is advocating, however, that readers develop a very fast, machine-gun type of reading style. The rate a reader reads will vary for different types of material and should demonstrate that the reader understands his own words. Rate should also naturally increase as the reader becomes more practiced and adept at the skills of reading. Hasbrouck and Tindal (2006) have estimated for example, that reading mid-year in appropriate grade-level material, average first graders will read 23 correct words per minute, average third graders will read 92 correct words per minute, and average fifth graders will read 127 correct words per minute. Reading quickly enough and accurately enough to make meaning from the text is the goal.

Prosody

Prosody is sometimes explained as reading with expression. It encompasses several components, such as correct loudness, phrasing and intonation. All of these lead to smooth and expressive reading that demonstrates understanding of the text.

While prosody is not as easy to judge as rate and accuracy which can both be measured quantitatively, most teachers recognize whether or not a reader is reading smoothly, with correct expression which attends to punctuation. For example, in the area of smoothness, less competent readers read word-by-word while the most competent readers read in phrases or sentences.

Just as with rate and accuracy, the concept of automaticity is also important in reading with expression. Until students can move away from laboriously sounding out or pondering every word, they cannot begin to look at the other features of written language, such as punctuation, that serve as cues to readers in how to phrase and express material for maximum meaning. Work in word attack skills, then, will precede fluency, and is an important first step. However, once these skills become automatic, instruction must shift from decoding to fluent reading. Figure 6.1 summaries the various components of fluent reading.

Figure 6.1: Components of Fluency in Reading

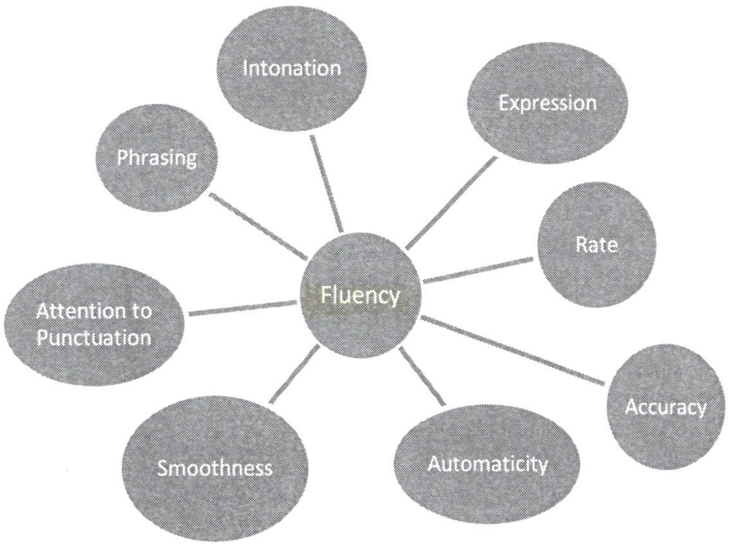

Why Fluency is So Important

Over the years, fluency as a reading skill to be developed has not enjoyed the same level of commitment from teachers as phonics or comprehension skills. However, the National Reading Panel (2000) established fluency as one of the five components needed in reading instruction. This was decided on the basis of research that showed clear and consistent correlations between fluency and comprehension. Comprehension of text is the true purpose of reading, so instruction should focus on anything leading to increased comprehension.

The idea of automaticity, discussed previously, gives us a clue as to why fluency and comprehension are related. When the brain must distract itself from the meaning of the text in order to sound out a word, for example, or struggle to remember a sight word, then the brain does not have the resources to continue to also concentrate on the meaning of the text. Further, what comprehension of the text that has been stored up so far in short-term memory may also be lost while the brain shifts its focus to decoding. Perhaps you have had the experience yourself of reading a very difficult textbook, in which you often had to ponder new terms, coming to the end of a page, and realizing you had no clue as to the meaning of the page you had just read.

So while reading aloud is not practiced much in the lives of 21st century citizens, the importance of developing the skills of fluency in your students goes far beyond any futures they may have as newscasters. Fluency skills are important to them (and to you!) right now so that they can understand the material they read. Let's look now at some principles and methods for developing reading fluency.

Principles of Fluency Instruction

Whatever methods you choose to use to help your students develop fluency, there are several underlying principles you should keep in mind to guide your work. Let's discuss a few.

- *Be Intentional.* While some students will develop into fluent readers with very little guidance from you, most will need for you to intentionally focus on the skills of fluency in order to become fluent. Just as you intentionally plan lessons in decoding or comprehension skills, you must intentionally plan for fluency instruction and allow time in your reading program for students to develop these skills.

- *Focus on the Big Picture.* While decoding skills and sight words are important to develop in readers, the extreme emphasis we often put on discrete skills leads some children to conclude that reading is really about just pronouncing all the words right. Accuracy, of course, is one of the skills of fluency. But an over-emphasis on accuracy will impede the development of overall fluency. For at least part of your reading time, stop correcting errors and instead focus students' attentions on reading smoothly without worrying about minor mistakes.

- *Model.* Some of your students will never hear fluent reading unless you provide it for them. Read to your students every day no matter how old they are. Let's say that again. *Read to your students every day!* There are many good reasons why you should read aloud to your students no matter what grade you teach, and one of the best reasons has to do with modeling reading fluency. Reutzel (2006), and others have shown through research that reading fluency in students is assisted by hearing an exemplary reader. You are the best reader in the room, and you must demonstrate this skill to your students, but you can also use excellent peer readers or older students as models of fluent reading. In our opening vignette, Miss Aylsworth was hoping that the fifth grade Reading Pals would be models of fluent reading for her first graders.

- *Use Repeated Reading.* Our opining vignette also demonstrates the importance of reading a text more than once. Most of us, if we were planning to read in front of a group, would want to see the text beforehand, read the text several times while working through any difficult parts, and perhaps even read the text out loud to a mirror so that we get the inflection just right. Unfortunately, in school life, children are not often afforded this opportunity. Yet fluent reading is developed by practicing the same text numerous times. Not everything in your curriculum needs to be read more than once, of course, but when you are focusing on fluency, repeated readings must take place. Both Mrs. Leffler and Miss Aylsworth in the opening vignette gave their students plenty of time and reasons to read the same material several times.

  Let's take one short side trip here to discuss the practice of **round-robin reading**. This outdated and ineffective method involves students going around the room, each reading a paragraph of the text in turn. While this practice is still sometimes seen in classrooms today, there is no evidence that it actually helps students become better readers. This could be because it violates all the steps that we normally take when we will read aloud to a group. Instead of a prepared reading which has been practiced enough to be smooth, in round-robin reading students are asked to do a cold reading of a text they have never seen before. Not surprisingly, this often leads to extremely dis-fluent reading which embarrasses the reader and does not help listeners comprehend the text. As an added drawback, the listeners in this situation have just had dis-fluent reading rather than fluent reading modeled for them. Avoid round-robin reading if your goal is fluency.

- *Encourage Reading Volume.* Reading **volume** in this context does not mean how loudly someone reads. Instead, here it refers to the amount of reading done. To become a fluent reader, children must read a lot! As an analogy, let's pretend you are a golfer. When you were learning to play golf, maybe you watched a video about how to play. Maybe you watched great golfers on television. Maybe you even took lessons where the club professional fixed your arm position and corrected your posture. While all of those things were probably helpful, if you can play golf today, it is not due to instruction or modeling or error correction. It is because you played a lot of golf, practicing your skills on a variety of courses under many different situations.

You learn to golf by golfing, and you learn to read by reading (Krashen, 1993). This seems obvious, but for some reason we ignore this fact and do not plan for adequate practice of reading with diverse materials in our classrooms. It is important to set aside time for free-reading (reading practice!) each day. And it is also important to guide students in their choices of appropriate texts. (For more information on this, refer back to Sustained Silent Reading in Chapter 5.)

LaBerge and Samuels (1974), in their work dealing with automaticity, have noted that an activity eventually becomes automatic when we practice it enough times in non-taxing conditions. Their use of the word "non-taxing" is important. Much of what we ask students to read during the school day is decidedly taxing to them. Many students struggle all day with grade level readers, science books and social studies texts. Hopefully, they are learning a great deal from this reading about these subjects, but it is unlikely this work will contribute to their reading fluency because it is such challenging reading for them. You will need to guide students, therefore, to appropriate materials for their free-reading.

There are numerous ways to determine whether a book is at a student's independent (non-taxing) reading level. For example, some textbook series come with sets of "little books" that have been leveled. There are lists of leveled trade books, such as Fountas and Pinnell (2006). And there are several readability formulas which you could use to level your own books. Perhaps the easiest strategy is the time-honored "Five Finger Method." To use this method, the child chooses a book and reads one page of it. Every time she comes to a word she does not know, she raises one finger. If she uses all the fingers on one hand before she reaches the bottom of the page, the book is probably too difficult, and she should choose another one. While this is not a very fancy system, it does seem to work well enough, and has the added advantage of making reasonable choices the responsibility of the child.

However you do it, the principle of Encouraging Reading Volume means you must give adequate time and adequate direction for students to engage in sustained periods of non-taxing reading each day if they are to become fluent readers. Mrs. Leffler did this in our opening vignette when she required her fifth graders to spend some of their free-reading time reading and re-reading a picture book they planned to share with their Reading Pal. Figure 6.2 summarizes these principles of good fluency instruction.

Figure 6.2: Principles of Fluency Instruction

Principle	Explanation
Be Intentional	Plan mini-lessons on such topics as attending to punctuation
Focus on the Big Picture	Supply unknown words quickly to children rather than asking for decoding
Model	Read aloud fluently to your class each day
Use Repeated Readings	Require students to read the same story several times for different purposes
Encourage Reading Volume	Set aside SSR time every day

Let's Talk Teaching

Keeping these five principles in mind, there are numerous ways to intentionally include teaching for fluency in your reading instruction. Here are some ideas:

Modeling
Anything that allows an adept reader to be heard by a less skillful one will work for modeling. The only requirement is that the reader is fluent. Try the following:

- You read to your class,
- An outsider reads to your class (principal, famous person, parent volunteer, etc.),
- An older student reads (Reading Pals),
- Students follow along with a book on tape,
- Students watch episodes of Reading Rainbow or other program of read-aloud fluent readers.

Repeated Reading
Anything that encourages/compels a student to read text several times will work. To encourage repeated reading try the following:

- Choral reading (everyone reads out loud together),
- Echo reading (adept reader reads a sentence and less skillful reader echoes it),
- Partner reading (readers prepare to read to a partner),
- Reading for different purposes (i.e. first time for skills; second time for comprehension; third time for prosody),

- Reading to a parent (send "Book Bags" home for family reading),
- Readers' Theatre (fully prepare a text as theatre to present to another class).

Reading Volume

Anything that allows and encourages a student to spend a sustained period reading a text will work to increase reading volume. Try the following:

- Sustained Silent Reading which requires everyone in the class, including the teacher, to read for a specified amount of time,
- Classroom Book Clubs (several students read the same book and meet to discuss it),
- Book Talks (read widely in children's literature yourself and recommend books either through a formal book talk to your class or an informal book conversation with one student),
- Author or Genre Studies (present the works of one author or several examples of one genre and then allow students to choose from these).

However you go about teaching fluency, it is clearly a skill too important to be left to chance. While beginning readers will necessarily focus most of their brainpower on decoding and word attack skills, very soon this focus must shift to smooth, expressive reading that emphasizes comprehension. If you want this type of fluent reader, you will need to intentionally plan time, instruction and activities designed to make this happen.

Summing Up

Chapter 6 focused on the important skill of fluency. Fluency includes reading accurately at an appropriate rate and reading with prosody. We discussed principles of teaching fluency which included being intentional, focusing on the big picture, modeling, using repeated readings, and providing for reading volume. All of these principles led to the automaticity needed by all readers if they are to shift their focus from decoding to comprehension. In the next chapter, we will look closely and specifically at the skills involved in reading comprehension.

Chapter 7

Comprehension: The Point of it All

Miss Dickinson is midway through a fairy tale unit with her third graders. Right now they are focusing on two variants of the Cinderella tale. At the beginning of the week, the students watched the Walt Disney movie version of Cinderella and completed a story grammar that listed the major components of this variant. In this graphic organizer, the class included the components of setting, characters, plot and theme based upon the Disney version of Cinderella.

Most of the students considered this to be the only version of the Cinderella tale, and so they were surprised when Miss Dickinson then read aloud to the class *The Rough-Face Girl* by Rafe Martin (1992) which is an Algonquin Indian Cinderella variant. The class repeated the exercise of graphically displaying the literary elements of *The Rough-Face Girl*. Here is what they came up with:

Story Grammar for The Rough-Face Girl

Setting	**Characters**	**Plot**	**Themes**
By Lake Ontario	The Rough-Face Girl-RF	Sisters are cruel to RF	Be brave
Long ago	Cruel sisters	Sisters get pretty clothes	Be kind and nice
	Father	Sisters try to marry IB	Don't give up
	Invisible Being-IB	Sisters can't see IB	Be pretty inside
	Invisible Being's Sister	Rough Face makes clothes	Depend on yourself
		RF can see the IB	
		RF answers questions right	
		RF marries Invisible Being	

N ext, Miss Dickinson led her class through a comparison of the heroine in these two variants using another graphic organizer, the Venn diagram. She put two very large, intersecting circles on the board and explained that the place where the two circles intersect shows how the heroines are alike, but the rest of the circles show how they are different. The class used their two story grammar charts to complete the Venn comparison. The finished graphic organizer looked like this:

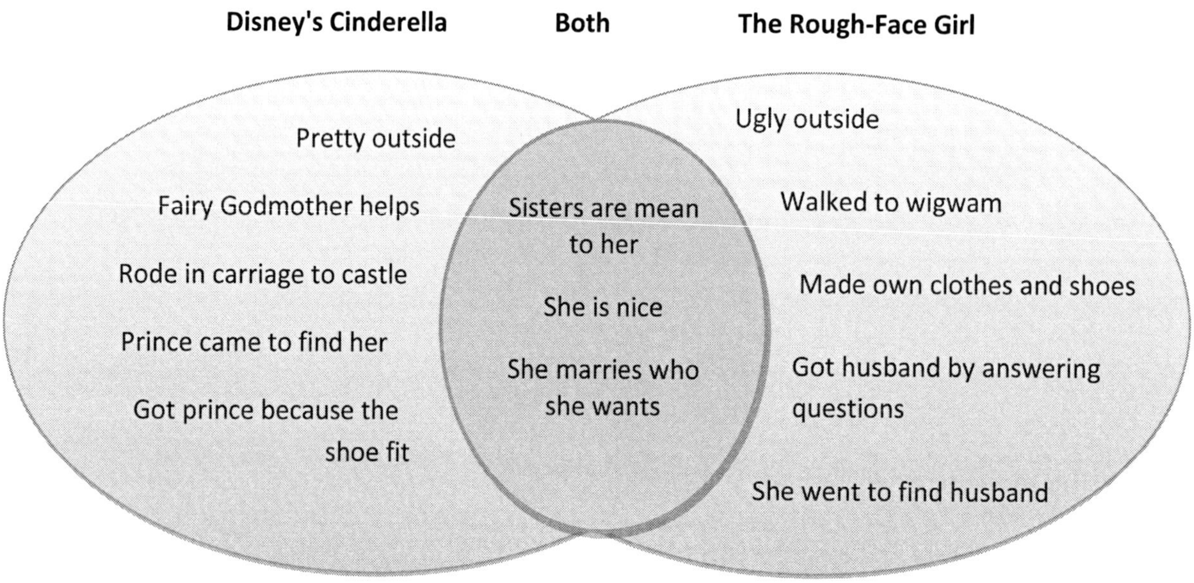

Throughout the four days that Miss Dickinson has been focusing on Cinderella variants, she has very intentionally been asking questions requiring different levels of thought. Many of her questions at the beginning of her work with each story were at the literal level. She knew her students must understand what literally happened in the stories before they could think more deeply about them. The story grammars often focused on literal understandings, such as who was in the story or what happened next. As soon as Miss Dickinson was comfortable that her students had literal understanding of the story, though, she quickly increased the complexity of her questioning to include inferential or critical thinking, asking her students, for example, to state one theme of the story or to compare the two main characters.

Finally, Miss Dickinson introduced a third Cinderella variant, *Yeh-Shen* by Louie (1982), a Cinderella tale from China. She reminded the class of the steps they had taken to compare the Disney movie with *The Rough-Face Girl* and then sent the students off in groups to repeat this process with *The Rough-Face Girl* and *Yeh-Shen*. The resulting Venn diagrams were impressive enough to display out on the hall wall!

Comprehension: The Point of it All

Bettelheim and Zelan wrote rather prophetically in 1982 that, "It is high time that children and teachers were freed of the yoke and the blinders that are the direct result of teaching reading as if its ultimate purpose is the acquisition of decoding skill" (p. 304). Certainly from the classroom practices today (and the first sections of this book!), it would be easy to conclude that word attack skills are the point of reading and reading instruction. That conclusion, however, would be a serious error.

Reading is for communication. It is so one person can understand, profit from, and engage with the thoughts of another person. The true purpose of reading and learning to read is comprehension of text. Decoding and other skills are only means to that end. As means to an end, word attack skills are important, but they should never be confused with the purpose of reading. The point of it all is comprehension.

Reading comprehension was defined by the National Reading Panel (2000) as "...intentional thinking during which meaning is constructed through interactions between text and reader" (p. 4). Unfortunately, the "intentional" part of that definition has seldom been apparent in lessons dealing with the comprehension leg of the balanced reading program. In a landmark study conducted in 1978, Dolores Durkin found that, while enormous amounts of classroom time were spent on activities labeled reading comprehension, only a tiny fraction of this time was spent on actually teaching the skills of comprehension. Most of those activities labeled as reading comprehension were actually testing rather than teaching. You will want to make sure this is not true in your classroom.

Think back to Chapter One of this book to the visual of the balanced reading program as a three-legged stool. Recall that one of the legs represented decoding and other work attack skills while another of the legs represented comprehension. This chapter will consider factors which contribute to reading comprehension. Then it will examine research-supported comprehension strategies. And, finally, it will look at methods for teaching these strategies. All this is to help you be more intentional in making the comprehension leg of your balanced reading stool strong.

What Factors Contribute to Understanding a Text?

Numerous factors will help or hinder a child (or anyone) in comprehending written material, and several of these have already been discussed in previous chapters. Please go back now to Chapter 3 and review Figure 3.1 (The Blessing Chart) because oral language skills will certainly influence how well a child understands a written text. You can see from this figure how interrelated the four types of communication are, and that the written forms use the oral forms as their base. A child with a weak or shallow oral language base may struggle with written text because, for example, they do not know the meanings of words in the text or they do not realize that stories conform to a recognizable structure. The strengthening of oral language that was begun in early childhood and the primary grades must be continued throughout the later grades if reading comprehension is the goal.

A second factor we have already discussed which influences comprehension is fluency. In Chapter Six, we especially considered how the concept of automaticity relates to comprehension of text. Take for example, the child, who reads a line of text like this: *The bird—no, b...b...ig—big house, no....horse, p..ooooolled—pooled, the hungry, w...w...water, no...wagon!* This child is unlikely to comprehend from this that the text is about a big horse pulling a heavy wagon. Repeatedly, the child has needed to distract his brain from the meaning of the text to concentrate on decoding skills. He has fairly good phonics skills, and sometimes eventually comes up with the correct word. However, the fact that he lacks automaticity in these skills and reads so haltingly means he has introduced numerous errors into his brain (bird, house, pool, hungry) before decoding the words correctly, and the thread of the line is completely lost by the end of the sentence. If a teacher wishes to help students with comprehension, work in fluency is a necessary first step.

A third factor that influences comprehension has to do with the information processing concept of **schema,** which is sometimes called background knowledge. Schema theory envisions the mind as a large filing cabinet (or computer storage system if this suits you better). Just like the filing cabinet in an office, your mind organizes the information it stores in different file folders. New information will be retained more easily if there is already a developed file folder (prior knowledge) in which to store it. And information will be accessed more readily if the file folders in your mind are orderly and appropriately titled. If information in separate file folders can be connected or cross-referenced in some way, both storage and retrieval will be easier.

Here is a demonstration of how schema theory works. Please read the following passage and decide where to store it in your brain:

> *First, you will probably need to leave your house, though some people are able to accomplish this task indoors. Next, you should clip your pants and possibly your hair if you have any. Third, you should check carefully for obstacles and remove or avoid them. You can begin this operation either by sliding through or by climbing over. Either way will work, so it is really your preference. Now, simply push hard and repeat as many times as necessary until you are finished. Enjoy!*

Probably your brain was not quite sure where to file this, and if I began to ask you questions (like what was the third step?) without allowing you to consult the passage, chances are you would not be very successful at answering these questions. Yet this is a short, easy passage about a common activity.

The reason you probably met with little success in filing this passage is because I did not help you identify the correct file folder of background knowledge in your head. Numerous ambiguous terms in the passage may even have sent you scrambling to incorrect file folders

Sidebar 7.1: Key Terms

Graphic Organizer: a visual representation that presents information in a picture or diagram to enhance understanding.

Metacognition: the act of thinking about your own thinking.

Modeling: showing students how something is done. Modeling can be implicit or explicit.

Picture Walk: a technique to activate schema by discussing the illustrations in a text.

Scaffolding: the process of providing students with strong support (such as modeling) as they learn something new, then gradually releasing responsibility for learning to students as they grow more capable.

Schema: file folder in the mind through which information is organized. Background knowledge. The plural is schemata.

Self-Monitoring: like metacognition, being aware of your own reading processes in order to correct problems.

Taxonomy: a classification system in which categories of information are listed sequentially, such as from lowest to highest only to have your brain realize it had made a mistake and scramble to a new folder. If, however, I had told you at the beginning that this passage was about riding a bike, you would have had no trouble at all understanding it and filing it for later reference.

This exercise demonstrates why schema theory is important in comprehension. It also demonstrates how easy it is for teachers to use schema theory to help children access their prior knowledge (the file folders) and connect new learning to old. Of course, if a child turns out not to even have a file folder (background knowledge) on a specific topic, schema theory also explains why it will be important for the teacher to somehow build and enrich a new file folder on the subject.

So, oral language skills, fluency, and schema will all influence the comprehension of written texts for children. We would do well, therefore, to include attention to these three general areas in our reading programs since comprehension is our final goal. Now let's look beyond these general influences and consider comprehension skills directly. When you begin to look at comprehension, you won't go very far until you come across the concept of higher-order thinking skills. Let's begin there.

Higher-Order Thinking Skills—Higher Than What?

The term higher-order thinking has become so commonplace in reading literature that we sometimes gloss over it without sufficient understanding. And while higher-order thinking implies there must be something lower, the literature never really discusses lower-order thinking skills. To try to address this confusion, let's look closely at a piece of foundational research about comprehension.

Benjamin Bloom et al. (1956) first addressed the idea that some understandings about a text will be more profound than other understandings. This rather obvious observation then led Bloom's committee to try to organize different types of comprehension into some sort of **taxonomy** from less profound to more profound. The result was the ubiquitous Bloom's Taxonomy of Cognitive Objectives that listed six levels of comprehension beginning with the lowest level of literal understanding, which was labeled "knowledge", through progressively harder skills labeled, "comprehension, application, analysis, synthesis and evaluation". Here is a summary of those six levels:

- Knowledge—remembering the information
- Comprehension—understanding the information
- Application—using information in a new way
- Analysis—pulling the information apart for better understanding
- Synthesis—combining several pieces of information
- Evaluation—critiquing the information

The higher levels of the taxonomy rest upon success at the lower levels. Yet, too often teachers stop at these lower levels, focusing on knowledge or comprehension for example, and never moving on to the higher levels. This is a mistake. While the lower levels are necessary before students can move on, the higher levels are how students comprehend material deeply. A visual of the six levels of comprehension in Bloom's Taxonomy which shows this relationship is in figure 7.1.

Figure 7.1: Bloom's Taxonomy

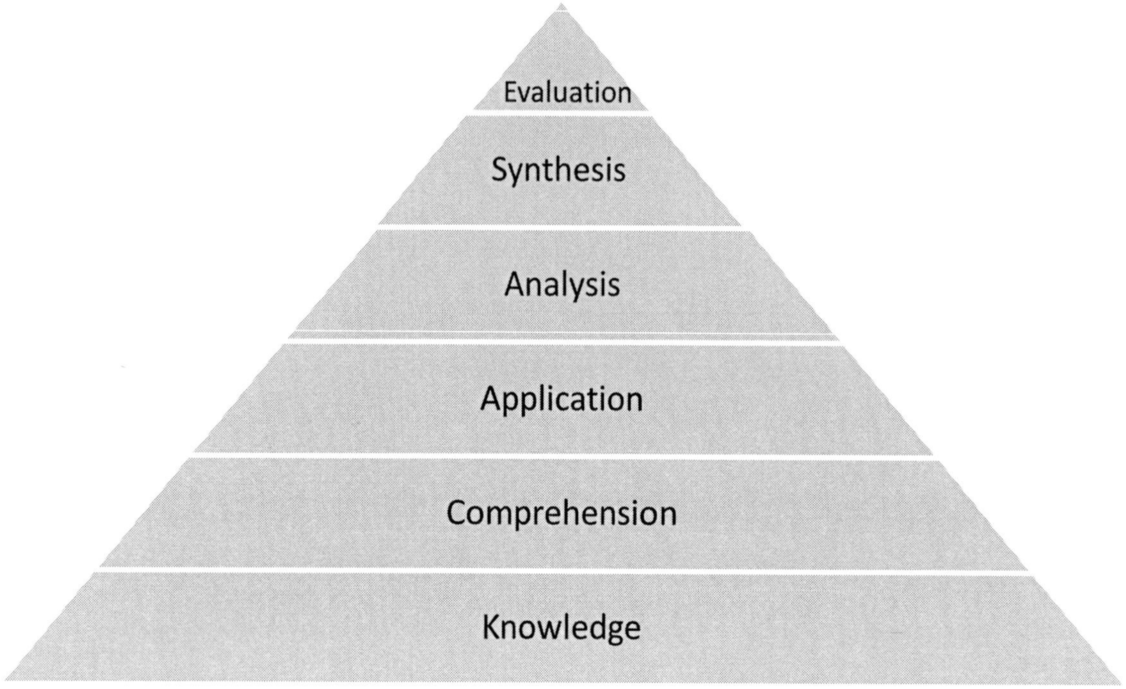

Once Bloom's Taxonomy became highly disseminated, several classroom consequences of it came about. First, there was a heightened awareness that indeed, there were different levels of comprehension of any text, and that children were mostly being asked to focus only on knowledge or comprehension of facts and were seldom being asked to ponder texts in any more profound ways. Teachers recognized this error and consciously began to try to lead their students to think with more complexity about their reading matter.

Another consequence of Bloom's Taxonomy was that the comprehension strategy of questioning was given heightened attention. It became clear that most of the questions teachers asked were clustered in the lower-level comprehension skills, and the higher-order thinking skills were often minimized or skipped altogether. This realization led to the design of various techniques to help teachers ask higher-order questions with greater regularity. Some techniques provided sentence stems for each level with the evaluation area, for example, asking such a question as: Do you agree with________________? Other techniques provided verbs at each level to aid teachers in designing questions. For example, verbs like create, design, or make might be good words to begin a synthesis level question.

A third consequence of all of this attention to Bloom's Taxonomy of Cognitive Objectives was that classroom teachers and researchers noticed that six levels of cognitive thought might be dissecting comprehension a little too finely to be practical in the classroom. While there was general agreement that some levels of thought were higher than others, there was also general confusion about how knowledge differed from comprehension, for example, or whether a particular question would be labeled application or synthesis. This led to a host of simplified taxonomies that remained committed to the importance of higher-level thinking skills, but did not demand such fine distinctions. Now, you will see widely used the three distinctions of literal, inferential and critical thinking. Figure 7.2 summarizes this simplified taxonomy.

Figure 7.2: Simplified Comprehension Taxonomy

Taxonomy Level	**Representative Skills**	**Motto to Remember**
Literal	Remembering, sequencing, re-telling, locating	Just the facts, ma'am.
Inferential	Interpreting, concluding, predicting, generalizing	Read between the lines.
Critical	Evaluating, responding, applying, analyzing	Go deep!

Literal Comprehension

Literal comprehension refers to lower-level comprehension skills roughly combining knowledge and comprehension from Bloom. This level asks students to remember or locate particular facts presented in the text. The emphasis is on working with the information actually presented on the page. Literal level questions almost always have only one right answer. For example, in reading *Brown Bear, Brown Bear* (Martin, 1967), if you ask a child for the color of the bear, you are asking a literal question. Only if the child responds, "brown" will you be able to count the answer correct.

Inferential Comprehension

Inferential comprehension is also sometimes called Interpretive Comprehension and asks students to read between the lines. The skills at this level ask for higher-level thought than literal skills, and could roughly correspond to Bloom's middle levels. Students now must do more than simply report what was written in a passage. Now they must look at what was reported and draw inferences or make predictions or interpret pictures, for example. A fourth-grader looking at the cover of *One Crazy Summer* by Rita Williams-Garcia (2010), for instance, might be asked to predict from the title that the story takes place in summer and, and from the cover illustration that the story will involve three African American girls in a city.

Critical Comprehension

Critical comprehension asks students to think very deeply and with complexity about what they read. It roughly corresponds to the highest levels of Bloom's taxonomy, and asks students to do such tasks as recognizing the mood of a story, identifying propaganda techniques, or deciding if characters acted ethically. Both inferential and critical questions will routinely have more than one correct answer. So when Miss Dickinson, in our opening vignette, asked her students whether both Cinderella and Rough-Face were "good" girls, she got numerous answers combining yes, no and sometimes in a variety of ways. Her only requirement was that students were able to justify their answers.

Bloom's Taxonomy and all the versions of simplified taxonomies that were generated by Bloom's early work, have helped teachers to identify different levels of comprehension and have assisted them in matching their questioning strategies to the level of understanding they have as a goal. Students can also be taught these taxonomies so that when they compose their own questions, they will also give attention to higher-order thinking.

Now that you know the basic theories behind comprehension, let's begin to look at what you can do in the classroom to increase your students' comprehension of their reading.

Research-Based Comprehension Strategies for All

There may be as many identified reading comprehension strategies as there are readers! Well, maybe not quite that many, but still a dizzying and overwhelming array of the many ways readers address a text in order to gain meaning from it. Teaching this multitude of strategies will leave children (and their teachers!) feeling muddled and fragmented. For everyone's well-being, then, let's focus on a few, research-supported, multipurpose comprehension strategies that can be used by most readers in various situations.

Five of the best researched and most effective comprehension strategies are: self-monitoring, accessing prior knowledge, questioning, summarizing and using graphic organizers. Let's discuss each strategy briefly. Keep looking back at Sidebar 7.1 for the important terms which are in bold print.

Self-Monitoring

Good readers are active and purposeful in their reading (Duke & Pearson, 2002). They consistently monitor their own reading to be sure they understand. The term often used for this is **metacognition,** which roughly means thinking about your own thinking. It is as if a reader engaged in metacognition has a little portion of the brain standing to the side consciously monitoring how well the text is being understood. The metacognitive reader is continuously asking such questions as they read like, "Did that make sense to me? Did I understand that? What did that section mean, and how does it connect to what I read earlier?" If the metaman (or woman) in the brain reports back that the reader is not understanding a part of the text, then a good reader will stop and somehow remedy the situation using some of the other comprehension strategies they have learned. Perhaps they will focus on an unknown vocabulary word and stop to define it. Or perhaps they will re-read a section and try to put the troublesome part into a better-understood context. Whatever action they take, the point is that they are not allowing poor understanding of the text to go untreated.

Self-monitoring, or metacognition, is an over-arching skill that precedes the use of other comprehension strategies. Until students develop the skill of self-monitoring, they will not be able to become independent readers. Instead, they will remain dependent on the teacher to monitor their comprehension through questioning or testing. Good readers eventually learn to serve this function for themselves. However, readers who have gotten the mistaken notion that reading is primarily about decoding will often pay little attention to whether they are understanding a text, and will happily read sentences like "A house ran down the road" without the slightest discomfort. The first step in teaching reading comprehension, then, must be helping students to monitor their own comprehension and take an active role in understanding what they are reading.

Accessing Prior Knowledge

Accessing prior knowledge relates directly to schema theory which was discussed earlier in this chapter. A good reader, upon beginning a new text, will ask herself what she already knows about the topic. If she has a file folder in her head for the topic, she will access this and bring all of that prior learning to bear on reading the new text. So much the better if that file folder is very rich, bulging with lots of information about the topic. If, however, the folder is thin (or non-existent), the reader starts this new text thinly-prepared to comprehend what she reads. As noted in the section on schema, it is the teacher's task to help students access prior knowledge, or build a new file folder if there is no background knowledge to access in a child.

Let's look at two examples of this. First, in the vignette in Chapter Two, Mrs. Emerson was teaching the book *If You Give a Mouse a Cookie* by Laura Numeroff (1985). Before reading the book, she held a lengthy discussion about real-life mice with her students. In doing this she, a) allowed those students who had prior knowledge about mice to access and refer to this background knowledge, and b) encouraged those students who had little prior information about mice to build and enlarge their MOUSE file folder through the information provided by other students.

Miss Dickinson in the vignette at the beginning of this chapter also made use of schema theory when she began her Cinderella unit by having her students watch the well-known Disney film. Many students already knew this version of the story well and were able to easily discuss the literary elements. The film only served to remind them of the CINDERELLA file folder already in their minds. When Miss Dickinson moved on to *The Rough-Face Girl* variant of the tale, students found it easier to consider this new and surprising version because they already had their CINDERELLA folders open on their desks, so to speak.

Questioning

Since reading comprehension involves an interaction between the reader and the text, good readers must constantly ask themselves multiple questions about the text. Teachers who are helping students to become independent readers consistently pose questions about a text in order to model for students what they will one day do for themselves.

Sometimes the questions teachers ask are relatively easy ones designed to help students with the literal meaning of a text. For example, Miss Dickinson began her Cinderella discussion in the opening vignette by asking students to name the characters and retell the plot. She needed to make sure students understood the story literally before moving on.

Sometimes, though, the questions teachers ask are harder, designed to delve into the deeper meanings of a text. These questions ask students to make inferences or interpretations of what they have read and to think critically about the text, such as when Miss Dickinson asked her students to compare the main characters in *The Rough-Face Girl* and *Yeh-Shen*. Regardless of the level of complexity, though, generating and answering questions are two comprehension strategies good readers use consistently. As such, they are strategies worth teaching and practicing in the classroom. Teaching students either Bloom's Taxonomy or a simplified one will help with this.

Summarizing

As a comprehension strategy, summarizing is a powerful tool to aid in the understanding and retention of information in a passage. New readers often think summarizing just means saying everything in the story over again in their own words. However, summarizing is actually a combination of skills that asks for much more discernment from the reader than just the regurgitation of facts. In summarizing, the reader must consider what was important in the passage and what was trivial enough to leave out. She must consider the purpose of the passage and her purpose for reading it in order to retain the most important information. And she must find generalizations or patterns in the reading in order to see the bigger picture of what the passage is trying to convey. While re-telling a story will be a helpful first step, moving beyond re-telling to summarizing will encourage students to actively engage with a passage by considering how best to condense or rearrange the material into something new.

Using Graphic Organizers

Putting information presented in written text into some sort of picture or graphic is the idea behind using **graphic organizers** for comprehension. This skill actually could be divided in two by thinking of a) the graphic material given to students by authors and b) the graphic interpretations students design on their own for understanding.

The first skill has to do with helping students understand how to use the graphic representations found in a text. This may take the very early form of doing a **picture walk** through an illustrated book in order to better understand the words of the text through the pictures. It can also take the progressively more difficult skills of understanding the charts, graphs and maps often found in the science and social studies texts older students read.

The second skill has to do with helping students form pictures, either in their minds or on paper, to actively engage them in better understanding of a text. There are many formats to do this, and we will discuss several later in this chapter. And you have seen several graphic organizers in use already in your vignettes. For example, Mr. Green in Chapter Five used a cluster to brainstorm vocabulary words about apples, and Miss Dickinson in this chapter used a literary elements chart and a Venn diagram in her lessons. Miss Dickinson then went one step further and asked students to design their own graphic organizers applying the models they had done as a class to a new story.

The five powerful comprehension strategies just discussed, self-monitoring, accessing prior knowledge, questioning, summarizing and using graphic organizers, can all be used by readers to understand text at any level of either taxonomy. Now let's focus on what you as the teacher can do to help stu(develop these strategies.

Let's Talk Teaching

Before we look at specific techniques for teaching the five strategies (and more!) that we discussed above, let's be sure to understand the difference between strategy and method. Strategies are techniques the reader uses to understand a text; methods are techniques the teacher uses to teach these strategies. All of the methods we are about to discuss can be used to teach any comprehension strategy.

Comprehension Strategies	Teaching Methods
Self-Monitoring	Think-alouds
Accessing Prior Knowledge	Mini-Lessons
Questioning	Reciprocal Teaching
Summarizing	Using Text Structure
Using Graphic Organizers	

Once you realize that there are specific comprehension strategies children need to learn to be effective readers, the question then becomes one of how best to teach these strategies. There are countless effective methods and techniques for teaching comprehension, and this section will focus on four fairly multi-purpose methods. These are: Think-alouds, Mini-lessons, Reciprocal Teaching, Using Text Structure. Each of these can be used at many grade levels with a variety of texts focusing on any of the comprehension strategies listed earlier. As such, they can be powerful methods for helping students develop comprehension skills.

Think-alouds

The Think-aloud technique (Roehler & Duffy, 1991) is connected to two powerful ideas about how learning happens. The first idea is the concept of **modeling.** Much of the learning we do, especially once we leave formal schooling, is based upon watching a more competent person perform some task and then copying what they do. They serve as a model for us as to what we are trying to accomplish and how best to go about it. In the classroom, the teacher serves all day as an implicit model of the "good reader" simply because she is the best reader in a room where reading routinely takes place. The Think-aloud method merely makes this implicit modeling more explicit.

The second concept related to think aloud is the idea of **scaffolding.** Just as a scaffold is erected around a new building to hold it up until it can stand alone, so too, the idea of academic scaffolding provides support for students as they learn a new skill. This support is gradually withdrawn as the students become more capable of using the new skill independently. The idea of scaffolding makes use of Vygotsky's Zone of Proximal Development that we discussed in Chapters 1 and 3 because the teacher provides enough support for students to work at a slightly higher level than they would be able to do alone. Miss Dickinson at the beginning of this chapter used scaffolding, for example, when she worked through a Venn diagram on Cinderella and *The Rough-Face Girl* with her students before she asked them to do a Venn diagram on *The Rough-Face Girl* and *Yeh-Shen* alone.

Now, back to the Think-aloud method. This method simply makes the implicit modeling and scaffolding the teacher routinely does explicit to students. It is a relatively straight-forward technique in which the teacher simply states what comprehension strategy he is employing, and then verbalizes his thoughts as he uses this strategy. By letting students see into his mind, so to speak, the teacher models a process that is usually hidden, showing how this comprehension strategy is being used more explicitly to students. The teacher then supports, or scaffolds, the students as they try to follow his example by using the strategy themselves. Here is a short example of how a Think-aloud might go if Miss Dickinson would have done one in the opening vignette:

> Miss D. says: *Today we are focusing on the skills of comparing and contrasting, and I am going to practice by comparing Cinderella with the main character in The Rough-Face Girl. I already know that this is a different version of the Cinderella story, but the girl here on the cover doesn't look like Cinderella at all to me. She has dark hair and dark eyes. I think she is Native American because she has a feather in her hair. And something is wrong with her hands because she has bandages on them. How can she be called Cinderella? I just don't know. Maybe the story will tell me. I think I will read it and see if this girl is anything like the Cinderella I know.*

In this example, Miss Dickinson has made the focus skills (compare/contrast) explicit to the students. She then lets students observe her thoughts as she compares the two main characters. Later, as students read the story, Miss Dickinson will ask students to make their own comparisons.

Mini-lessons

Much of your work with comprehension will naturally be integrated within authentic literacy activities. You will model the strategies, and use them regularly in the course of actual reading and writing during the day, such as when you are doing a DRL as explained in Chapter 2. However, sometimes you will want to focus very intentionally on one specific comprehension skill. Perhaps you wish to focus on a skill because this is one of your grade-level standards. Or perhaps you have determined through observation or testing that students lack a particular strategy. Whatever your reason, when you wish to focus in a laser-like way on one skill, a mini-lesson is a good way to do this.

As suggested by its name, a mini-lesson is very short—perhaps ten-twenty minutes. It can be used for any skill, vocabulary or phonics for example, though we will be considering it here in teaching comprehension strategies. When you design a mini-lesson, it is helpful to keep the acronym TPA in mind. In this acronym, the T stands for Teach; the P is Practice; and the A stands for Apply. (Look back in Chapter 5 to see a TPA lesson for vocabulary.) Not all of these steps may be completed during the actual mini-lesson, but it is useful to keep the acronym in mind to connect the mini-lesson to later classroom work. Let's look at the three steps individually.

TEACH. Several activities appropriately go in the Teach portion of the mini-lesson. The teacher should:

- Decide on the skill to be taught.
- Select a book or passage which will allow this skill to be demonstrated.
- Explicitly name, define and explain this skill for students.
- Read the passage and model the use of this skill with this passage.
- Repeat this modeling and direct instruction until students understand the concept.

PRACTICE. During this portion of the mini-lesson, responsibility for using the new skill is gradually transferred from the teacher to the students. The teacher scaffolds, or supports, students at whatever level is necessary for students to be successful with the new skill. This section of the mini-lesson may include:

- Guided Practice in which the teacher helps students as they work with the new skill.
- Peer Practice in which students help each other either in pairs or small groups to practice the new skill.
- Independent Practice in which students practice the new skill alone.

APPLY. Often this is the part of the mini-lesson most likely to connect the skill being taught to the wider world of authentic reading. Before this section, then, or whenever the teacher decides to end the mini-lesson and send students off to use the new skill, she should provide a summary review of what the skill was, and how and when it should be employed. After this review, numerous activities may logically be used to help students apply their new skill in their real reading. Some of these would include:

- Use the strategy with a new text.
- Demonstrate the strategy in their writing.
- Take turns using the strategy with a partner.
- Design a graphic organizer that demonstrates use of the strategy.
- Apply this new reading strategy to work in content areas (science, social studies, etc.).
- Take the role of the teacher to present the strategy to a Reading Pal (Chapter 6).

A sample mini-lesson Miss Dickinson might use to teach the skill of sequence is in Figure 7.3

Figure 7.3: Sample Mini-Lesson on Sequence

Teach: "Today we are going to focus on the skill of sequence. This means the order in which something happens. We often use words like first, second, next, after that and finally to show the order of events. Let's look at The Rough-Face Girl and list the steps she took to marry the Invisible Being." This is the list the class made together:

1. Made her clothes and decorated them
2. Made her shoes
3. Walked to the Invisible Being's wigwam
4. Answered his sister's three questions
5. Met the Invisible Being
6. Married him and lived in great gladness

Practice: "Now in your table groups, I want you to take these other picture books (provide some with clear sequence of steps), and list the steps the main character takes to get what he/she wants." Miss Dickinson monitors groups, and then they all discuss their lists together.

Apply: "We know the sequence of events for Rough Face to get what she wanted and the sequence for these other characters to get what they wanted. Now it is your turn. In your journal, put something you want at the top of your page. Then list the steps you will need to get this. Be sure your steps are in the right order—the right sequence."

Reciprocal Teaching

The Reciprocal Teaching Method, designed by Palinscar and Brown (1984), makes use of two concepts already discussed, modeling and scaffolding. It also builds upon Pearson and Gallagher's (1983) concept of gradual release of responsibility in which responsibility for using a comprehension strategy gradually transfers from the teacher to the student. In Reciprocal Teaching, the teacher takes more responsibility for the skill at the beginning of the lesson, but gradually students take on more and more leadership until they actually assume the role of the teacher. Reciprocal Teaching is usually done with small groups, though it does not have to be limited to these, and it usually takes approximately 30 minutes to complete. This method focuses very intentionally on four specific comprehension skills: Predicting, questioning, clarifying, and summarizing. Teachers using this technique can focus on teaching only one of these at a time or may use some or all of the skills together in their lesson. Comprehension skills used in conjunction with each other are the mark of a good reader, and the goal of Reciprocal Teaching, but for beginners it may be better to start with only one or two skills.

At the beginning, the lesson is teacher directed. He states the skills to be learned, reads a passage, and models the use of these skills with this passage. The goal, however, is to help students become independent users of the four targeted comprehension skills, so as soon as possible the teacher begins to turn over leadership of the group to one or more of the students. This student then takes on the teaching role and uses the four strategies to work through another passage. At first, the teacher monitors this closely, and redirects as necessary, but eventually students become able to predict, question, clarify and summarize in groups of peers or independently.

Reciprocal Teaching has been widely researched and found to be especially effective with struggling readers. Other researchers have also created ways to improve the original Reciprocal Teaching design. One promising technique for this comes from Oczkus (2003) who suggested teachers use a graphic organizer listing the four strategies to display the steps students might take when leading each strategy.

Text Structure

Most of the text students read fits into two different types, narrative and expository. If students can be taught to recognize the underlying structures of these two types of text, they can use these predictable structures to better comprehend what they read. Let's look at the two types separately, since the structure of each type is quite different from the other.

NARRATIVE TEXT. Narrative writing is typically called a story. As children listen to many stories being read to them, they gradually develop a sense of how a story should go. This is called their story schema (remember that file folder in the mind). In the story schema, students notice that stories follow a predictable pattern. They have a beginning, middle, and an end. Somewhere there will be a problem or issue that comes to light. There will usually be some buildup of excitement while this problem is confronted, which will then lead to a climax in the story. Finally, there will be a resolution of this problem leading to the ending of the story.

Besides recognizing how stories move along, students also have in their story schema the fact that stories contain various similar features. There will be a setting, characters, plot and theme, for example. Recognizing the existence of these literary elements, helps students to expect and identify them in a story, which in turn helps students recall and understand the story better.

Any of the methods already discussed (Think-aloud, Mini-lesson, Reciprocal Teaching) could easily be focused on helping students identify and work with story structure. Discussions of plotline, for example, could naturally be included in the prediction section of Reciprocal Teaching. Or a teacher could easily use a Think Aloud to consider the traits of one of the characters in a story. So any of the previously given methods can address story schema.

Besides these methods, though, understanding the structure of narrative seems to lend itself extremely well to the use of graphic organizers. One type of graphic organizer for story structure is variously called a story map, a story grammar or a literary elements chart. Whatever the name, this graphic organizer uses the predictable features of a story to map a story visually. Miss Dickinson, in her Cinderella lesson, used the literary elements of setting, characters, plot and theme to summarize both Disney's Cinderella and *The Rough-Face Girl*. She then helped students combine both of these separate charts into a Venn diagram comparing the various elements of each version. The use of story grammar (the various elements) gave her students a way to organize their understandings of these two stories.

An additional graphic organizer useful with narrative text is the story frame/story board or flowchart. In this organizer, students display visually, either in pictures or in words, the events which happened in the story. A story frame will usually be guided through short connecting phrases that pull the reader along through the action. Here is a sample story frame:

This story takes place________(where and when)______________________________.
It starts because ____________________(main character)____________has a problem.
This problem is ______________(plot)____________________________________.
The problem gets worse when_________________(plot)______________________.
Then______________________________________(plot)_______________ ________.
The problem is solved when __________________ (plot)______________________.
This story taught me ___________________(theme)____________________ ____.

EXPOSITORY TEXT. Much of what children read in school will fit into story structure. However, not everything they read is in the form of a story. The informational reading they do in their science and social studies textbooks, for example, will not follow story grammar because the writing is expository rather than narrative. Expository, or informational writing, has a very distinct structure from narrative, and children need to also develop an expository schema if they are to understand informational writing well.

Features of expository writing include prose with a very dense introduction of ideas and lots of details. This style makes use of headings and subheadings. It often introduces many terms and demands a closer style of reading than narrative. Since it does not have a storyline to carry it along, it is often more difficult for students to sustain interest and to discern the most important facts. We will discuss expository text in more detail in Chapter 11 when we consider content area reading, but for now, let's look at one strong method for helping students work with informational text.

The KWL Method was designed by Ogle (1986) specifically to help students deal with expository writing. In the acronym, the K stands for "What I Know," the W stands for "What I Want to Know", and the L stands for "What I Learned". These three steps are taken individually and displayed on a graphic organizer. The first two steps (K and W) are pre-reading steps, with the last section (L) taking place after the selection is read.

The K (What I Know) section is designed to do several things for students. It introduces the topic, allows students to access prior knowledge, encourages them to build knowledge together and motivates them to read the selection.

The W (What I Want to Know) step involves generating questions about the topic. This helps students focus their efforts as they read the selection. It also helps them decide the most important facts and features of what they are about to read.

The L (What I Learned) section takes place after students have read the text and is a natural outgrowth of the first two steps. As students record what they learned from their reading in the L column of the chart, it is easy for them to see how their W questions were answered and to determine whether they have some questions that did not get answered and will need further investigation. A sample KWL chart on drought is presented in Figure 7.4.

Figure 7.4: KWL Chart on Drought

What I Know (K)	What I Want to Know (W)	What I Learned (L)
A drought means no rain. A drought kills things. A drought happened last year in our town. A drought can cause fires, too.	Why do droughts happen? Where have the really bad droughts happened? How do people live during a drought? What can we do to prevent droughts?	Droughts happen when no rain or snow falls for a long time. Droughts have happened all over the world. People and animals can die in a drought. Poor people suffer more during a drought than rich ones. Global warming might cause droughts.

The entire KWL method can be used in a whole class, small group, or individual setting. These grouping options could also be combined, with the K and W portions being done with a small group and the L section being completed individually, for example. In the example given in Figure 7.4, the K and W columns began the lesson. Then the students read *Droughts* by Judy and Dennis Fradin (2008) to complete the L column.

A Final Thought

Comprehension is the point and purpose of reading, and as such we must help children to become skillful at using the strategies of comprehension to understand what they read. This chapter has discussed multiple comprehension strategies worth teaching, and has presented numerous methods for teaching those strategies.

The teaching of comprehension, though, is somewhat of a paradox. It is important for the individual skills to be identified, focused upon, and taught intentionally. Yet good readers do not use comprehension strategies one at a time. They use the strategies in endless and complex combinations in response to what they are reading. So while it is important to teach the skills individually, it is just as important to help children use the skills in an integrated way. In order to do this, a good plan is to choose a few comprehension skills you want to focus upon, introduce all of these skills early in the year, and then spend all year using, reinforcing and refining these skills in every text your students read.

Summing Up

This chapter began by reminding us that comprehension is the real purpose for reading, and that good comprehension will depend upon a student's oral language skills, fluency and schema. Higher-order comprehension skills along with various taxonomies were discussed. Five important comprehension strategies, self-monitoring, accessing prior knowledge, questioning, summarizing and using graphic organizers, were presented. Finally, we looked at lots of teaching techniques. Now it is time to connect all of these good ideas about reading to the fourth quadrant of the Blessing Chart—writing. Chapter 8 will do just that.

Chapter 8

Writing: What Does it Have to do with Reading?

Several years ago, the teachers at Heron Creek Primary School decided to become very committed to writing skills with their students. It was a concerted, school-wide effort that meant all children at every grade level wrote often and widely. It also meant that some of this writing was saved each year for every student so that growth in writing could be documented. In every child's cumulative folder, there was a section called "**Portfolio**" that contained these saved writing samples so that they were available to next year's teachers. Whitney, the emergent reader you met in Chapter 1, has attended Heron Creek Primary School since kindergarten. She is now moving up from third to fourth grade, and her new teacher, Mrs. Fox, is taking some time to study Whitney's writing portfolio from her first four years of schooling.

Beginning with the Kindergarten samples, Mrs. Fox noticed that Whitney used very strong phonics skills even early in the year. Her story about the black cat (Figure 8.1) was phonetically accurate enough for Mrs. Fox to read.

Figure 8.1: Kindergarten Work Sample (Once Upon a Time)

Furthermore, her Thanksgiving story (Figure 8.2) showed rapid improvement in both creative production and correct conventions. Letter formation was legible indicating good fine motor skill development.

Figure 8.2: Kindergarten Work Sample (Thanksgiving Story)

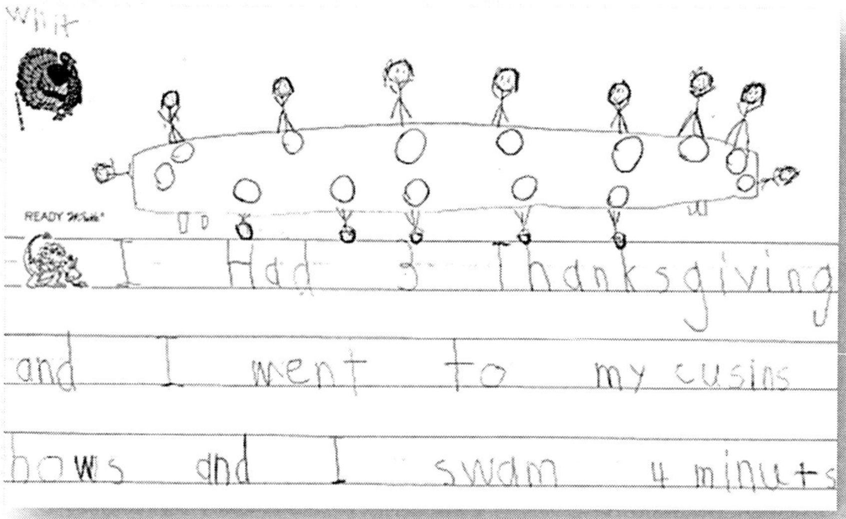
I Had a Thanksgiving
and I went to my cusins
hows and I swam 4 minuts

Moving to the first grade samples, Mrs. Fox saw even more creative production. Whitney's story, "My Bad Day at School" (Figure 8.3), was a full page long and entirely legible. While she still used some invented spellings, these were rare and reserved for relatively uncommon words.

Figure 8.3: First Grade Work Sample (My Bad Day)

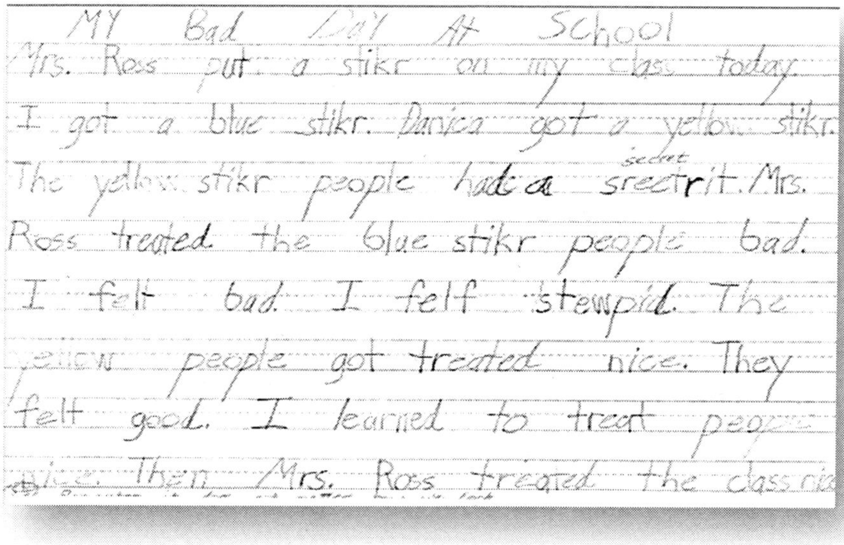
MY Bad Day At School
Mrs. Ross put a stikr on my class today.
I got a blue stikr. Danica got a yellow stikr.
The yellow stikr people had a srectrit. Mrs.
secret
Ross treated the blue stikr people bad.
I felt bad. I felt stewpid. The
yellow people got treated nice. They
felt good. I learned to treat people
nice. Then Mrs. Ross treated the class nic

Mrs. Fox also saw in Whitney's literary element chart about a book (Figure 8.4) that she was able even in first grade to use writing to organize her thoughts. However, this sample also showed that Whitney still needed clearly lined paper to help her with legibility.

Figure 8.4: First Grade Work Sample (Literary Elements Ch

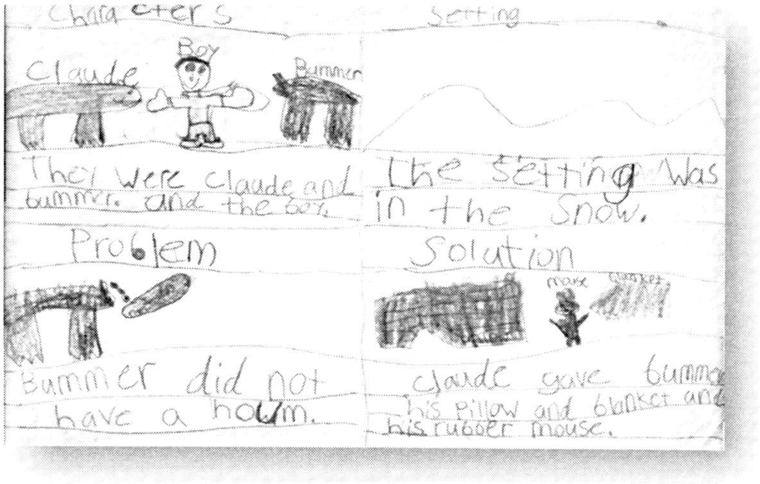

Figure 8.5: Second Grade Work Sample (Land of Candy)

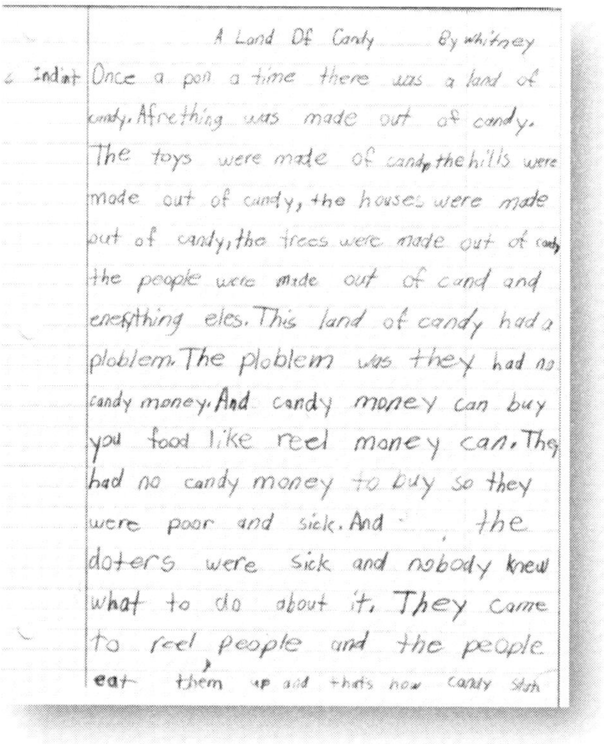

By second grade, Whitney's writing samples showed a student who was continuing to make steady progress in writing. Her "A Land of Candy" story (Figure 8.5) showed that she had graduated to regularly lined paper instead of specialized primary print lining. She was able to tell a well-constructed story that demonstrated an understanding of narrative structure. Her invented spellings continued, though, and some punctuation was in error.

Looking at both of Whitney's third grade samples, though, Mrs. Fox noticed that Whitney's writing had improved a great deal during this last year in numerous ways (Figures 8.6 and 8.7). First, she had moved from printing to **cursive** handwriting, and the transition had gone fairly well, with Whitney's samples still being legible. Next, both samples showed a refinement in creative writing skills with more complex use of language, economic sentence structures, and clear organization. Finally, errors in conventions were few with most spelling, punctuation and capitalization being done correctly. The two writing samples also showed that Whitney could use her writing for different purposes.

Figure 8.6: Third Grade Work Sample (Fields)

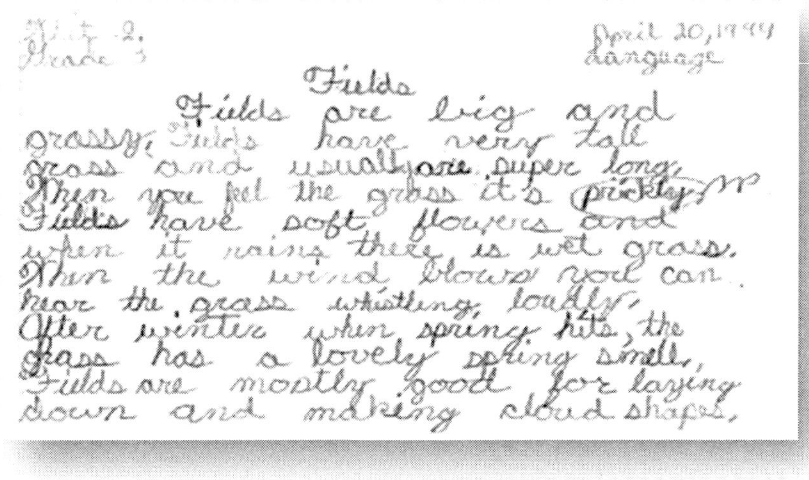

Unit 2.
Grade 3
April 20, 1994
Language

Fields

Fields are big and grassy. Fields have very tall grass and usually are super long. When you feel the grass it's prickly. Fields have soft flowers and when it rains there is wet grass. When the wind blows you can hear the grass whistling loudly. After winter when spring hits, the grass has a lovely spring smell. Fields are mostly good for laying down and making cloud shapes.

Figure 8.7: Third Grade Work Sample (Joyful Noise)

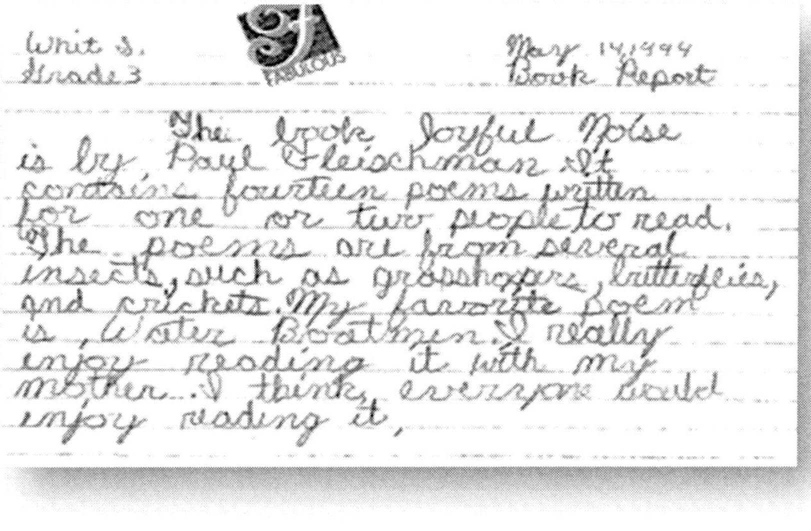

Unit 3.
Grade 3
May 14, 1994
Book Report

The book Joyful Noise is by Paul Fleischman. It contains fourteen poems written for one or two people to read. The poems are from several insects, such as grasshoppers, butterflies, and crickets. My favorite poem is, Water Boatmen. I really enjoy reading it with my mother. I think everyone would enjoy reading it.

Mrs. Fox was pleased to see the skills in writing that Whitney was bringing into the fourth grade, and she began to make plans for helping Whitney improve her writing further.

The Reading/Writing Connection

In any program designed to help children become better readers, it would be very unwise to ignore the place of writing instruction. Cullinan (1993)has called reading and writing two sides of the same coin, and Reutzel and Cooter (2012 have referred to these two skills as mirror images. Figure 3.1 in Chapter 3 (also shown in Chapter 5) demonstrated how these two modes of communication are related. This figure (The Blessing Chart) is reproduced here as Figure 8.8 for your easy reference. Look at how reading and writing are related because they both use written symbols to communicate, and how they are reciprocal because one is a receptive skill and the other is expressive. Additionally, this figure makes clear that writing is also related to the oral language modes of listening and speaking that serve as foundations for the written communication modes.

Figure 8.8: Oral and Written Language Modes (The Blessing Chart)

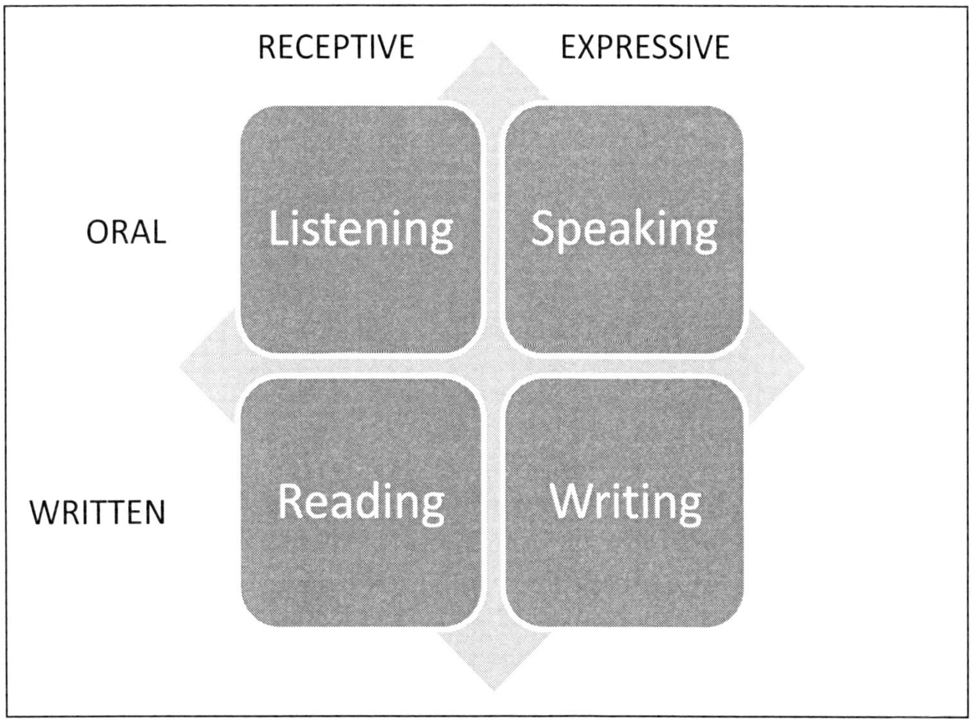

The four modes of communication are related to each other in rather obvious ways as shown in this figure, and these relationships are borne out by research. Tierney and Shanahan (1991) reported that both reading and writing shared similar thought processes and both depended on critical thinking. These researchers, as well as Olness (2005) found that teaching reading and writing together actually helped students become better at both. In other words, as children learn to write better they become better readers and vice versa. Further, as written language skills of any sort improve, oral language skills benefit, and vice versa. Receptive or expressive, oral or written, communication is a finely integrated web of reciprocal and supporting skills upon which the whole endeavor rests. If competent reading is your goal, you must pay attention to all four quadrants. In this chapter, we will focus carefully on the fourth quadrant of writing.

Stages of Writing

Just as emergent readers learn early to recognize the Golden Arches of "McDonald's" in their quest to obtain French fries, emergent writers also focus their concentration on ways to communicate with the wider world. As these emerging readers go through clear stages in making sense of the images they are receiving in their lives, so they also go through stages in their attempts at expressive communication. And these stages of written communication (reading and writing) echo the stages of oral communication (listening and speaking) that children engaged in years ago.

Numerous researchers (Gentry, 1982; Temple et al., 1993; Rubin & Carlan, 2005) have studied the stages that children go through on the way to becoming conventional writers. Each of these researchers has given slightly different names to the various stages, but the stages themselves are remarkably similar. We looked at these stages briefly in Chapter 3, but let's look at a synthesis of this research in examining in more detail the following five stages as representative.

- *Scribbling and Drawing Stage.* Just as babbling and cooing infants apparently recognize that the sounds they are hearing are keys to oral communication and attempt to replicate these sounds, however imperfectly, so too do early writers recognize that the marks they see everywhere have something to do with written communication. They begin to try to replicate these marks, however imperfectly, in attempts to join in the communication game. Very early, children will scribble on any surface they can find, and soon they begin to make primitive drawings that attempt to convey meaning through pictures. Both the drawings and the scribbles are often incomprehensible to adults (just like babbling), but children often will be able to tell you what the marks "say".
- *Pre-Phonetic Stage.* Children in this stage are beginning to realize that particular marks on the paper may carry particular meaning. They are, however, very unclear as to exactly how this works. In this stage, children will write random letters on paper and ascribe to them any meaning they desire. For example, a child in this stage may write AMTR and say that this says, "I love you, mommy."

Sidebar 8.1: Key Terms

Conventions: spelling, grammar, punctuation and other skills considered acceptable for correct writing

Cursive: commonly known as handwriting as opposed to the printing used in primary grades

Invented Spelling: spelling that shows sound/letter relationships but is not considered conventionally correct

Portfolio: a collection of a student's actual work samples, often used to document progress in writing

Process Writing: a belief that writing follows many steps from planning to final product

Rubric: a tool that spells out acceptable levels of achievement for an assignment

- *<u>Phonetic Stage.</u>* Children at this stage of writing are beginning to crack the code of written language. In the early part of this stage, a child may write *I lv u m* to mean I love you, mommy. Later the child may write *I luv u mome* to say the same thing. In the first example, it is clear the child is beginning to put sounds and symbols together, but the result still lacks some of the sounds. In the second example, all of the sounds are perfectly represented, though most of the words are still misspelled. The term **invented spelling** is often used to describe the writing of children in the phonetic stage. They spell words, progressively more accurately, as they sound. But since English is quite irregular in its sound/symbol relationships, many spellings are invented rather than conventional.
- *<u>Transitional Stage.</u>* In this stage, children continue to use what they have learned about sound/symbol relationships, but they also begin to use some of the **conventions** of written language. A child in this stage might say "I love you, mommy" by writing *I luv you momy.* This child has kept correct sound/symbol relations, but also demonstrates that she knows the conventional spelling of you and the conventional punctuation that marks the end of a thought.
- *<u>Conventional Stage.</u>* This stage is often what we call correct writing. The words are spelled correctly even if they are phonetically irregular, and grammar and punctuation usage follow the correct conventions of written communication. Handwriting is also considered a convention with students moving from primary printing to **cursive** writing as they progress.

Figure 8.9 is a graphic display of the stages of writing.

Figure 8.9: Stages of Development in Writing

In the vignette at the beginning of this chapter, we saw that Whitney entered kindergarten at the phonetic stage with most of her writing being readable by an adult. By third grade, she had moved to the conventional stage, with most of her writing exhibiting the correct conventions of English. Just as babies do not produce grammatically correct, perfectly articulated utterances when they first begin to speak, so children's written communication also begins with numerous imperfect attempts before they finally become correct writers of the language. No one would consider telling babies to remain silent until they can speak perfectly, and we should also honor young children's developmental attempts as they progress through many stages in learning to write. This is what Whitney's early-grade teachers did while simultaneously helping her to become a conventional writer.

The Writing Process

For many years the term "writing" was considered a noun, a product. Students would turn in their writing, and teachers would judge the product as either adequate or not. Then in the 1980's, the ground-breaking work of Donald Graves (1983) led teachers to begin to think of writing less as a noun and more as a verb, less as a product and more as a process. The term **process writing**, which is widely used today, came from this pioneering work.

The idea behind process writing is that whatever a student writes does not come full-blown and correctly articulated all at once during the first try. Students, unfortunately, often tended to treat writing assignments this way, dashing off ill-conceived and error-ridden essays and turning them in, mostly unread, to teachers. Teachers were then supposed to revise and edit these hurried compositions and notify students through a letter grade whether they were good writers. The idea of process writing shifts the emphasis from this one-shot idea of writing to a multiple-step process, and it also shifts the responsibility for perfecting writing from the teacher to the student.

Here are the steps in the writing process:

- *Prewriting.* Experienced writers spend about 30% of their time in the prewriting stage, planning what they want to say and how best to say it, before they ever begin to actually write. Beginning writers, on the other hand, tend to skip right over this stage, spending almost no time at all planning, rushing instead to put something—anything—onto paper. This lack of advance planning shows in the quality of students' writing products, but students often do not know how to plan their writing and must be taught these skills. Prewriting is technically anything that comes before the first draft. It may include brainstorming techniques, such as the cluster of the apple Mr. Green used in Chapter 5. It might include a quick write in which students get their ideas onto paper haphazardly. It may include information gathering about the topic to be addressed. During this stage, students should be selecting a topic for their writing and coming up with a rudimentary organization for their paper before they ever start to work on a product.
- *Drafting.* As the name implies, this stage does not aim for a final product. Instead, during this stage, the first of perhaps several drafts is put on paper. The idea here is to get all of the student's ideas down without undue worry about perfect organization or mechanics. During this stage, students follow their rudimentary organization, changing it as they see fit as they go along. They might write alternate beginning sentences or try out different outlines for the content. Organization of the writing will differ by genre, so students who are writing a narrative may want to organize by the literary elements of setting, characters and plot while students writing exposition might use a graphic organizer that lists main topics with supporting details.
- *Revising.* This is another stage that beginning writers would like to skip. Beginning writers tend to think whatever they have written is very good—except for maybe a slight error here or there in spelling or punctuation. They want to move directly to these small errors in mechanics, but that is not what the revising stage is about. During this stage, writers look at

their own work in terms of the big picture. Content of the writing is what is important. Writers may ask themselves such questions as:

- ✓ Did I say what I meant to say?
- ✓ Is there anything I left out?
- ✓ Does my organization flow well?
- ✓ Can people understand what I wanted to say?

Writers should ask themselves these questions, but it is often hard to see your own writing clearly. So during the revising stage, it is also helpful to have others look at the writing, too. Writing peers can often serve as mentors to help their friends improve their writing. One method for peer revision has small groups of students meeting to read their compositions out loud and then respond to each other using these three prompts:

- ✓ The thing I liked best about your writing was_______.
- ✓ The most important change I would make is ________.
- ✓ The part I didn't understand was _______.

In addition to peer revising, this stage is also a natural place for teacher/student writing conferences where the same sorts of prompts can direct the changes needed for clarity, completeness and fluidity. The main idea to keep in mind during this stage is that the focus is on the content. All revisions are meant to make the content more understandable and readable. The focus is not on small errors. That comes next.

- *Editing.* Finally, we come to the stage that previously occupied all of the attention of both writer and teacher. The emphasis during this stage is on perfecting the mechanics of the paper. Spelling, punctuation, grammar, usage, and the like are all addressed during this penultimate stage of the writing process. If a piece of writing is to reach the final stage of the writing process, which is publication, then it must undergo strict editing designed to correct any and all errors against convention. Peer and teacher editors are often quite helpful here, as are computer programs which point out misspellings or grammatical errors. Another helpful tool during the editing phase is a checklist reminding students to check for such things as capital letters, punctuation, paragraph use and the spelling of common words. However you help children edit their writing, it is important to remember that the revising stage looks at the big picture of meaning and the editing stage focuses on the tiny details of conventions. Both are important, but editing comes last.
- *Publishing.* The final stage of the writing process is getting student writing out to a wider public. The term, publishing, often has too formal a connotation, though, for what really happens at this stage of the writing process for students. All writers want to be read, but the "publication" of student writing can be much less formal and grand than being published in the *New York Times.* Here are some "publishing" ideas:
  - ✓ *Authors' Chair or Authors' Tea*. Have an Authors' Chair in the classroom which students can take when they have something to share. A more formalized way to do this is to

have an Authors' Tea to which parents or students from other classrooms are invited so that all students can share their writing.

- ✓ *Wall and Hall*. Display students' finished writing products either on the walls of your classroom or in the hallways between classes.
- ✓ *Writing Groups*. Functioning much like adult writing groups, these groups of peers meet regularly to share what they have written.
- ✓ *Classroom or School Literary Magazine*. Students select examples of their best work to be published in a local literary magazine. These publications do not need to be very costly. Spiral binding, the use of notebook rings or stapling can all be used to "bind" the book.
- ✓ *School Publishing Company*. A slightly more elaborate idea is for a school to arrange for students to make a cloth book each year. Once the work is word-processed, students can illustrate their work before it is bound. Parent volunteers can help with the typing and binding. The finished products could be read at an Authors' Tea. One ambitious school that followed this process, also double published the fifth-graders' books each year. These second copies were housed in the school library and well-read by students year after year.
- ✓ *Outside Publishing*. Not all publications of students' writing must remain in-house. There are multiple contests and opportunities for students to truly publish their work either online or in children's magazines. Venues for student publication include www.amazing-kids.org and www.cyberkids.com and www.newmoon.com

Figure 8.10 summarizes the steps in the writing process.

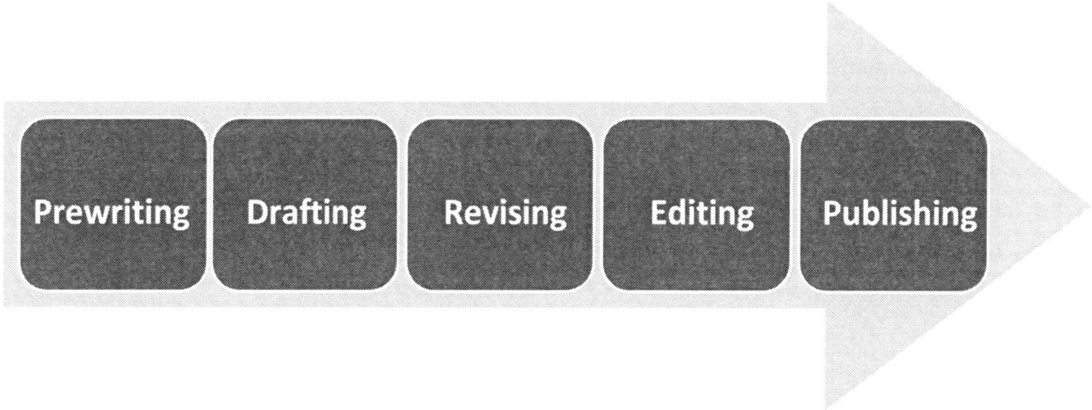

Let's Talk Teaching

When you think about teaching writing, there are really two quite different components to keep in mind as you teach. The first component is the expressive or creative component. This involves the skills that allow children to say what they want to say in concise, creative and comprehensible ways. Most of the stages of the writing process which was described above deal with this component. Helping children select a topic, organize their paper and choose creative wording all deal with the expressive side of writing. And all of these stages should take place at every grade level, though obviously the products will be increasingly complex as students age.

There is another component to writing well, too. That component deals with the mechanics of conventional written language. These mechanical aspects, such as spelling, punctuation, capitalization and penmanship are also important in helping students become good writers. While these aspects are much more detail-driven and less exciting for children to learn, they are extremely important for comprehension. As the recent book, *Eats, Shoots and Leaves* (Truss, 2003) illustrates so clearly, one misplaced comma can change the entire meaning of a sentence.

It will be important then, as we teach writing, that we address both the creative side and the mechanics side of the writing process. Let's look now at three different methods for teaching writing that can each be used to teach both of these aspects in an integrated way. The three methods we will examine are: shared writing, guided writing and the writing workshop. All of these methods are useful at any grade, though the second grade teacher will certainly be focused on different skills than the fifth grade teacher.

Shared Writing

As its name suggests, shared writing is a method in which the teacher and the students share in the task of writing. This method is somewhat like the Think Aloud method discussed previously in that the teacher says out loud what is going on in her head while she takes her students through the complete writing process. Students see the writing process modeled for them in this way. An example of shared writing might go like this:

1. *Prewriting.* The teacher has just finished an author study of children's author, Beverly Cleary. She reads the beginning of *Dear Mr. Henshaw* by Cleary (1983) to her students in which the main character writes to his favorite author. The teacher says she would like the class to write to Mrs. Cleary. Together they brainstorm things they might like to tell this author.
2. *Drafting*. Students dictate sentences they would like to see included in the letter. The teacher writes these on large chart paper for all to see.
3. *Revising*. After the class is satisfied with what they have said in their letter, the teacher models ways in which to improve the organization, tighten the prose, choose more descriptive words, etc. until the letter satisfies everyone. The teacher writes the changes right on the original manuscript, and speaks out loud the thought processes going on in her head as she revises.
4. *Editing*. Now is the time to bring in the mechanics of writing. The teacher Thinks-aloud as she ponders whether a sentence should say, "We would like to meat you" or "We would like to meet you." She considers aloud whether a sentence should end with a period or exclamation point. She might use teachable moments that present themselves here to focus on one or two identified conventions.
5. *Publishing.* The letter is copied neatly and mailed to Beverly Cleary.

After doing a shared writing lesson, it is important to then ask students to use this knowledge in their own writing. After the next author study, for example, students can follow this same procedure to write their own letters to that author.

Guided Writing

In this method, designed by Sharan Gibson (2008/2009), the focus is on giving support and guidance about writing skills AS students are doing their own writing. Here is an explanation of the guided writing process:

1. *Prewriting*. The teacher provides a small group of students with a brief shared experience (perhaps a walk on the playground). Teacher and students talk together about this experience. During this conversation, the teacher helps each student choose one interesting observation he/she made during the experience to write about (perhaps one child found an unusual shiny stone).
2. *Composing, Revising, Editing*. All of these stages happen nearly concurrently. As each student writes about his/her interesting observation, the teacher offers individual comments that support, model and scaffold writing skills (Can you think of another way to say "shiny"?). The emphasis here is on guiding writing as it is happening. Gibson uses a very provocative term to describe this. Instead of offering feedback, she says teachers should offer "feed forward".
3. *Publishing*. Students in the group share their writing with each other, and perhaps with other students who did not have this group's experience.

Writing Workshop

In some ways, the Writing Workshop is more of a philosophical belief than a teaching method. While the Writing Workshop does include distinct teaching steps, its most important feature is that is creates extensive time in the classroom for writing to take place. Much like Sustained Silent Reading respects and encourages students' own reading, the Writing Workshop respects and allows time for a student's own writing. The three main portions of the Writing Workshop are the mini-lesson, workshop time and sharing.

1. *Mini-lesson*. Each Writing Workshop begins with a mini-lesson (Calkins, 1994) in which a very short lesson is given by the teacher on a writing topic. (Look back in Chapter 7 for a sample mini-lesson.) The writing topic may be one the teacher has observed her students are finding difficult. Examples of mini-lessons for writing could include such diverse topics as choosing a good topic sentence, making characters more believable, or the correct use of capital letters. This lesson is focused on the students' writing needs and takes only about ten minutes.
2. *Workshop*. This time is the core of the entire method and the lengthiest portion. Teachers often allot between 30 and 60 minutes each day to workshop time. Work on any part of the writing process may take place during this time. Some students may be brainstorming or composing first drafts. Others may be meeting in peer writing groups or with the teacher to revise and edit their work. Still others may be perfecting a final draft. The keys to this portion are that students have enough time to really make progress in what they are writing, and that they have the support of peers and the teacher as they work through the inevitable writing problems they encounter.
3. *Sharing*. The final stage of the Writing Workshop is the opportunity for students to share what they have been writing. A brief period of perhaps ten minutes each day is set aside so that students who have finished a writing project can share this with peers to receive encouragement and feedback. Writing can also be shared in a more formal way using some of the publishing ideas given earlier in this chapter.

Writing and Assessment

In this section we will talk about two distinct topics relating to writing and assessment. As a teacher you will need to assess the writing your students do, and we will discuss how to do that first. But you can also use your students' writing samples to assess their literacy development, and in the next section we will discuss that. First, let's turn our attention to how to assess all that writing your students are doing.

Assessment *of* Writing

Whether you use shared writing, guided writing, writing workshop or some other method to help your students improve their writing, you will soon have numerous writing products that must somehow be assessed. Of course, it is always wise to attend to your core, state or local standards when deciding what writing skills should be your focus. Beyond these, though, there is always the question of how best to judge student writing for quality, and how best to offer feedback designed to help students improve their writing.

Graves, et al. (2011) list several overarching principles that can guide teachers as they respond to student writing. These guidelines include among others:

- Be positive
- Don't try to respond to every piece of student writing
- Focus your response on only a few matters
- Mostly comment on works-in progress, not finished products
- Deal with content before mechanics
- Make use of peer editing

In addition to these general guidelines, many teachers make use of a **rubric** to judge and give feedback on writing. A rubric is a tool designed to provide a qualitative assessment of a product and then assign a quantitative grade to it. In a rubric, the skills to be assessed are listed along one axis of a chart, and narrative descriptions of what constitutes excellent, good, and poor attainment of these skills are listed under each of these designations for the skills being assessed. For example, one axis of a writing rubric might list such skills as clear content, appropriate organization and correct punctuation. The quality narratives would then delineate the standard to which this paper must attain if it is to be judged excellent, etc. An example of a writing rubric for fifth grade is in Figure 8.10, but writing rubrics can be designed for any grade level. Just change the skills and descriptions of quality to fit the writing objectives in your grade level.

Figure 8.10: Sample Writing Rubric for Fifth Grade

Skills	Excellent	Progressing	Needs Work
Content	*Very clear thesis, well-supported by details *Close focus on topic *Purpose clear to reader	*Thesis & purpose mostly clear *Mostly focused on topic *Thesis mostly supported by details	*Thesis or purpose missing or unclear *Shifting focus
Organization	*Clear, logical progression of ideas to support thesis *Smooth transitions	*Organization mostly easy to follow *Some points may lack support or clarity	*Lack of clear organization *Points do not seem to follow or support each other
Words and Sentences	*Creative choice of words *Smooth sentence structure *Correct use of language	*Some repetition in words or sentence structure, but mostly smooth and correct	*Repetitive choice of words or sentences *Errors in sentence structure
Conventions	*Punctuation, grammar and spelling are all correct	*A few errors in punctuation, grammar or spelling that do not inhibit understanding	*Numerous errors in punctuation, grammar or spelling that inhibit understanding

Assessment *Using* Writing

The preceding section discussed ways to assess writing products in order to give students feedback and help them improve their writing. But there is one more important topic dealing with writing and assessment, and that is how to use a student's writing to learn more about their other literacy skills.

A child's writing is like an open window to his brain, and if we are alert, we can gain a great deal of knowledge about his literacy skills simply by carefully analyzing his writing. As an example, let's look closely at an additional writing sample from Whitney's portfolio. This page was completed in kindergarten just after she returned to school from winter break. Look carefully now at Figure 8.11 before moving on to the list of discoveries that follow it.

Figure 8.11: Writing Sample (I stayed home for Christmas.)

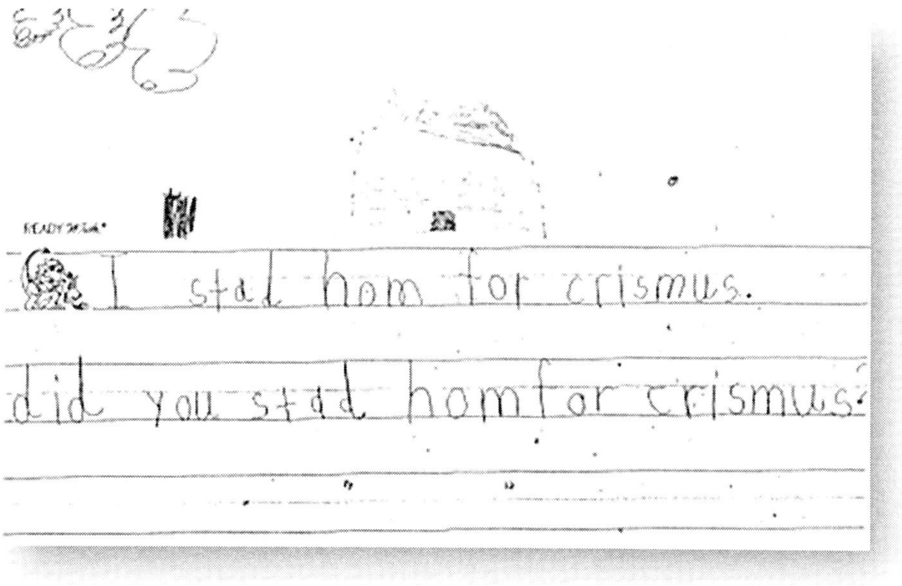
I stad hom for crismus.
did you stad homfor crismus?

STOP here and think before moving on!

Now that you have pondered Figure 8.11, consider for yourself what you now know about Whitney's literacy skills from this brief writing sample.

Did you notice these strengths for Whitney?

- Has excellent sound/symbol relationships; virtually no phonics errors
- Understands that I must be capitalized
- Understands the punctuation marks of period and question mark and their correct use
- Understands some conventions of the language (you) that do not necessarily conform to phonics rules
- Has clear understanding of the concept of a word
- Spaces words appropriately for reader understanding
- Has good enough penmanship for legibility; all letters formed correctly

Perhaps you also noticed the following needs for Whitney:

- Does not know that first letters of sentences (except I) must be capitalized
- Does not know that proper nouns (Christmas) must be capitalized
- Does not appear to be aware of the silent e rule
- Does not know how to spell stay, stayed, home or Christmas
- May have a deviation from standard English syntax (Did you stayed)

All of those strengths and needs are an enormous amount to learn about a child from only two lines of writing. Since it *is* only two lines, some of the needs may prove to be untrue upon further investigation, and luckily, longer writing samples from older students will yield even more information. Yes, writing as a window to the brain, is an easy way for the alert teacher to learn a great deal about a child's literacy needs without resorting to additional testing.

Let's Talk Teaching—Again

Writing, as the fourth quadrant in the modes of communication, is as important to include in the school day as listening, speaking and reading. And remember, research shows that work in any quadrant often improves skills in reading. However, time being what it is in the school day, many teachers find it hard to include writing in an already full schedule. So we will close this chapter with a handful of quick ideas for incorporating writing throughout the school day.

1. <u>Journals</u>. Journaling is perhaps the easiest and most unobtrusive way to get children writing every day. There are virtually no hard and fast rules about journaling. Some teachers have students write in their journals when they arrive each day. Other teachers have students journal as part of literacy time or whenever they have free time. Students often choose whatever they want to write about in their journals, but sometimes teachers will assign a topic as when everyone has been on a field trip or the like. Sometimes journals are private, but sometimes they are read by others. And as evidenced by the page from one of Whitney's journals (Figure 8.3), even very young children can keep and profit from a journal. In addition to a straight-forward journal, there are also lots of subtypes of journals. A *response journal*, for example, asks student to respond to the literature they are reading. And a *double-entry journal* asks students to draw a vertical line down a piece of paper and write quotes from a book on one side and their thoughts about those quotes on the other side. However you do journaling, it is a quick and effective way to incorporate more writing into the school day.
2. <u>Quick Writes</u>. Beginning any lesson with a five minute Quick Write helps students focus their thoughts on the topic at hand, and also lets them access whatever background knowledge they already have about this topic. The method for doing a Quick Write is very simple and can be used for nearly any topic. Tell students, for example, that today they are going to be reading about magnets in science and they should write whatever they want about magnets for five minutes without stopping. Instruct students that they should not stop writing even if they have to repeat something they have already said. Spelling and other conventions are of no importance in this method. After the five minutes, begin the regular lesson knowing that students have already focused themselves on your topic. Quick Writes are particularly useful in the content areas (Science, Social Studies, Math, etc.), and we will talk about them again in Chapter 11.

3. Functional Writing. The main reason we write is to communicate with someone else, so it is fairly easy to include lots of instances of functional writing in any classroom. Examples of functional writing would include a morning message written on the board, a quote for the day on the classroom door, student mailboxes which house notes from peers and the teacher, and bulletin boards focusing on new words. Besides including some or all of these ideas, you can encourage children to "put it in writing" by telling others things they want them to know through written communication rather than oral.
4. Literature Connections. Since reading and writing are reciprocal processes, it is easy and appropriate to connect what students are reading to their writing. For example, the young students in Mrs. Emerson's class in Chapter 2 might write their own never-ending story using the shared writing technique after reading *If You Give a Mouse a Cookie* (Numeroff, 1985). Or older students could use *Jacob Have I Loved* by Katherine Paterson (1990) as a springboard to write their own thoughts on sibling rivalry. Connecting nonfiction or informational reading to writing is particularly fruitful. Students may begin, for example, by reading a biography about sharp-shooter, Annie Oakley, and then progress through the entire writing process to research and write about another influential woman in U. S. history. Literature is also a natural place to find examples of exemplary writing. Pointing out these models of good writing to students, and encouraging them to find their own examples, is a good way to connect literature to writing. A rule of thumb in any reading you ask students to do is to consider how a writing topic or a writing experience can be incorporated into that reading.
5. Writing Center. In order for children to become productive writers, they need time and space to write. They also need something to write about. A Writing Center in your room can provide that space and inspiration. The Center should have lots of different materials for use in writing, such as different types of markers and different colors and sizes of paper. It should have comfortable but productive seating and lighting. Most importantly, it should contain lots of inspiration to help students begin a writing project. Some of this inspiration could include:
    - Provocative pictures from magazines showing people in different situations and displaying different emotions
    - Story starters or story enders
    - Books that use language in interesting ways, such as *A Chocolate Moose for Dinner* by Fred Gwynne (1976)
    - Reference books, such as a dictionary, a thesaurus, and a writer's guide
    - Literary elements spinners in which Who, What, When and Where spinner boards each list interesting literary elements. Students spin each spinner and then write a story using the selected elements.
    - Models of poetry and instructions on various forms

    All of these components can be changed periodically so that a student could always go to the Writing Center for fresh inspiration. Figure 8.12 summarizes these three methods.

Figure 8.12: Summary of Sample Methods for Teaching Writing

Teaching Method	When to Use
Journaling	Every day. Can either be self-chosen by student or teacher-directed
Quick-Write	Brief writing used to brainstorm or collect thoughts. Correct conventions are not important
Functional Writing	Writing used to really communicate with another, such as letters, morning messages, mailbox notes
Literature Connections	Writing done in conjunction with the study of a book. Should be incorporated in every book study
Writing Center	Area devoted to writing. Can be used as one of several centers in a room.

Summing Up...and Moving On

As we complete this section on Developing Readers in this book, let's keep in mind that these students are also developing writers. As they become more comfortably literate, they will increasingly call on their skills in reading and writing, in addition to their skills in listening and speaking, to communicate. This chapter dealt with the stages of writing development, the steps in the writing process, various techniques for teaching writing, and ways in which to assess writing.

Most of your third through fifth grade students are now moving onward to becoming independent readers. Yet it is abundantly clear that students do not all progress in lock-step fashion at the same rate. Before we discuss the skills and needs of independent readers as a group, we will spend some time in the next section of this book considering the needs of individual readers.

Section Four

Individual Readers:

Meeting Diverse Needs

Section Four consists of two chapters:

Chapter 9: Assessment:

How do We Know What to Teach?

And

Chapter 10: Differentiated Instruction:
Treating Students as Individuals

Chapter 9

Assessment: How Do We Know What to Teach?

Nicholas Perez arrived in Mrs. Carpenter's second grade classroom the day after Halloween. All the other children were still excited about the holiday when Nicholas slipped quietly into a new desk hurriedly moved into the back of Mrs. Carpenter's room. Mrs. Carpenter noted that he came with no accompanying school records. Maybe they would catch up with him in time. She assigned Nicholas a buddy to help him through the first few days, and began to plan how to integrate him into her classroom.

Normally, she would have consulted his cumulative record from his old school soon. This record usually told her a student's scores on standardized tests, and their academic progress in kindergarten and first grade, including anecdotal records, or teacher comments, from prior teachers. The cumulative file would also have told her a student's first language and whether there were serious health problems to accommodate. Finally, it would have had notations about prior referrals and testing for special needs. Since this treasure trove of information was unavailable to her, Mrs. Carpenter began to develop her own "Nicholas File" in order to know how to best meet his needs.

The easiest place to start was with a student interview. During this very brief and congenial "Getting to Know You" talk, Mrs. Carpenter found that Nicholas' family had just moved to town after living for several months with his grandparents. The only language anyone spoke in his family as far as he knew was English. In his old school, his reading book had been called *Reading Wonderland* which Mrs. Carpenter knew to be the name of the third grade reader in the basal reading series also used in her school. Nicholas had a dog named Squeaky and a new baby was on the way. He especially missed his grandmother since the move. Mrs. Carpenter followed up on her interview by giving Nicholas a written interest inventory through which she learned, among other things, that Nicholas "read all the time," really liked *Encyclopedia Brown* books, and would read "anything that had to do with weather."

Next, Mrs. Carpenter decided to give Nicholas an informal reading inventory (IRI). Tipped off by the fact that in his previous school he had been placed in the third grade reader and by the knowledge that *Encyclopedia Brown* books were challenging for most second graders, Mrs. Carpenter suspected that Nicholas would be reading above grade level. The results of the informal inventory, though, were astounding. Nicholas' instructional reading level was fifth grade. He did not hit his frustration level until sixth grade, and then was able to continue two more years with good comprehension when Mrs. Carpenter read the passage aloud to him. In doing a miscue analysis of the errors Nicholas made during the informal reading inventory, it was clear that he had strong phonics skills that he used well. He self-monitored continuously for comprehension, and took action when he did not understand what he was reading. Consequently, he was able to answer even some of the more challenging comprehension questions on the inventory. He read fluently and with expression, further demonstrating his understanding. About the only area Mrs. Carpenter found where Nicholas needed work was with the decoding and understanding of some of the more advanced vocabulary words. She also thought it might be helpful to him if he slowed down somewhat in his oral reading.

With many new second graders, Mrs. Carpenter would have given a phonics inventory, but her miscue analysis on the informal reading inventory showed her that phonics skills were not a problem for Nicholas. In the end, she decided to do just one additional test, a cloze procedure, to determine if the second grade science and social studies materials would be suitable for Nicholas. Predictably, even these content area texts were very easy for him to handle.

For now, Mrs. Carpenter placed Nicholas in her highest reading group *(Reading Wonderland),* found a new book on meteorology to give him, and went home pondering the situation. If she were to meet the needs of this exceptional reader, it would take much more than placing him all day in non-challenging materials and hoping for the best. She had enough information from her various assessments to know what Nicholas needed. The hard question now was how would she provide it? Nicholas Perez was turning out to be a challenge —a cute, engaging and articulate challenge—but a challenge just the same.

Assessment: A Help or a Hindrance?

All good teaching begins and ends with assessment. Without accurate knowledge of what a child knows and needs to know, how can a teacher plan appropriate lessons and activities? Indeed, assessment might be called home base in any reading lesson because the teacher will need to keep returning to assessment in order to teach well. Figure 9.1 is a visual image of assessment's role in the teaching process.

Figure 9.1: Assessment Baseball

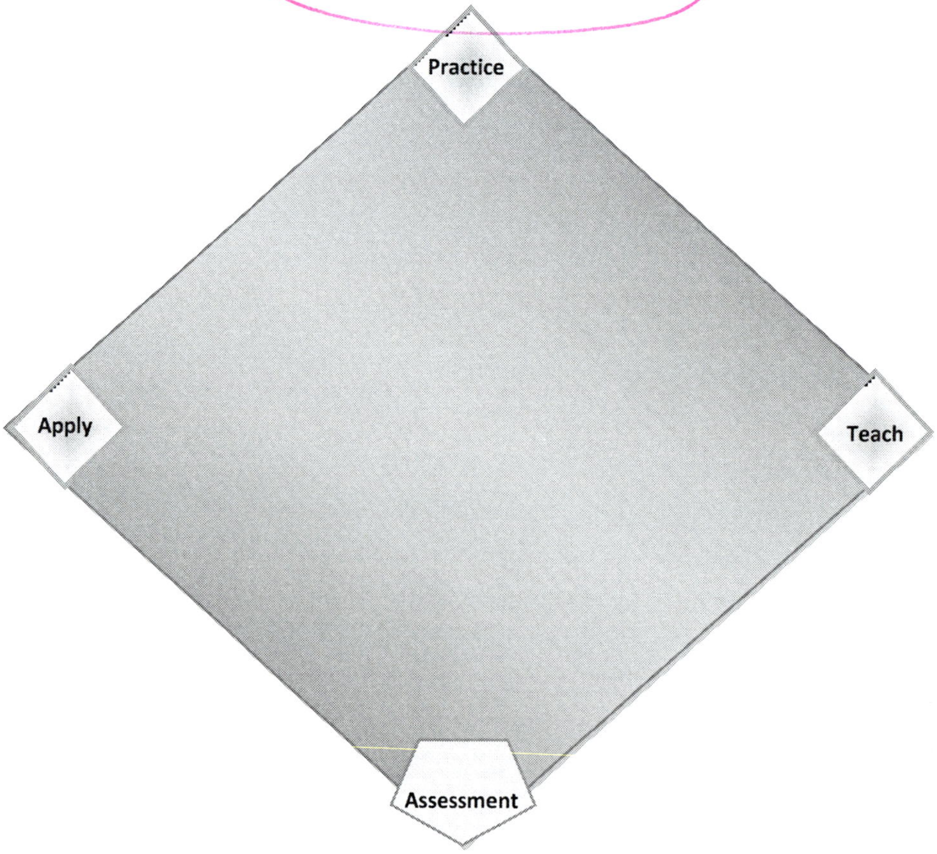

To neglect to begin or end a lesson with assessment means you may end up wandering around and around the wrong diamond. Without assessment, for example, Mrs. Carpenter may have placed Nicholas in the second grade reader and worked with him on word families as the rest of that group was doing. This would have been inappropriate instruction for Nicholas.

Mariotti and Homan define assessment as "the ongoing systematic collection of information on students (2010, p. 1). Using this definition, it is clear that assessment is integral to high-quality teaching. This collecting of information cannot be skipped. Both before and after (and sometimes during!) any teaching, it will be important for the teacher to assess what the students know and need to know in order to proceed efficiently.

One of the ways we decide what students should know is by establishing the goals and objectives we hope students meet. The current emphasis on standards, benchmarks, common core, and the like is just putting different terminology on the idea of establishing goals for students. Once a standard (goal) is established, it makes good educational sense to find out whether that standard has been met. Knowing where you are going is essential to actually getting there, so the establishment and assessment of goals (standards, benchmarks, or objectives) is a positive step. The problem comes in when assessment becomes more important than instruction and actually begins to take the place of good teaching. Green (2002) has termed this "accountability run amok."

In today's school environment, it does seem that assessment has run amok. With the job security of teachers and principals resting on successful year-end test scores showing adequate yearly progress (AYP), and children as young as eight years old threatened with retention if they do poorly on their achievement tests, it is no wonder emphasis on assessment has gotten woefully out of balance. Samuel Johnson was reported to have once said, "The prospect of hanging concentrates the mind wonderfully."

This is just what has happened in schools with all constituencies focused on successful test completion. Instructional time is being used for "bubbling" practice or other test-preparation activities, for example. And the curriculum is being narrowed or "cannibalized" (Kohn, 2001), with subjects like science and social studies not being taught because they are not on the test. The popular children's book, *Testing Miss Malarkey* (Finchler, 2000) illustrates the level of anguish this over-emphasis on testing has produced for everyone concerned when the author says underneath a humorous picture of the nurse's station, "That morning there were more teachers than kids waiting for the nurse."

It is clear, then, that assessment can be misused and abused. Yet it is too important a component of good instruction to discard out of hand. Let's discuss a few guidelines that might help us to keep assessment in perspective and use it for the good of students.

Principles of Good Assessment

- *Avoid high-stakes testing.* A high-stakes test is one in which something very important is decided on the basis of that one test. For example, a year-end achievement test that decides whether a child will be retained in grade is a high-stakes test. The fields of education and psychology are united in stressing that nothing of real importance should ever be decided on the basis of one test, and many of the current abuses of assessment could be mitigated by adhering to just this one principle.
- *Use a variety of assessments.* This goes along with and extends the first principle. While you will not be depending on one test to make decisions, it also does not make sense to just keep giving the same type of assessment over and over. Objective tests, writing samples, interviews, observations, and authentic reading tasks would give a teacher a broader, more accurate, picture of a student's needs than the results of five similar multiple choice tests.
- *Keep assessment and instruction connected but not confused.* As Jonathan Kozol pointed out (2001), it does not make a sheep any fatter to weigh it over and over. Today's testing climate means teachers waste many days weighing their students instead of feeding them. To avoid this, nearly all assessment activities should be for the purpose of planning appropriate instruction. Assessment should function as home base (Figure 9.1) in an overall lesson plan or it is taking time that could have been better spent on teaching. The International Reading Association states this succinctly in their Standards for Reading Professionals (2010) www.reading.org. Their third standard states, "Candidates use a variety of assessment tools and practices to plan and evaluate effective reading and writing instruction." Figure 9.2 summarizes how assessments can be effectively used or abused.

Figure 9.2: Uses and Abuses of Assessment

Abuses of Assessments	Better Uses of Assessments
Using one test to determine something very important (high-stakes tests)	Using multiple tests to guide instruction or report progress, and making no life-altering decisions based upon one test
Using only one type of test to make decisions	Using multiple types of both informal and formal tests to gain a complete picture of student's needs
Focusing mostly on summative assessments	Using mostly ongoing formative assessment in order to guide instruction. Summative testing is mostly only useful for reporting progress,
Focusing on test-taking skills like bubbling or multiple-choice formatting	Focusing on authentic, valuable learning goals, such as competence in reading or mathematics

One Size Fits Nobody: Different Assessments for Different Needs

Adhering to the three principles listed above should help teachers avoid contributing to the worst of the assessment abuses occurring today. This will allow assessment to take its rightful place in the classroom for informed instruction. Different needs in the school day and school year will call for different assessments useful for various needs. The main levels of assessment include the following phases:

- *Screening.* Screening tests are those assessments given to a large group of students in order to determine which students may be at-risk for failure. These assessments, because they are given to large groups, must be relatively quick and easy to administer. For this reason, they are not as illuminating as more individualized diagnostic tests, but they do give a teacher generalized knowledge about all students' skills. For example, Mrs. Carpenter, in the opening vignette, always administers a phonics screening test to all her students at the beginning of the school year. This tells her quickly which of her second graders still need instruction in phonics.
- *Diagnosing.* Diagnostic tests are generally only given to those students who puzzle the teacher for one reason or another. Diagnostic measures are much more time-intensive because they are usually given individually, but they yield much more specific information about a particular child's needs. An example of a diagnostic tool is the Informal Reading Inventory (IRI) that Mrs. Carpenter gave to Nicholas in the opening vignette. Diagnostic tests guide a teacher in providing appropriate instruction for a child, and any child who needs special handling for any reason will benefit from diagnostic assessment.
- *Monitoring.* As instruction takes place, it will be important for a teacher to constantly monitor whether students are learning the concepts being taught. There are numerous informal ways to do this, such as *Kidwatching* while the lesson is in progress, or giving a quick survey at the end of the lesson. Monitoring assessment is the quick and repeated return to assessment home base to be sure students are learning the concepts being taught.
- *Evaluating.* This testing usually comes at the end of a unit of study, a semester or perhaps a whole year. Evaluative tests sum up the progress a student has made and often assign a grade of some sort to it. For example, the end-of-year achievement tests given to students in the United States assign grade-level designations or percentiles to students in order to judge whether these students have made adequate progress during the year.

Figure 9.3 summarizes the four types of assessments we have just discussed.

Figure 9.3: Types of Assessments

Type	Who	When	What	Why
Screening	All	Beginning of year or whenever needed	Quick group test to determine skill levels	Establish At-Risk; Determine skills
Diagnosing	Students who puzzle the teacher	Whenever student is identified	Individual and intensive	Establish strengths and needs
Monitoring	All	Regularly as instruction continues	Curriculum-based tests	Plan effective instruction
Evaluating	All	At the conclusion of teaching	Curriculum-based tests or standardized exams	Determine progress or grade

Types of Tests for Different Goals

Two terms which are routinely used to describe the purposes of all these various types of tests are formative assessment and summative assessment. It will be important to understand the differences, and this is quite easy to do if you examine the roots of each word.

Formative Assessment

In formative assessment, the root is form. These tests are used to inform a teacher's instruction. They are used in the formation of lesson plans, and in the formation of students. Formative assessments come periodically during instruction, and are used to help both teacher and student plan next steps. The first three types of assessments listed above, screening, diagnosing and monitoring, are usually formative tests in that they are used to inform instruction rather than assign a grade.

Summative Assessment

In summative assessment, the root is sum. Just like a sum in addition, summative evaluation produces a summation, an ending evaluation, a grade. The last type of assessment above, evaluating, is generally a summative evaluation. It comes at the end, and rather than informing further instruction, it summarizes a student's progress. This summary often takes the form of a numerical or letter grade or a grade-level designation.

Both formative and summative evaluations are valuable when used appropriately. Yet, it will be very important to discern your purpose when you choose a test. If your purpose is to plan appropriate instruction, then formative assessments should be used. If, however, your purpose is to communicate progress to someone (student, parent, government), then a summative assessment is well-suited for this.

Beyond these four types of assessments (screening, diagnosing, monitoring and evaluating), and the two general purposes (formative and summative), there are two other assessment terms it is important to know: formal assessment and informal assessment. Please do not confuse these with formative assessment, which is easy to do! In order to remember this new distinction, it might be helpful to keep in mind the difference in dress required at a formal (black-tie) affair and an informal party. Let's look at both types of assessment a bit more carefully beginning with formal assessment.

Formal Assessment

Formal assessment refers to the standardized tests so prevalent in schools today. Just as the dress is rather tightly regulated at a black-tie, formal affair, formal assessments are also tightly prescribed. Formal assessments are written and validated by experts in test design, and are usually multiple choice examinations meant to be scored by computer. These assessments are developed with great rigor, and they have tightly controlled administrative constraints. While they are not very useful for the day-to-day diagnostic instruction teachers do, they can serve as a summative evaluation of a student's progress. Unfortunately, today they are often misused as high-stakes tests which can lead to the abuses mentioned earlier in this chapter. It is important, though, to understand the basic terms and concepts relating to these formal assessments, and the correct ways to use them. Let's look first at the difference between norm-referenced and criterion-referenced examinations.

Norm-Referenced Tests

A norm-referenced test is one that has been given to a large norming population in order to establish what the average score is for that group. This results in the well-known bell curve in which the 50th percentile is considered average and half of all students fall above and below this line. Figure 9.4 is a visual of the bell curve.

Sidebar 9.1: General Assessment Terms

Formative Assessment: tests given by teachers for the purpose of informing instruction

Summative Assessment: tests given at the end of learning in order to assign a grade or other evaluation

Formal Assessment: rigorously standardized tests given under tightly controlled conditions

Informal Assessment: tests that have not been rigorously standardized and depend on teacher knowledge and skill

Norm-Referenced: tests based upon the average scores of a norming population. Placement on the bell curve results in students being seen as above or below the "norm".

Criterion-Referenced: tests based upon a set of criteria such as objectives or standards. Students either meet or do not meet the established criterion

Validity: whether a test measures what it says it measures

Reliability: whether a test performs consistently time after time

Figure 9.4: The Bell Curve

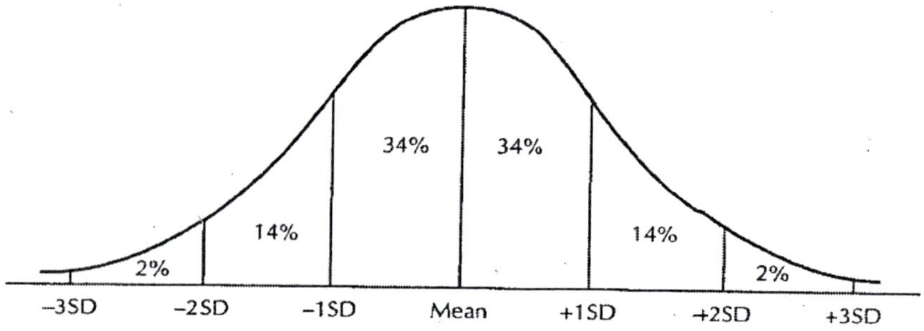

In a norm-referenced test, a student's individual scores are compared to those of the norming population, and these scores are then expressed in several ways. They can be given as percentile scores with students at the 50th percentile being average and students at the 90th percentile being far above average, for example. They can be expressed as stanines, which divide the scores into nine equal parts making 5 the average score. Or they might be expressed in grade level equivalents. A fifth grader scoring 3.4 (third grade, fourth month) is obviously below average, while one scoring 7.2 (seventh grade, second month) is above.

No matter how these scores are reported, it is important to remember that they are based on only ONE multiple choice test and are much less revealing than individualized assessments. Using the fifth grade student above who achieved a 3.4 grade level equivalency as an example, we do not know from this number what specific skills that student knows or needs to know about reading, and we have no inkling as to why the student is so far behind.

Criterion-Referenced Tests

The other type of standardized test is the criterion-referenced test. These are also rigorously designed and controlled, but instead of looking at norming populations, these tests are based on set criteria. These criteria are usually curricular goals for which a mastery rate is set. If a child fails to achieve this rate, they fail this criterion. For example, a criterion for first grade could be that students know the sounds of all long vowels. A student who cannot do this does not meet this standard.

Criterion-referenced tests are somewhat better in providing diagnostic data to a teacher because these tests speak specifically to what skills a student knows and needs. Critics of these tests remind us, though, that mastery of discrete reading skills does not always lead to good reading. In other words, a child may know all the sounds of the long vowels, but still be unable to apply that knowledge in an authentic reading situation.

Two final terms are important to understand in order to use standardized test results wisely. These terms are validity and reliability. **Validity** means that the test actually measures what it says it measures. The example just given above illustrates this point. That criterion-referenced test might very validly measure knowledge of long vowels. However, this does not necessarily make it a valid measure of reading ability which is much more than phonetic knowledge.

Reliability means that the test measures whatever it purports to measure over and over consistently. Results do not swing wildly from one test administration to the next. Test designers will provide voluminous data on the validity and reliability of their tests. However, teachers much always ask themselves how valid and reliable this test is for their own students. If the norming population differed widely from the teacher's student population, for example, the results may not be valid or reliable in this instance.

Standardized, formal testing has its place in the assessment program of schools, yet in today's "accountability run amok" climate, it is being seriously abused. The clutching onto a one-test number to compare students, teachers and schools is an abuse. The use of these tests to establish the "value-added" by a particular teacher or school is a use for which these tests were not designed. Using time on "bubbling practice" instead of instruction in reading defeats the entire purpose of these or any assessments. Teachers must think very critically about these tests and be as careful as they are able in sheltering their students from the worst of their abuses. Keep in mind the three principles of assessment with which we began this chapter to guide you. Now let's turn our attention to *Informal Assessment.*

Informal Assessment

Informal assessment does not mean the testing takes place while lounging in your pajamas, drinking tea and listening to soft music, though come to think of it, all of these would add appeal to any testing! And informal assessment does not mean poorly organized or unsystematic testing. Think back to the analogy of the black-tie affair and the informal party in which the dress at the black-tie affair is strictly regulated while the dress for the informal party is much more flexible. Just so, informal assessment refers to all of those ways of assessing students that, in direct contrast to formal assessments, have not been so rigorously standardized. In addition, informal assessments have less prescribed administration procedures than formal assessments, and they depend more on teacher judgment and training. In thinking about informal assessment, do not think about the school-administered end-of-year achievement tests. Instead, think of the myriad ways throughout the year that a teacher determines what her students need. These might range from simple observation techniques to more highly refined tests like an Informal Reading Inventory. Let's look at a few of these informal techniques.

Informal Reading Inventory (IRI)

This general, all-purpose test is perhaps the best assessment available for giving a teacher detailed information about a student's reading skills. There are numerous commercial IRI's available, such as *Analytical Reading Inventory* by Woods and Moe (2011), *Classroom Reading Inventory* by Silvaroli and Wheelock (2004), and *Informal Reading Inventory* by Roe and Burns (2012). Alternatively, it is possible for a teacher to design her own IRI. All of the commercial IRI's differ slightly, but they usually have in common word lists and short reading passages at various reading levels, and comprehension questions at various levels of difficulty. Some of the IRI's also include instructions for doing fluency checks and retellings.

The IRI is given individually, which makes it a wonderful diagnostic tool, but very time-consuming as a general screening instrument. To administer an IRI, the teacher first asks the student to read from the graded word lists in order to get a general idea of where to begin with the student in the graded passages. Once beginning the reading passages, the student reads the passage out loud while the teacher makes note of any miscues (errors in reading) the student makes. After the student finishes reading, the teacher asks the comprehension questions, or sometimes asks for a retelling. Errors in comprehension are also noted to be analyzed later. The student can also be asked to read the passages silently which will not, of course, reveal oral miscues, but can still be useful for analyzing comprehension skills.

By counting the oral reading miscues and the comprehension errors, the teacher will establish three reading levels for the student. These levels are usually determined as follows:

Reading Level	**Word Recognition**	**Comprehension**
Independent	99% or higher	90% or higher
Instructional	95%	75%
Frustration	90% or lower	50% or lower

The *independent* reading level is that level at which a student can read during recreational reading, or any other time when he will not have someone helping him. This level is helpful in guiding a student's book choices in the library. The *instructional* level is the level at which a student can be successful with guidance from the teacher. This is the level at which a student should generally be placed during any part of the school day involving instruction with the teacher, such as during small group reading time, or social studies lessons. The *frustration* level is just what it sounds like. At this level, a student will be too frustrated to learn, so this level should be conscientiously avoided by the teacher for this student.

In addition to revealing the reading levels for a student, the **miscue analysis** that the teacher does on the oral reading miscues a student makes during the IRI will reveal patterns in how well a student applies their reading skills in actual reading. While the student is reading, the teacher quickly makes notations about the miscues made. In order to efficiently record miscues, teachers generally use a shorthand code similar to the one shown in Figure 9.4.

Figure 9.4: Sample Miscue Scoring Guide

Type of Miscue	Code	Text Said	Student Said
Omission	Circle omitted word	John ran home quickly.	John ran home.
Substitution	Write in substitution	The horse ran. [house]	The *house* ran.
Addition	Write in addition	The car was big. [very]	The car was *very* big.
Repetition	Underline repeated words	*Jane was* worried.	*Jane was—Jane was* worried.
Reversal	Draw wavy line around reversed letters/words	The snow lay on the ground.	The snow lay *no* the ground.
Hesitation - Fluency	Draw slash mark at hesitation	The dog was/vicious.	The dog was...*vicious*.
Self-Correction	Write SC after error	Jim went home. [want SC]	Jim *want—went* home.
Teacher Pronounced	Write TP over word	Janet waited patiently. [TP]	Janet waited_____.

After the miscues are noted, the teacher analyzes the miscues in several ways. First, she looks to see whether the miscue is graphophonically similar. Substituting the word *house* for *horse* in the example above is a very graphophonically similar substitution. Next, the teacher asks whether the miscue is syntactically reasonable. In other words, does it work grammatically? In the same substitution of *house* for *horse*, both words are nouns, and so syntactically they are compatible. Finally, the teacher asks if the miscue is semantically accurate. In other words, does it make sense? In this area, substituting *house* for *horse* is a grievous error indeed because it makes the sentence nonsensical. Since the student did not go back and correct this miscue, we must assume he is not self-monitoring for meaning.

In this miscue analysis, the teacher is looking for patterns, and she is especially worried about meaning-changing miscues. However, one miscue does not a pattern make! Even in the substitution of *house* for *horse*, if the student did not make this type of error again, we might assign it to haste or inattention and not worry unduly about it. However, a meaning-changing miscue like this, if repeated several times, tells the teacher something about the student's comprehension skills.

Information from the miscue analysis is corroborated and enlarged by the answers the student gives on the comprehension questions. These answers are also analyzed for patterns as much as possible. For example, the teacher might notice the student consistently answers lower level questions based upon facts well, but struggles with higher level questions calling for critical thinking. In addition, the teacher looks at both the miscue analysis and the comprehension answers together. The student who is able to sound out most words and has few miscues but does not understand what he is reading, for example, has different needs than the student who makes many small errors but comprehends well.

The IRI, then, gives the teacher independent, instructional and frustration reading levels. It establishes comprehension strengths and weaknesses. And, through the miscue analysis, it demonstrates what word attack skills a student knows and uses. As an all-purpose, diagnostic assessment, it is hard to beat. Its one drawback is that it is time-consuming. Teachers who would like a similar, but more quickly administered assessment should also investigate the **Running Record** designed by Marie Clay (1985) which uses a simplified technique to match children to texts and analyze miscues.

Inventories, Surveys, Conferences and Interviews

All of these techniques are informal ways of simply asking students for the information you want. These can be done in writing or orally. They can be individual, small group, or whole class. For example, students might take a written reading interest inventory to help the teacher suggest appropriate books, or form interest groups. Or a student might meet individually with the teacher to discuss the book he is currently reading. Or a teacher might survey a small group about their reading habits. While there are some published interest inventories and reading surveys available, most teachers design these instruments on their own to meet their specific classroom needs.

Cloze Procedure

In this procedure the teacher selects a 100-300 word passage from a grade-level textbook or story that the students have not yet read. She retypes the passage leaving the first and last line intact but leaving out every fifth word in the rest of the passage. Students fill in these blanks. To count as correct, the exact word must be used—not a synonym or other acceptable word.

To get a score, the teacher divides the number of correct responses by the number of blanks. For a student scoring above 57% the material is at an Independent level. Students scoring between 44 and 57% are at Instructional level. And students scoring below 44% are at Frustration level (Bormuth, 1968). This informal method is especially useful for determining whether a student will be able to

Sidebar 9.2: Types of Informal Assessments

Cloze Procedure: an assessment tool that omits every fifth word in a passage to check for comprehension

Curriculum-Based Tests: Tests designed to measure specific curricular skills

Informal Reading Inventory (IRI): an individually administered test involving graded passages and comprehension questions. Determines reading levels and literacy strengths and weaknesses

Inventories and Surveys: written or oral questionnaire designed to reveal reading interests or attitudes about reading

Miscue Analysis: analysis of a student's oral reading errors in order to determine strengths and weaknesses in student's reading skills

Observation: watching of literacy events by an astute teacher in order to determine student needs. Sometimes called Kidwatching

Portfolio: a collection of a student's written work. Reflection on this work shows literacy progress and needs

Running Record: a simplified method for recording student miscues in reading. Similar to an IRI in some ways read grade-level textbooks in content areas like social studies and science. The method assesses comprehension skills by focusing on context clues, syntax and semantics. Figure 9.5 shows a sample Cloze passage.

Figure 9.5: Sample Cloze Passage

Not many people get an entire period of history named after them, and yet that is exactly what happened to Queen Elizabeth I of England. The nearly 45 years _______her reign have been _______ the Elizabethan Age. This_______ true not just in _______, but in many other _______, as well. We in _______ United States also refer _______ the years between 1558 _______1603 as the Elizabethan _______. Since Elizabeth was so _______ to the making of _____ England we cannot really _______much about how life _______ then until we know _______ about her. By all _______she was a remarkable _______complex woman who had _______talents but also many _______. All this probably started _______she was a very _______ child. Let's get to know her now.

Scoring: To receive credit, a student must insert these exact words. The words that go into the blanks in order are: *of, termed, is, England, countries, the, to, and, Period, important, Elizabethan, know, was, more, accounts, and, many, flaws, when, little.*

Since there are 20 blanks in this 100 word passage (5 points each), the approximate reading levels are as follows:

Independent Level:	12 or more correct answers
Instructional Reading Level:	9-11 correct answers
Frustration Reading Level:	8 or fewer correct answers.

Curriculum-Based Tests

Since there are so many discrete skills in reading, it is a very common practice to use teacher-made curriculum-based assessments for these skills. For example, a teacher who has been teaching the sounds of initial consonants will devise a test (oral or written; individual or group) to assess whether students now know the sounds of the initial consonants. Textbooks also often come with informal skills tests designed to test the curriculum contained in the text. Many specific skills tests have been published, though, and a few are widely enough used to deserve mention here. These are:

The Concepts About Print test designed by Marie Clay (1993) assesses a student's knowledge of print concepts as title, author, front of the book, top of the page, directionality and the concept of a word. These skills are all necessary for emergent readers.

The Yopp-Singer Phonemic Awareness test (Yopp, 1995) assesses whether a student can hear the sounds that make up a word. Skills such as blending, segmentation, and rhyming are assessed by the Yopp-Singer. These skills have also been proven to be necessary for emergent readers.

The Dynamic Indicators of Basic Early Literacy Skills (DIBELS) test battery provides very short assessments in such areas as alphabet knowledge, phonological knowledge and fluency. These tests can be accessed on the DIBELS website http://dibels.uoregon.edu/. Their use is free.

Observation

Perhaps the most ubiquitous type of informal assessment is astute observation by a trained teacher. Sometimes called **kidwatching** (Goodman, 1978), this technique simply means the teacher knows what she is looking for and takes pains to observe it. Simple though it might sound, there are several aspects of kidwatching that make it much more complex than it sounds. First, the teacher must actually know what she needs to see and be able to recognize it. This assumes a fully-trained, intelligent teacher who understands both her curriculum and her students. Second, the teacher must be systematic in her observations making sure that she observes all children on a rotational basis and observes the specific skills she hopes to see. Finally, she must be intentional and systematic in recording these observations. This might be done on an index card for each child, on sticky notes placed on a class roster or in a variety of other ways. It is important, though, that astute observations are not forgotten, and that they eventually make it into an organized record of the student.

Portfolios

A portfolio is simply a collection of student work samples organized in such a way as to show progress. Whitney's writing portfolio, discussed in the vignette of Chapter 8, is an example of such a document. There are two features of portfolios to keep in mind, though, to prevent them from becoming mere scrapbooks.

First, the portfolio is not a dumping ground for any and all work a student does. Both teacher and student must be very selective in what they choose to include in the portfolio. Establishing goals in the beginning will help to guide this selection process.

Second, reflection is the key to a useful portfolio. Dropping a work sample into a folder and never thinking of it again until it is sent home is not a portfolio. To qualify as a portfolio, both teacher and student must reflect on the entries. Why is a particular artifact included? What does it demonstrate? How is progress evident through this artifact? This reflection can sometimes be oral, but at least sometimes there should be written reflection on the artifacts in the portfolio. The teacher's reflection is valuable, but the student's self-reflection on his own work is more valuable still.

Once you have met these two requirements of selectivity and reflection, the portfolio can be organized in many ways. Folders, accordion-style containers and notebooks can all be used effectively. Many schools are now moving to the use of electronic portfolios. How students store and organize their portfolios is less important than actually using the portfolios to guide teaching and enhance learning. Their real values are in using authentic reading and writing work samples to document, explain, and direct student progress.

Both informal and formal assessments will be necessary features of any classroom. And it is clear that a teacher will need to be selective and thoughtful in choosing when and why to use different assessments. The Let's Talk Teaching section which comes next will give you some help with this.

Let's Talk Teaching: Playing Assessment Baseball

Go back to Figure 9.1 at the beginning of this chapter now, and recall the place of assessment in the teaching process. In this figure, we used the metaphor of a baseball diamond and referred to assessment as home base. In order to teach reading well, the teacher must begin and end with assessment, and this chapter has given you many ideas for techniques to use in assessing students. That is appropriate for a chapter on assessment, however, if you stand continuously on home base, you won't score any runs.

The whole point of home base is to leave it and run to the other bases. In Figure 9.1, those bases are labeled *Teach, Practice* and *Apply*. It will be important to remember that the point of assessment is to decide what should be taught and then do it. Reutzel and Cooter (2012, p. 449) refer to this as IF-THEN Thinking. In other words, IF a student knows or needs to know________, THEN I am going to teach them ___________. Finding out what a student needs without taking this next step defeats the entire purpose of assessment and turns it into a time-wasting exercise. Whenever you have taken the time to give any sort of assessment, you must then use these results to teach, practice and apply whatever those results indicated the student needed.

So let's return briefly to Mrs. Carpenter's quandary with Nicholas in the vignette that began this chapter. Listed on the next page is the information Mrs. Carpenter now knows about Nicholas. Use your teacher brain to consider what Mrs. Carpenter should do now to meet Nicholas' needs in reading.

What Mrs. Carpenter Knows	What Mrs. Carpenter Should Do
Nicholas reads significantly above grade level.	
Nicholas can handle above grade level content area text.	
Nicholas needs help with reading and understanding advanced vocabulary.	
Nicholas likes Encyclopedia Brown books.	
Nicholas has an interest in meteorology.	
Nicholas misses his grandmother.	

Summing Up

This chapter dealt with the values, types and terms of assessment. We began with specific assessment principles that will help you avoid the abuses of testing. Then we discussed formative and summative testing and the uses of each. Both formal and informal assessments are valuable, and we discussed the strengths and weaknesses of each type. We talked about the terms of formal testing like norm-referenced, criterion-referenced, validity and reliability. And we looked at several informal assessments, such as the IRI, miscue analysis, kidwatching and the cloze procedure. The metaphor of assessment baseball demonstrated how assessment should be used to direct classroom instruction. In Chapter 10, we will use all of this information about assessment to consider how to meet the special needs of your students in the regular reading classroom.

Chapter 10

Differentiating Instruction: Treating Students as Individuals

It is mid-July, and Miss Starkey has begun to plan reading instruction for her new fourth graders. This will be Miss Starkey's very first year as a teacher, and she wants to do a really good job. But as she bends over the cumulative folders of the 27 children who have been assigned to her classroom, a rising feeling of worry and dismay invades her cheerful enthusiasm. She had thought when she got this job as a fourth-grade teacher, that most of her students would be quite similar. She had lots of ideas for teaching units and word-study activities geared toward fourth grade abilities and curriculum. Yet looking at the records of her students, it was becoming clear that the only attribute these children had in common was their general chronological age. And nowhere was this diversity more apparent than in their literacy needs.

First, there was the awesome range of reading abilities. According to the test scores in the folders, some students in Miss Starkey's class were virtually nonreaders, while others read at the seventh grade level. It appeared that nearly 30% of the students in her new class were reading below grade level. Some of these students had been identified as having special needs and were receiving special services. But despite very low reading scores, several of her new students had never been diagnosed as having special needs, and their instruction would fall completely to her. The same would be true for the students reading significantly above grade level. Since the gifted program in her school had been discontinued several years ago due to lack of funding, Miss Starkey knew the instruction of these very able readers would also fall completely to her.

Second, compounding and complicating the range of reading abilities was the fact that many of Miss Starkey's students were English language learners. The cumulative folders listed Spanish as the language spoken at home for four Hispanic students, and two Asian students listed Hmong as their first language. Miss Starkey might be able to remember a smattering of her high school Spanish, but she had never even heard of Hmong before. Further, it was impossible to tell from these cumulative folders just how far along these students had progressed in learning English. Just as the reading abilities of this group were diverse, Miss Starkey suspected their language abilities would also differ widely.

Looking about her at the stacks of cumulative folders and test results, Miss Starkey had the slowly dawning realization that this information was only the tip of the iceberg. These written materials could report such information as reading level, special education diagnosis and first language, but they said nothing about the various specific skills of students, or their interests or their motivation levels. All of these would, no doubt, be as diverse as the information she already had, and they would all make a difference in Miss Starkey's reading instruction. And despite all this diversity in her incoming class, Miss Starkey knew that national and local guidelines insisted that all of her students MUST leave fourth grade reading at grade level.

As the full impact of all this settled onto Miss Starkey's thin shoulders, she slowly lowered her head in despair to the stack of papers on her desk. She remained there for several minutes, breathing quietly and waiting for inspiration. Suddenly she knew exactly what she should do. She lifted her head defiantly and went out for ice cream.

Differentiation—Meeting the Literacy Needs of All Students

Let's begin this chapter with a very obvious statement: children differ from one another. This statement is so obvious that most people would never even think about it. It is apparent to everyone that some children are boys and some are girls. Some children are tall, stocky and have red hair, while other children are short, slim and have brown hair. Beyond these easily observable physical differences, we also routinely recognize emotional, social and maturity differences in children. Some children are talkative, active and have difficulty tying their shoes, while other children have wonderful fine motor skills but cry easily at the slightest provocation.

For some reason, we have no trouble acknowledging these very real physical, social and emotional differences in children, but we are slow to apply this same clear vision to cognitive differences. No one, for example, would advocate that all fourth graders must be 4'2" (the average height of nine year olds in the United States) by the end of 4th grade, but many people would advocate that all nine year olds must be reading at the 4.9 reading level (somewhat arbitrary designation of fourth grade, ninth month) before leaving fourth grade. Further, people who would not think of treating all fourth graders as if they are 4'2" (making taller children stoop and shorter ones jump, for example) often do just this sort of thing in the cognitive realm by expecting all children to profit from identical lessons.

Let us go back to our original obvious statement: children differ from one another. And nowhere is this truer than in the area of learning to read. While the entire beginning of this textbook dealt with the general teaching of reading skills as if all children learn these skills in roughly the same way in roughly the same amount of time, real children quickly show us that this will never be the case. Knowledge about general philosophies and methodologies of literacy instruction must now be applied to individual student needs. Good teaching is differentiated teaching. Building upon the information about assessment we acquired in Chapter 9, let's consider now how to use that assessment data to provide **differentiated instruction**. While there are many areas of literacy, like learning styles and reading preferences, which will enter into your literacy instruction, in this chapter we will especially consider the two areas of reading levels and English language skills.

Reading Levels

The rule of thumb for range of reading levels in any classroom is that students will differ in reading levels by roughly twice whatever grade level you teach. For example, if you teach third grade, there will be a six year range (3x2) of reading levels in your students. Miss Starkey's class in the opening vignette roughly conformed to this because as a fourth grade teacher she had students who were virtually nonreaders (4 minus 4), and a student reading at seventh grade level (almost 4 plus 4), leaving her with a nearly 8 year (4x2) range in her classroom.

In an average classroom, many children will read at or near grade level. While these grade-level readers will have numerous different reading needs in say phonics skills, comprehension levels or reading motivation, they will at least all be able to profit fairly well from grade level materials. But what of the readers on the edges of the range? For the challenged readers (those reading significantly below grade level) and for the gifted readers (those reading significantly above) grade level materials and instruction will fail ever more to meet their needs the farther these students are from the mean. Let's take a closer look at our challenged readers.

Challenged Readers

There are many reasons why children may find learning to read difficult. Some of these reasons could be physical. For example, visually impaired and hearing impaired students will need different instruction in reading in order to work around their physical impediments. Some of the reasons students are challenged may be due to emotional or behavioral disabilities, such as attention deficit disorders that make it hard for the students to concentrate. Cognitive ability may also be a reason, with cognitively delayed students progressing more slowly than their age-mates. Finally, there is the vast, complex area of learning disability which includes diagnosed disabilities such as dyslexia, but also extends to conditions for which diagnosis is elusive, but the student's reading ability is nevertheless impaired.

It is quite likely that a single teacher will have students in every one of these categories among her challenged readers. To further complicate matters, some of these students will be receiving services from a variety of special education professionals, but other students in this group will be receiving no special services at all. A short side trip into the alphabet soup of special education law might be helpful here.

In 1975, the United States Congress passed PL 94-142 (Education for All Handicapped Children Act) to address the educational needs of exceptional children in public schools. From this legislation, several philosophical ideas became part of public acceptance in how children with exceptionalities should be educated. The idea of **least restrictive environment** became the norm for placing exceptional students in the free and appropriate education to which they were entitled. This law also instituted the idea of the **individualized education plan (IEP)** to guide teachers in their instruction of exceptional learners, and it called for a team approach to meeting the needs of these students with parents, classroom teachers, administrators, and special educators all having a role.

In 1997, Congress passed the Individuals with Disabilities Education Act (IDEA) which re-affirmed and broadened the scope of PL 94-142. Subsequently, this law was re-authorized in 2004 as the Individuals with Disabilities Education Improvement Act (IDEIA). All three of these laws further interacted with NCLB (No Child Left Behind, 2001) legislation. The intent of all these laws was to

Sidebar 10.1: General Differentiation Terms

Acceleration: Moving through curriculum at a faster rate.

Differentiated Instruction: Instruction designed around the individual needs of students.

Enrichment: Teaching curriculum topics with more depth or breadth than usual.

Individualized Education Plan (IEP): Plan for the successful education of a special needs student.

Least Restrictive Environment (LRE): Placement of special needs students in the environment as close to the regular classroom environment in which they can be successful.

Response to Intervention (RTI): a system of tiered instruction designed to prevent student failure.

protect and well-educate students with special needs. The effect of the laws, however, tended to be increasingly standardized and rigid instruction not based upon individual needs. This was especially apparent in the murky area of learning disabilities.

Since many of these learning disabilities were difficult to diagnose, struggling readers were required to follow a deficit model. In this model, these students would only be entitled to special services when they had fallen at least two years behind grade level. Most people can readily see the inadvisability of requiring a child to fail for at least two years before providing any special assistance. And, indeed Juel's (1988) research showed that struggling readers in first grade would still be struggling readers in fourth grade if no action was taken to help them. Luckily, IDEA and IDEIA contained provisions to allow for additional flexibility in meeting special needs. These eventually led to RTI or Response to Intervention. Let's look at this differentiation scheme more closely.

Response to Intervention (RTI) is a philosophical approach to meeting special needs that contends that differentiated instruction should not rest on a student's continuing failure. Instead, RTI focuses on early intervention at the first sign of reading trouble. RTI is firmly based in the regular classroom and on regular assessment activities within that classroom.

Look back now in Chapter 9 at Figure 9.2 which depicts the different levels of assessment. Of these different levels of assessment, screening, diagnosing, monitoring and evaluating, RTI makes use of the first three. Early screening assessments identify students who may be at risk for reading difficulties and diagnostic assessments further illuminate where these difficulties may lie. On the basis of these early assessments, students are placed in one of four tiers for instruction.

Tier One is the good classroom instruction provided normally for all students by the regular classroom teacher. All students in the classroom will benefit from Tier One instruction which may be whole group at times, but will also include small group and individualized differentiated instruction. For most students, Tier One instruction will be adequate for their success in reading.

For those students who do not meet with success in Tier One, though, Tier Two provides additional small group instruction. This normally takes place in the regular classroom and may be given by the classroom teacher or by a reading or special education teacher.

Students for whom Tier Two instruction proves inadequate move to Tier Three with even more time provided for reading instruction in even smaller groups. This instruction is usually provided by a specialist in reading or special education.

Finally, the student who fails to thrive in Tier Three can be placed in Tier Four which is generally a pull-out special education program. At every level of instruction, ongoing progress-monitoring assessment guides teachers in how well a particular student is responding to the level of intervention being offered. Figure 10.1 summarizes the four tiers of RTI.

Figure 10.1: RTI Triangle

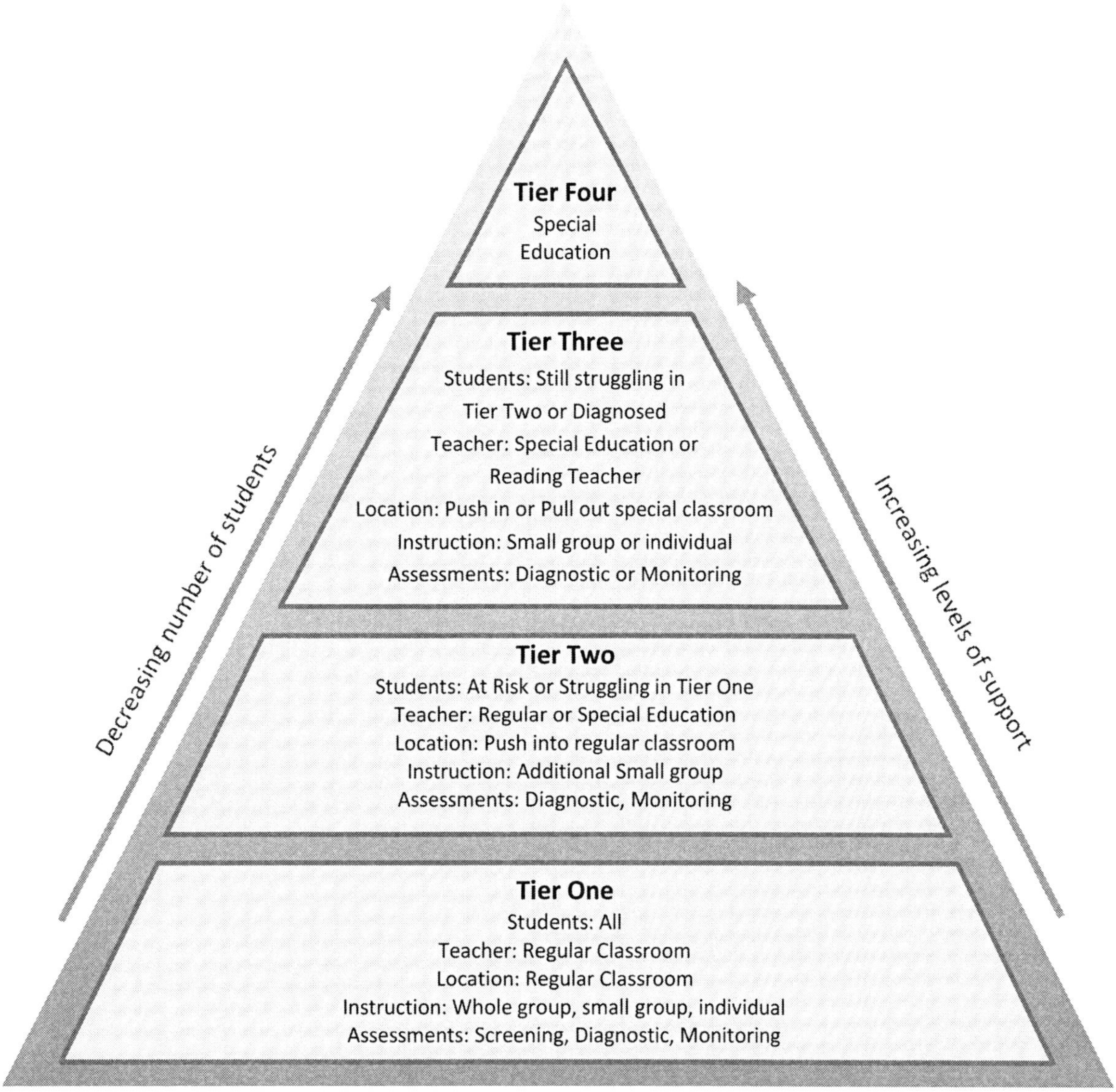

Response to Intervention has several advantages over traditional methods of addressing special needs in literacy. The first advantage is the one already mentioned of not relying on the prolonged student failure of the deficit model before intervening. RTI also has the advantage of focusing nearly all of its efforts in the regular classroom so that students remain part of this classroom and do not suffer the isolation sometimes inherent in pull-out programs.

Finally, the regular classroom teacher in RTI is the first-response teacher, and her instruction must be sound, research-based methodology incorporating differentiation. This focus on improving regular classroom instruction while providing the needed support from reading specialists or special education teachers means that not just challenged readers, but all readers can benefit from RTI. This brings us to the topic of readers who are not struggling, those gifted students reading significantly above grade level.

Gifted Readers

Theoretically, students reading significantly above grade level are also included in all the previously discussed legislation as students with special needs. In practice, though, due to differences in state definitions of giftedness, gifted students are often provided with minimal and sporadic special services. Friend (2008) found that on average only 12% of gifted students are being served in the United States. Yet students reading three years above grade level are just as inadequately served by grade level materials and tasks as those reading three years below grade level. Just as with the challenged readers, the farther from the mean the gifted reader is, the more imperative differentiated instruction will be. Unlike the needs of challenged readers though, meeting the needs of gifted readers will fall almost exclusively to the regular classroom teacher.

Definitions of gifted learners cite such characteristics as advanced vocabularies, general knowledge and reading levels, the ability to complete tasks quickly and independently, and advanced complexity in thought. Renzulli and Reis (2003) use the three criteria of above-average ability, high motivation, and high creativity to define giftedness.

Gifted students also tend to work very hard at any task which does not bore them. Because grade level materials and learning may fall far short of challenging these students, undifferentiated instruction for them may mean they not only do not reach their literacy potential, but also they may become progressively less motivated to learn. It will be just as important, then, for you to address the special needs of your gifted students as you do those reading below grade level. Research has focused on two main ways to accommodate the special needs of gifted readers in the regular classroom. These two ways are acceleration and enrichment.

Because one of the characteristics of gifted readers is that they learn more quickly and effortlessly, a common way to meet the needs of gifted readers is to move them along more quickly than other students in the class. Feldhusen, Van Winkle and Ehle (1996) considered **acceleration**, or curriculum compacting as it is sometimes called, to just be appropriate instruction for gifted students. Since these students learn quickly, it is a fairly easy task to compact the curriculum they must learn letting them move forward through grade level and above content at a faster rate than the other students. This increase in pace of learning will then free up time for additional learning beyond the core curriculum. This quite naturally will lead to the need for enrichment.

Another way to meet the needs of gifted readers is to offer them an enriched curriculum (Renzulli & Reis, 2003). This can be done either with or without acceleration. Since gifted readers are more capable of complex, independent and creative thinking, just speeding up the general curriculum may not provide for their need for greater depth. **Enrichment** programs generally challenge gifted learners to go beyond the understanding demanded of average students.

One easy way to include this sort of challenge in any lesson is to ask gifted students to work on questions dealing with the higher levels of cognition in Bloom's taxonomy that we discussed in Chapter 7. Another common way to enrich the regular curriculum is to encourage gifted students to complete independent projects dealing in more depth with grade level topics.

Whether you decide to do acceleration, enrichment or a combination of both there is one undeniable fact which must be addressed for gifted readers. That is: grade level materials will be mostly inappropriate. These readers, like all others, must be placed for most of the day in books at their instructional levels. This means you must assess the reading levels of these students and then find materials that match these levels just like you will for your challenged readers. Miss Starkey's fourth grader who is reading at the seventh grade level will not benefit from staying in unchallenging grade level materials all day, and Nicholas (in Chapter 9) cannot stay in *Reading Wonderland* very long if he is to thrive.

English Language Learners

Schools in the United States have always needed to find ways to accommodate students who were just learning to speak English. Our immigrant population came from a variety of non-English speaking countries, and our Native American inhabitants spoke many different native languages. Followed far enough into the past, most of our ancestors were once **English language learners (ELL)**, and teachers have always needed to somehow work around this.

While *how* to teach English language learners (ELL) is an age-old issue for schools in the United States, the importance of this dilemma has increased dramatically in recent years. This is due to the tremendous increase, in only the past two decades or so, of numbers of students who speak English as a second language. For example, according to Goldenberg (2012) in 1990, only about 5% of students did not speak English well enough to fully participate in school, but today that figure is nearing 10%.

While Border States like California have always had high numbers of English language learners, states not generally concerned about second language, like Georgia, have sometimes seen an increase of more than 400% in their English language learner student population between 1994 and 2004. Almost three-quarters of these English language learners speak Spanish as a first language (Kamil & Bernhardt, 2004), but the rest of these English language learners may speak one of perhaps 400 other languages now found in the population of the United States.

To further complicate matters for teachers, their English language learners may be more different from each other than alike. Not only may they speak different first languages, but their facility with that home language and with English may vary widely. A child who has been in the United States for several years will have made gains in learning English that a newly immigrated child will not. And a student who has had excellent academic opportunities in his home country and who is fully literate in his home language will be able to transfer those skills to English more quickly and easily than a student who is not so well-educated in a first language.

Many reasons may explain why ELL students differ so widely, but suffice to say they are not going to all be alike. Miss Starkey in our opening vignette is coming to that realization though she does not have enough information to act yet. At least she is aware that four of her students speak Spanish and two speak Hmong at home, and that she will need to accommodate these students in her literacy instruction.

Acquiring a New Language

In order to begin thinking about English as a second language, it would be wise to remember what you learned in Chapter 3 about language acquisition. Go back now to Figure 3.1 (The Blessing Chart). This figure displays the four modes of language and their relationship to each other. Young students acquire a second (or third!) language in much the same way as they acquired their first one. When these children first began to learn a language, they concentrated on the oral portions of The Blessing Chart. This was done in a reciprocal way through listening and speaking with others in day-to-day activities. And not only was the emphasis on oral rather than written language at first, this beginning language learning was focused on concrete vocabulary and the making of meaning. Grammatical learning was de-emphasized in favor of comprehension. Additionally, the grown-ups with these children modified their own speech, using fewer words and shorter, less complex sentences for example, in order to help new language learners understand.

All of this knowledge about how a first language is acquired can be applied to the acquisition of any subsequent languages, so bring to mind again now any toddler you may have watched as they learned English. Their listening skills developed first, and they could understand much more than they could say. Their first attempts at expressive language were telescoped bits of speech riddled with errors. And it was years later, when their oral language was quite firmly developed, that someone began to teach them to read and write. Then their written language went through the same error-ridden stages as their oral language had done before they began to be literate individuals.

We naturally allow many years for this developmental process to be completed for first language acquisition in young children, and research has shown that second language acquisition will also be a lengthy developmental process. Cummins (2001) identified two levels of language learning in this process. The first

Sidebar 10.2: English Language Learner Terms

Affective Filter: The mechanism in the human brain that forces a person to concentrate on survival when threatened

Basic Interpersonal Communication Skills (BICS): Enough facility with a language to engage in routine social interactions

Cognitive Academic Linguistic Proficiency (CALP): Facility with a language needed to go beyond routine social interactions

Comprehensible Input: Receptive language (oral or written) that is understandable to the receiver

English Language Learner (ELL): Student whose first language is not English. ELL's can be at radically different stages of development.

Language Acquisition: The natural development of a language that happens mostly without instruction

Scaffolding: Technique of providing strong teacher support for learning when students are beginners with a gradual release of responsibility to students as they gain competence. Sheltered English and Specially Designed Academic Instruction in English (SDAIE) are two examples.

Transfer: the idea that knowledge or skills already held in one language are more easily learned in a new language level, **Basic Interpersonal Communication Skills (BICS)** takes students about two years to acquire. With this level of language facility, these students will be able to get by in most daily social interactions. These students may sound fairly fluent in English, but may be struggling in grade level work. This is because Cummins' second language level, **Cognitive Academic Linguistic Proficiency (CALP)** is necessary in order to succeed in anything more complex than a daily social situation. CALP can take a further five years to develop in students. Again, imagine that toddler who can communicate their daily needs fairly well, but would not yet be able to discuss democracy or understand what the teacher wants done when she says, "Define the following."

As students move through this developmental continuum to gaining a second language, they will naturally be at different stages along the way. These stages have been labeled by linguists as the *preproduction stage*, the *early production stage,* the *speech emergent stage,* the *intermediate fluency stage* and the *fluent stage.* Naturally, students at different levels will need different instruction. For example, students in the preproduction and early production stages will say very little but will be active listeners. Their teacher will need to shorten and simplify her speech and use many gestures to communicate. Students at the intermediate fluency stage, though, will talk much more and be able to discuss classroom topics well, but may still need additional help to do written assignments. These variations in student needs are why Miss Starkey must find out much more about the skills her English language learners possess before she can hope to provide appropriate differentiated instruction for them. Figure 10.2 summarizes these stages of language acquisition.

Figure 10.2: Stages of Language Acquisition

Stage	**Student Attributes**	**Teacher Accommodations**
Preproduction	Attentive listening; almost no speaking	Teacher does all the speaking using short, simplified speech with many gestures
Early Production	Uses one word or telescoped concrete speech; Understands more than says	Teacher still does most of the talking; Speech is concrete
Speech Emergent	More extended and complex speech; May combine both languages	Teacher accepts errors and combinations of language
Intermediate Fluency	Able to get by socially and in most classroom situations	Teacher especially continues to support student during abstract assignments
Fluent	Approaching native speaker abilities	Teacher makes use of student's particular gift of two languages

First Language/Second Language Connections

Up until now you have been thinking about second language learners regardless of age, as preschoolers going through the stages of language acquisition that normally happen during the first five to seven years of life. That is not quite the whole story. While research shows that a second language is acquired in much the same way as a first, these second language learners are not starting from scratch in language learning as a toddler would. English language learners already know at least one other language, and the research is very strong that literacy in a first language transfers to literacy in a second language (August & Shanahan, 2006; Genesee, et al., 2006). In other words, once a student knows how to read in one language, they do not have to learn to read again. They only have to transfer their literacy knowledge to a new language.

This idea of **transfer** is explained by Cummins (1981) by using the analogy of the iceberg. Cummins calls the large part of the iceberg that lies hidden under the water Common Underlying Proficiency (CUP). If this base is broad and strong, then many tips of the iceberg can extend from it, one in the first language (L1) and others in any subsequently learned languages (L2, L3). No matter how many new languages (tips of the iceberg) are learned, the base of the iceberg (CUP) does not have to be reformed.

This has obvious applications to classroom instruction for English language learners. For if Miss Starkey's ELL students have had the advantage of excellent schooling in their first language so that they are literate in that language, and have a broad knowledge base (CUP), she can expect them to transfer those skills quite readily to English. If, however, her English language learners have had limited educational opportunities and are not yet literate in their first language, there is no literacy skill to transfer and her task will be much harder.

The research about the importance of literacy in the first language is so strong that Goldenberg (2012), in a synthesis of many research articles states unequivocally, "Teaching students to read in the first language promotes higher levels of reading achievement in *English*" (p. 137, italics in original). While we can readily see the practical problems of this (Miss Starkey does not speak or read Hmong), it is still the research-based standard to which we must aspire in our second language teaching.

Some Basic Principles for Effective Teaching of ELL's

While it might be the ideal to teach second language learners to read first in their own language, this is often not possible in the practical world of public schools. Both teachers and schools are often completely unequipped to deliver any sort of instruction in any language other than English. Yet there are intermediate steps that classroom teachers can take to help their English language learners succeed. Let's look at five guiding principles.

- Provide an accepting, non-threatening climate in your classroom. Krashen (1982) has talked about the concept of the **affective filter**. This filter is a mechanism in the brain designed to help humans survive when under threat. Because of this filter, if a student feels threatened he will not learn efficiently. In a high-anxiety classroom environment, for example, the affective filter of students is raised and this means that all thoughts except those involving survival are filtered out. If English language learners (and all other students!) are to be able to think about language learning, the affective filter must be lowered. This is done by making the classroom and instruction as low anxiety as possible.
- Remember that good teaching is good teaching. Numerous authors (Graves et al., 2011; Robinson et al., 2012; Genesee et al., 2006) stressed that a teacher skilled in teaching literacy to

English speakers can use the same good teaching skills while instructing English language learners. General teaching techniques like clear goals, explicit instruction in skills, clear sequencing of instruction and effective use of assessment are as important for English language learners as they are for other students.

- Keep your focus on comprehension. Krashen's (1982) term **comprehensible input** explains what should be the clear focus of any English language learner's instruction. Rather than worry unduly about grammar, spelling, error-correction, and the like, focus instead on helping English language learners understand what is happening in the classroom. Graves (2006) suggested that one way to emphasize comprehensible input is to focus on vocabulary instruction. This vocabulary work should begin with oral understanding before proceeding to written vocabulary work.
- Accept that English language learners will need some modifications in their instruction if they are to be successful. August and Shanahan (2006) stressed that the older the student the more modifications they may need because of the increased complexity of the upper grade curriculum. **Scaffolding, Sheltered English** and **SDAIE** are different terms to explain how to provide this differentiated instruction. Here are a few specific tips:

    - Give extra time and extra practice for English language learners.
    - Assign a buddy to help English language learners navigate through their day.
    - Use the student's first language whenever possible, and point out similarities and differences in phonology or syntax between the languages.
    - Use gestures and graphic organizers to help with comprehension.
    - Adjust your own speech by slowing down and using simpler sentence structures.
    - Use English reading materials at the appropriate instructional level for English language learners and use books in their first language as possible.
    - Above all, have respect for the task these English language learners have undertaken. The vast majority of teachers in the United States today are monolingual. These young students are undertaking something most of their teachers have never achieved.

It is quite likely that the English language learners in any classroom will have very different needs from each other and will fall at various reading levels. As such, they may be either challenged or gifted readers as well as having special language learning needs. Chart B (below) summarizes some of the many educational acronyms you will find in this field. In the next section of this chapter we will consider ways to differentiate instruction for all students.

Chart B: Handy Educational Acronyms

Acronym	English
PL 94-142	Public Law 94-142 (Education for All Handicapped Children Act)
IDEA	Individuals with Disabilities Act
NCLB	No Child Left Behind
LRE	Least Restrictive Environment
IEP	Individualized Education Plan
RTI	Response to Intervention
ELL	English Language Learner
BICS	Basic Interpersonal Communication Skills
CALP	Cognitive Academic Linguistic Proficiency
CUP	Common Underlying Proficiency
SDAIE	Specially Designed Academic Instruction in English

Let's Talk Teaching: Differentiation in the Regular Classroom

Keep in mind that good teaching is differentiated teaching. Instruction cannot be a one-size-fits-all affair because children come in a wide variety of literacy "sizes". Regardless of whether a school is following the RTI model, regardless of whether a child is a challenged reader or a gifted one, and regardless of whether a teacher teaches first grade or fifth, good teaching must be differentiated in order to meet the literacy needs of every student. Since this is such an important concept, numerous researchers have endeavored to discover what effective intervention looks like. Here are a few of their findings:

- Effective Interventions: take place in small groups or in individualized settings (Graves, et al., 2011; Cooper et al., 2012). In RTI, the groups of students get smaller as the needs of students become more pronounced. General classroom teachers should be sure to incorporate flexible small groups in their reading instruction. These groups should be formed and reformed on the basis of assessment information.
- Effective Interventions: make use of explicit skills instruction which includes well-planned, reasonably sequenced lessons (Kame'enui, et al., 2001; Cooper et al., 2012). Kame'enui's team also mentioned the need for accessing the student's schema and providing for review. Cooper's team added the use of leveled texts to insure sequencing of lessons for difficulty.
- Effective Interventions: integrate the use of various reading strategies through the use of authentic reading and writing tasks (Kame'enui, et al., 2001; Strickland, 1994/1995). While small group activities may begin with explicit skills instruction of somewhat isolated reading skills, it should not stop there. Effective differentiated instruction includes lots of opportunity and support for the reading and writing of connected text.

- Effective Interventions: are delivered by fully trained and skillful teachers (Snow et al., 2005; Cooper et al., 2012). Even the best methods of differentiation are unlikely to be successful if delivered in an inept way. Teachers must be knowledgeable of reading skills and the sequence of these skills. They must have ready reference to different methods for teaching these skills. And they must know how to assess their students' literacy needs and match these with appropriate instruction. Needless to say, the interventions most likely to succeed rest on the shoulders of this highly qualified professional.

Assuming the classroom teacher *is* this highly qualified individual, the question now becomes a practical one of how best to organize the school day in order to provide for differentiated literacy instruction. There are many ways to do this. Beck (2001) recommended using student learning styles as a way to organize differentiation. The Teacher Keys Effectiveness System (Barge, 2012) differentiated instruction by content, process and product. And Graves, Juel, Graves and Dewitz (2011) recommended considering differentiation in terms of time, texts and tasks. Since this 3T format is easy to remember, let's consider what it might look like to implement.

- *Time.* Challenged readers will need more direct instruction time from their teacher, and this time will need to be spent on more explicit skills instruction. Gifted readers will not need as much time with the teacher, but they will need extended time to work on more complex tasks, such as research reports. English language learners will almost certainly need additional time to read texts written in English. Adjusting just the time provided for different tasks based upon the different needs of students is a good beginning toward differentiated instruction.
- *Texts.* Many reading programs provide leveled-readers in the form of little books to read along with the core reader. Additionally, websites like the Foutas and Pinnell leveled books website (www.FandPLeveledBooks.com) provide approximate reading grade levels for a variety of children's trade books. Matching students to appropriate texts, then, is a relatively easy task. Using an assessment tool like the IRI which was discussed in Chapter 9, the teacher can determine the levels at which the student can read independently and with instruction. Guiding students in their recreational reading to books at their independent reading level, and placing students in small groups at their instructional reading level then become reasonable tasks for the teacher. And differentiating just the student's texts in this way means that a student performs all day with challenging but not frustrating materials. Obviously, text differentiation works well for below and above grade level readers as well as English language learners.
- *Tasks.* Reading is a set of small, fairly easy tasks that somehow, almost magically, finally combine into the large and complex act of drawing meaning from the printed page. The skills of reading are well-known, and the sequence of teaching these skills is fairly well-accepted. Likewise, the strategies for using these skills in an integrated way are well-established. It is a straightforward task, then, for the knowledgeable teacher to know which skills and strategies to teach her students. Since not all students will be in the same place

along the sequence of learning these skills and strategies, the tasks the teacher will assign to various students will necessarily be different. For example, some challenged readers may still be working on rudimentary phonics skills in their flexible reading groups. Yet gifted readers (like Nicholas in the vignette of Chapter 9) may need to work not on phonics skills needed to decode simple words but on the morphological skills necessary to attack unknown big words like tricycle, triangle and tricornered. And English language learners may be able to answer similar comprehension questions to other students, but may need to do this orally rather than in written form.

While thinking about instruction in terms of time, texts, and tasks is a reasonable way to go about differentiation, teachers also find lots of other ways to accomplish this. Regardless of how you organize your classroom for literacy instruction, though, the tasks can seem daunting with so many student needs and so many district requirements. Some days it will feel as if you are managing a three-ring (or more!) circus instead of a classroom. In order to make organization of your classroom for differentiated instruction a little less overwhelming, now think in terms of the various groupings available to you and the types of tasks best suited to each grouping.

- *Whole Class.* Part of your day will surely be spent in whole class instruction. A good rule of thumb is that anything all (or almost all) of your students need to know should be taught to the whole class at once. There is no need to break into smaller groups unless you are doing different teaching with these groups. The types of activities that lend themselves to whole group instruction are such things as shared reading, introduction of a new unit, teaching of a skill most children do not know, or generalized assessment activities.
- *Small Groups.* Another part of your day should include small groups. These groups should mostly be flexible in that students can move in and out of a group as their needs dictate. Small groups are extremely useful for differentiated instruction in which several students have similar learning needs. During small group time, students might read in leveled texts or work with a teacher on specific reading skills.
- *Individual Work.* Finally, every literacy classroom schedule must include ample time for students to practice and apply their newly-gained skills in reading. Sometimes this is done through the use of reading centers. Such centers as the listening center, the vocabulary center and the writing center can contain organized activities for practicing these various skills. Sometimes this practice work is done through specific activities selected and assigned as seatwork by the teacher to be completed individually by the student. Most importantly, this practice and application portion of your schedule must contain extended time for students to read and write connected texts. Authentic reading and writing tasks should make up the bulk of this individual work time.

There are countless ways to organize all of this into a cohesive classroom day, but to simplify matters for you somewhat, figure 10.2 displays one way you might organize your literacy classroom for differentiated instruction.

Figure 10.2: Miss. Starkey's 4th Grade Core Reading Groups

Student Level	Above Grade Level	On Grade Level	Below Grade Level
Whole Class	Mini-lesson on finding details in story. Introduction of new unit using shared reading.	Mini-lesson on finding details in story. Introduction of new unit using shared reading.	Mini -lesson on finding details in story. Introduction of new unit using shared reading.
Small Group	Text level—4.5 New vocabulary words using morphology skills. Silent reading of text and discussion with teacher focusing on critical comprehension. Assignment connecting social studies with reading. Two students reading above this core group may be able to work together at times	Text level—4.0 New vocabulary words focusing on prefixes. Read silently then orally Discuss in sections with teacher. Begin written assignment together on literal and inferential comprehension.	Text level—3.5 New vocabulary words focusing on decoding skills. Partner, echo and shared reading of story twice. Begin worksheet on decoding skill together. Students reading below this core group may sometimes be able to be grouped together
Individual	Spend time in technology center doing research for project. Work on writing assignment with peer. Sustained Silent Reading and Journal Writing.	Complete comprehension assignment. Spend time in writing center working on graphic organizer of story. Sustained Silent Reading and Journal Writing.	Complete worksheet. Spend time in the listening center reading along with story. Sustained Silent Reading and Journal Writing.

Rescuing Miss Starkey

While this chapter has not been able to examine all the many ways in which children's literacy needs may differ, such as learning styles, reading preferences and motivation, it has addressed two of the most difficult problems literacy teachers face: widely differing reading levels and the difficulty of teaching reading in English to non-English speakers. As it happens, these are the two areas most worrying to Miss Starkey in our opening vignette. Assuming that Miss Starkey does not intend to spend the rest of her life eating ice cream, she is going to need to figure out a way to address the different literacy needs in her classroom. Let's return to that opening vignette now and try to be helpful to Miss Starkey by giving her a plan of action.

Step One. *Assess.* While it appears to Miss Starkey that she has a dizzying array of information about her students, she really does not have the specific information she needs to efficiently plan instruction. The first thing she should do is review the information in Chapter 9 about assessment and plan how she will find out what her students really need. She will probably do a few screening tests for everyone, may decide to do an IRI on a few of the students, and may refer for further testing the one or two students who appear to have been overlooked for special services. She will need to be especially pointed in testing her English language learners to see how far along they have progressed in becoming bilingual and biliterate.

Step Two. *Form flexible groups.* From the information she already has and the information she will get from her additional assessments, Miss Starkey will be able to form her small groups. While these will change over time, for now she has clusters of students reading at the 3.5 level, the 4.0 level and the 4.5 level. These can form three core groups. Two additional students reading at sixth and seventh grade levels can possibly work together. Four students reading significantly below grade level will form an additional group and receive both regular classroom reading instruction and additional resource time through RTI with the reading specialist. The English language learners appear to be able to fit well into these various groups, though Miss Starkey suspects she will occasionally need to meet with some of these students about specific literacy skills they are lacking.

Step Three. *Plan the texts and tasks for each group.* From her assessments, Miss Starkey knows that two of the groups still need work on word attack skills, though they will be placed in two different leveled-readers. She knows her grade-level groups need work on syllabication, and affixes, and she plans to teach these skills using materials at somewhat different difficulty levels. Finally, with her gifted readers, Miss Starkey develops a list of interesting trade books having to do with the state history they will study this year in social studies. She plans to give these students an in-depth research and writing project using these books. Through all of these groups, Miss Starkey will need to constantly monitor and scaffold the special reading comprehension needs of her English language learners in each group.

Step Four. All this is looking a little more possible for Miss Starkey, but just in case it might be wise for her to keep ice cream in her freezer!

Summing Up and Moving On

In this chapter we considered all the ways students may differ from one another, especially focusing on differences in reading levels and in English language skills. We had a very short introduction to special education legislation and RTI which led into a discussion of how to differentiate instruction for students reading below or above grade level. Then we considered ways to effectively teach English language learners. Finally, we looked at numerous ways in which to organize your classroom for differentiated instruction.

Chapter 10 concludes this section of the book on meeting the individual needs of readers. In Section Five, we move on to thinking about how to help students continue to develop in reading by using other content areas and by becoming lifelong readers.

Section Five

Independent Readers:

Literacy as a Life Skill

Section Five consists of two chapters:

Chapter 11: Intermediate Readers:
Helping Students Read in the Content Areas

And

Chapter 12: Making Lifelong Readers

Chapter 11

Intermediate Readers: Helping your Students Read in the Content Areas

Ms. Morgan teaches fifth grade in a school where all of the fifth grades are departmentalized. Ms. Morgan teaches only social studies to three different groups of fifth graders throughout the day. Today she is beginning a unit on immigration with all of her groups, but she has actually been laying the groundwork for this unit for several weeks as she read aloud the book, *Esperanza Rising*, by Pam Munoz Ryan (2000) to her students each day. In this story, Esperanza is a Mexican girl who immigrates to California after her father dies. Ms. Morgan plans to refer back to Esperanza often during this unit.

To begin her lesson, Ms. Morgan knows the importance of introducing the vocabulary words her students will need to understand their textbook. She introduces words like immigrant, citizen, allegiance, integration and prejudice first by using a vocabulary worksheet that asks her students to state whether they have heard each word and whether they already know the meaning. She then places each word into the context of a short sentence, and she and the class discuss each word using the students' prediction worksheets as a guide. Together they decide on short definitions for these words which will later be copied into each student's social studies notebook.

After this careful vocabulary work, Ms. Morgan wants to awaken any background knowledge students already have. She does this in two ways. First, she refers students back to Esperanza. Together they make two lists about Esperanza's immigration experiences. The first list contains the problems or issues Esperanza and her family faced as immigrants. The second lists Esperanza's feelings as she faced these problems. Finally, Ms. Morgan asks her students to do a five minute quick write about a time when they had gone somewhere new and how they felt about that experience.

With vocabulary taught and schema accessed, Ms. Morgan now asks her students to open their social studies textbooks to the new chapter on immigration. They take a quick text walk through the chapter noting headings, looking at pictures and reading the summary at the end. Next, Ms. Morgan leads her students through the text section by section, asking them to change each heading into a question and then read to find the answer to that question. She is careful to include higher level questions calling for interpretation and critical thinking as she guides the discussion through the chapter. During this chapter discussion, Ms. Morgan slowly relinquishes control of the discussion to the students as they gain more skill in posing and answering their own questions. When they begin to work on the end-of-chapter questions together, it is clear that most students have understood the content of the chapter.

After this carefully guided reading of the chapter, Ms. Morgan wants to spend some time teaching her students to interpret bar graphs. Using the bar graph provided in the textbook delineating numbers of immigrants from different countries, Ms. Morgan shows her students how to interpret this graph. They also go beyond what the graph says to considering the meanings behind the graph. Ms. Morgan knows that her teaching partner, Mr. Cole, who teaches all the fifth grade mathematics sections, has had students make bar graphs representing ethnicities in the school, and she reminds her students of these.

Finally, Ms. Morgan wants to help her students extend the knowledge they have gained about immigration from the textbook. She offers her students a choice of three culminating activities:

1. Students can use their own quick write and make a Venn diagram comparing the time they went somewhere new to Esperanza's experience.
2. Students can choose a concept in the textbook and present it in a graphic way, for example the process for becoming a citizen could be represented by a sequence train.
3. Students can choose one of the trade books provided and report on this book relating it to what they learned in the textbooks. Sample books provided are: *Grandfather's Journey* (Say, 1993), *Immigrant Kids* (Freedman, 1980), *Under the Blood-Red Sun* (Salisbury, 1994), and *Inside Out & Back Again* (Lai, 2011).

At the end of all this activity, students will display their work. Ms. Morgan will use these projects and a short objective test to determine whether she has met her goals for the immigration unit.

Intermediate Readers

During the primary grades, the emphasis in instruction is firmly on becoming literate. Primary teachers spend nearly all day focusing on reading and writing skills. Almost no other content, besides a bit of mathematics, is stressed in these early grades. If a primary teacher does include some social studies or science content, she is likely to use hands-on activities rather than a textbook, and the content itself is usually quite easy. For example, a first grade teacher may include a unit on community helpers or the five senses. This content will not be taxing for students to understand, and the vocabulary and language used to discuss these concepts are probably already in the students' oral vocabularies.

A marked shift in emphasis takes place in about fourth grade, however. Intermediate grade teachers (roughly grades 4-6) expect that their students are firmly literate now. They do not always feel the need to keep such a strong focus on reading and writing skills, and instead they move increasingly to teaching other content. This content is often not so easy to understand as that in the primary grades, and the language needed to discuss this content is often not yet in the students' oral vocabularies. Viewed in this way, it is not very surprising that some students who have been able to passably keep up with the work through third grade may begin to struggle in fourth grade. Teachers even have a name for this phenomenon. They call it the "Fourth Grade Slump."

Sidebar 11.1: Key Terms

Advanced Organizer: A technique which presents students with short ideas or questions before they read a text in order to focus comprehension

Content Area: Any subject area not specifically devoted to instruction in literacy. For example, Social Studies, Science, English or Mathematics

Context: The larger setting in which a word or idea occurs

Expository Text: Factual writing meant to explain or inform. Not a story.

Narrative: A story

Quickwrite: Very brief period of writing to brainstorm or collect thoughts

Readability Level: The grade level or difficulty of a particular text

Research Aids: Features of expository text that assist in understanding, such as a glossary, or index.

Semantic Map: A graphic organizer based upon meaning

Summarizing: Condensing a text by stating only the most important ideas it contains

Text Attack Skills: Techniques for helping students make sense of a passage. Similar to the way word-attack skills help students decode words

Text Walk: A technique used to survey expository text. Similar to a picture walk for narrative text.

There are many reasons for this slump, and we will discuss some of them in this chapter. Your main goal, as an intermediate grade teacher, though, is to make sure your students make it through this transition well by continuing to develop and increase their literacy skills while also focusing on broader content. To do this, you must commit firmly to the following phrase: All teachers are reading teachers (Bell, 2013). Committing to this phrase involves a disposition on your part that helping students become better readers and writers is your job no matter how old your students are or what content you teach. Even if you teach in a departmentalized situation like Ms. Morgan's and teach science or social studies all day, you are still a teacher of literacy. Accept this role now so that we can move on to how to teach reading and writing through the content areas.

Literacy in the Content Areas

When we speak of **content areas** we are generally considering any subject that is not the straight-forward teaching of literacy skills. Examples of content areas include mathematics, science, social studies, English, music, art, physical education, and the like. Each of these fields has a body of knowledge and a specialized vocabulary that we want students to learn. Often teachers use a textbook specially designed to impart this knowledge, and they expect students to be able to deal effectively with these textbooks. A catchy phrase sums this up nicely: In the early grades students learn to read, but after that they read to learn.

It is your job to help students make this transition. Yet, just as some students had difficulty moving from emergent literacy and crossing into Literacy Land, now some students will also find it difficult to move beyond basic reading skills to the application of higher level literacy skills. There are many reasons this might be true. If you will spend a few minutes examining a fifth grade textbook you may readily see the following challenges:

- <u>*Vocabulary.*</u> There are many new, specialized words like, *treaty, negotiate*, and *impeach* introduced in quick succession. Unlike stories in core readers, these words are not repeated numerous times. These new words are less likely to be in a student's oral vocabularies so the teacher must teach not only how to read the words, but also what they mean. And to make matters more complex, even those words that are already in students' oral vocabularies may be used in unfamiliar ways leaving students doubly confused over a term like *pitch* or *scale*.
- <u>*Concepts*</u>. Just like the differences found in textbooks relating to vocabulary, these books also begin to introduce unfamiliar and increasingly abstract concepts. The young child studying community helpers can bring to mind background experiences she has had with a letter carrier or a fire fighter. A fifth grader studying the concept of manifest destiny in social studies has no such cache of prior knowledge to draw upon. Lack of schema will inhibit any reading, and this is particularly true in the content areas.
- <u>*Writing Style*</u>. The writing style of most textbooks is rather abrupt and to the point, and new ideas are introduced quickly. This density of concepts can leave a student's head swimming with all the many ideas given in only a few paragraphs that he must understand and remember. Students not only have had little practice with this rapid-fire introduction of information, but they often cannot even discern patterns in the writing that would help them. The narrative reading they have done previously with its story structure using literary elements and a beginning-middle-end format, will not help them very much with the expository style and structure of textbooks.
- <u>*Graphic Material*</u>. The narrative writing students have encountered up to this point will usually have had many pictures which helped students understand the story. The same is true of content area textbooks, but students often do not know how to make use of this different style of illustration. For example, they do not know how to read a chart or use the legend of a map or interpret a graph. Since this graphic material is confusing to students, they often skip right over it missing out on valuable information
- <u>*Readability Level.*</u> **Readability level** of a text is assigned by publishers by taking random passages from the text and testing these using a formula which usually involves the length of the sentences and the length of the words in the passages. From this, a grade level, such as fifth grade, is then assigned to the text. But it is extremely difficult to write consistently in one reading level especially about increasingly complex topics. So it is common for the reading levels within any one text to vary widely. Therefore, even students reading firmly at the fifth grade level, for example, could still struggle with parts of a fifth grade textbook in science.

These are the main reasons why students who were fairly competent readers when facing the third grade curriculum may begin to struggle with the greater literacy demands of the intermediate grades. We will address some specific ways in the next section for you to help students become competent readers of content material, but first it will be important for you to realize that what you have learned in previous chapters of this book should still generally be applied to these older readers.

Good teaching is good teaching. Knowing the importance of schema, remembering to make your lessons as concrete as possible, integrating content across the curriculum, and differentiating your lessons according to student needs are skills you already learned in this book. Apply this same general learning now as you think about how to teach older students, but also consider how what you learned about teaching beginning readers might be differently applied to these intermediate readers. To help you in making these connections, in the rest of this chapter the places where concepts have previously been introduced are given wherever they apply.

Vocabulary and Word Attack Skills

In the early chapters of this book, we discussed the three-legged stool as a metaphor for a balanced reading program. One of those legs referred to reading skills such as vocabulary development and phonics. The methods you used for younger readers to help them with discrete reading skills are even more important now. For example, it will be crucial now that you introduce new vocabulary in context, not just as a list of new words. And it will continue to be important that you explicitly teach word attack skills so that older readers become ever more independent. In other words, you will keep doing the good skills teaching you have been doing. Yet there are important differences in focus, too, for the skills leg of the intermediate reading stool.

One important difference is in the vocabulary words you will be teaching to these older students. In the past, most of the vocabulary words students met were already in their oral vocabularies. All you needed to do was teach students to recognize these words in print. For example, while you probably awakened the schema of students when you introduced the word *cat,* you also probably found that students had lots of prior knowledge about a cat, and you could move right on to teaching the word attack skills necessary to sounding out this word. This is often not the case for intermediate-level vocabulary.

Now the vocabulary words you introduce to students may be terms like *photosynthesis* or *suffrage.* These terms may be completely foreign to students, or they may be familiar in other contexts (like the words *crust, core* and *plates* in earth science), but confusing in this new one. These words are not in the oral vocabularies of students, and there will be scant prior knowledge to awaken. Your task then is quite different from teaching the word cat. You must now not only teach students to recognize these words, you must also teach them what these words mean. It will be even more important, then, for you to introduce new words in meaningful **context**, and to provide ample opportunities for students to practice and apply these words. (See also Chapter 5.)

Not only will the new words introduced often not be in students' listening and speaking vocabularies, but these new words tend to be much longer and, therefore, resistant to phonetic analysis. The third grader who has had good success in memorizing and applying phonics rules to read short phonetically regular words, can easily turn into the struggling fourth grader when faced with words like *isthmus* or *allegiance* that are not readily decoded using phonics skills alone. In order to help students decode these bigger words, you will need to move their attention away from tiny sound/symbol relationships (phonics) that they employed as beginning readers to larger chunks of meaning (morphology). (See also Chapter 4.)

Remember that morphology deals with the morphemes (meaning units) in a word. The skills often taught in morphology include roots, affixes, compounds, contractions and the like. You taught these in simplified fashion to beginning readers, but with older readers the use of these skills will become much more important. For example, it will be very hard for a student to sound out a word such as *reconstruction.* It is just too long and too fraught with opportunities for error (should that e be long or short??).

Additionally, since this word may not be in the students' oral vocabularies, even if they do sound it out correctly they may not recognize that they have done so since it matches no word already in their heads. But if the teacher has taught students that the prefix *re-* means to do again, if she has already taught several other words using this prefix, and if she brings attention to the students' prior knowledge of the root word *construct*, the word *reconstruction* becomes much less problematic. Students are helped to chunk this big word into manageable meaning units rather than attack it letter-by-letter. Morphology study also has the added benefit of providing understanding of the word while it is being decoded for literacy.

Many of the tried and true methods used to teach vocabulary to beginning readers can be easily adapted for use in the content areas. For example, the word wall which is the staple of primary classrooms can now contain much larger words, and these can be categorized in ways other than alphabetically. For example, you may do a science word wall and have headings such as plants, earth and space to categorize the words.

Another strong method for word study is the **semantic map**. Just as Mr. Green in Chapter 5 used a semantic map to help students develop a depth of understanding for the word *apple*, so now Ms.

Sidebar 11.2: Helping ELL Students in Content Areas

It is quite likely that your English language learners will struggle in the content areas even if they appear to have good conversational skills. This is due to the difference between Basic Interpersonal Communication Skills (BICS) and Cognitive Academic Linguistic Proficiency (CALP) as discussed in Chapter 10. If you have second language learners in your classroom, especially if they are at or below the intermediate fluency stage, you will need to make modifications to your instruction. Try these ideas:

1. Limit new vocabulary as much as possible, and teach new terms very carefully using context and connections to first language as possible.
2. Spend additional time activating background knowledge and showing how this prior knowledge connects to new information. This will make your entire lesson contain more comprehensible input.
3. When possible, use texts, trade books, and other materials in the student's first language. These can be paired with materials in English so that students do not miss out on content learning just because they are not yet adept at English.
4. Allow English language learners to do at least part of their written work in their first language. Students may be able to demonstrate a great deal of content knowledge when writing in their first language, but may be so constrained in writing in English that it looks as if they do not understand the content.

Morgan can use the same clustering technique for the word *immigration.*

Finally, now is the time to help students learn to use both print and on-line dictionaries for word study. While it is not an effective educational practice to give students a list of terms to look up and copy the definitions, teaching students dictionary skills and modeling their use will be helpful for your class.

However you teach vocabulary and word attack skills to your intermediate learners, now is not the time to abandon the teaching related to the first leg of the balanced literacy stool. In fact, these skills remain so important that Roe and Smith (2012) unequivocally state, "A good way to decrease the difficulty of content passages for students is to teach the content vocabulary thoroughly before the material containing that vocabulary is assigned to be read" (p. 467). And this advice will be especially important for English language learners who may have good conversational English skills (BICS), but have not yet attained academic language in English (CALP). (See also Chapter 10.) Sidebar 11.2 also has other specific ideas for helping English language learners in content area study.

Text Structure

One of the aspects of textbooks and other nonfiction books that make them particularly puzzling to students is the fact that the **expository** (explanatory) style they employ differs a great deal from the narrative style to which young children grow accustomed. Through third grade, most of the writing students encounter either in their own reading or the shared reading adults do with them comes in the form of a story. We teach our young students to use the **narrative** (story) structure of this reading to organize their own thinking. For example, we ask them to look for literary elements such as setting and characters, or we ask them to attend to the plotline as having rising action, then a climax, and finally a resolution.

Young children can become very adept at using story structure to further their comprehension, yet when they try to apply this structure to writing that is not a story, they find it is less than helpful. Expository structures are much more varied than the regular predictable structure of a story, but students who are taught to use the major expository structures will be assisted in their comprehension and retention of factual material (Pearson & Duke, 2002). (See also Chapter 7.)

Some of the main expository structures you might teach, according to Cook & Mayer, (1988) are:

- Enumeration: Important information is listed either with actual numerals or with implied numerals.
- Sequence: Information is presented in a series. Marker words like first, next and finally may be used. Sometimes a sequence can show cause and effect.
- Generalization: A main idea is established and then explanation, examples and additional information about that main idea are presented.
- Classification: Information is divided into separate groups and examined as part of these categories.
- Comparison: Two or more categories or ideas are considered in relationship. Comparison structures can examine either similarities or differences.

To further complicate matters, textbooks generally do not employ only one or two of these styles. They may use all of these structures and move rather freely between structures in the course of only one chapter. For example, in a unit on plant life, a textbook may use a generalization structure to introduce the basic needs of plants, switch to a sequence structure to discuss the cycle of plant growth, and then use a comparison structure to consider the similarities and differences of various plants. This will make identifying and using expository structures more difficult for students.

One technique for teaching these structures is the use of various graphic organizers. According to Marzano, Pickering, and Pollock (2001), graphic organizers are one of the most effective ways to make relatively abstract concepts more concrete. Each of the text structures given above could be represented graphically for better clarity.

Here are some examples of graphic organizers that could be used for the various expository structures:

Figure11.1: Enumeration--The Grocery List: (The Known Planets)

1. Mercury
2. Venus
3. Earth
4. Mars
5. Jupiter
6. Saturn
7. Uranus
8. Neptune
9. Pluto

Figure 11.2: Sequence--The Sequence Train: (Events leading to the U.S. Revolutionary War)

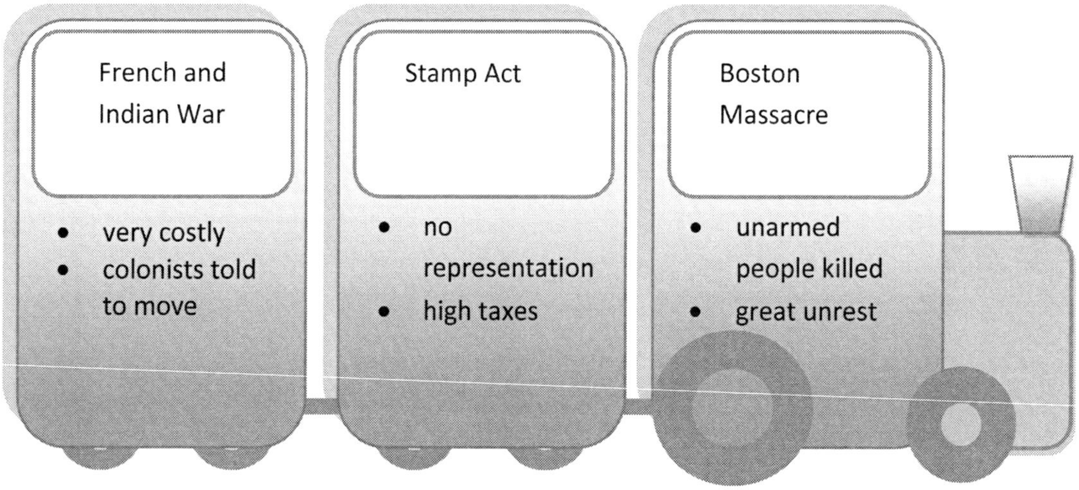

Figure 11.3: Generalization--The Cluster: (Good Nutrition)

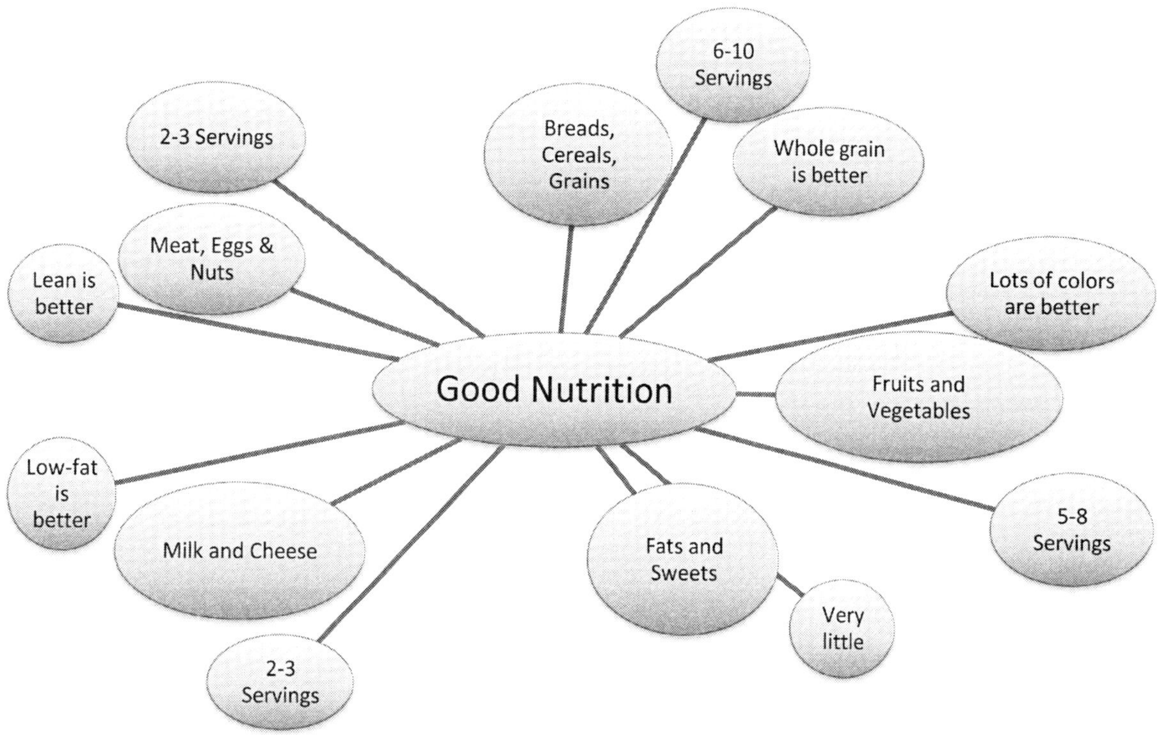

Figure 11.4: Classification--The Tree Map: (Objects and Light)

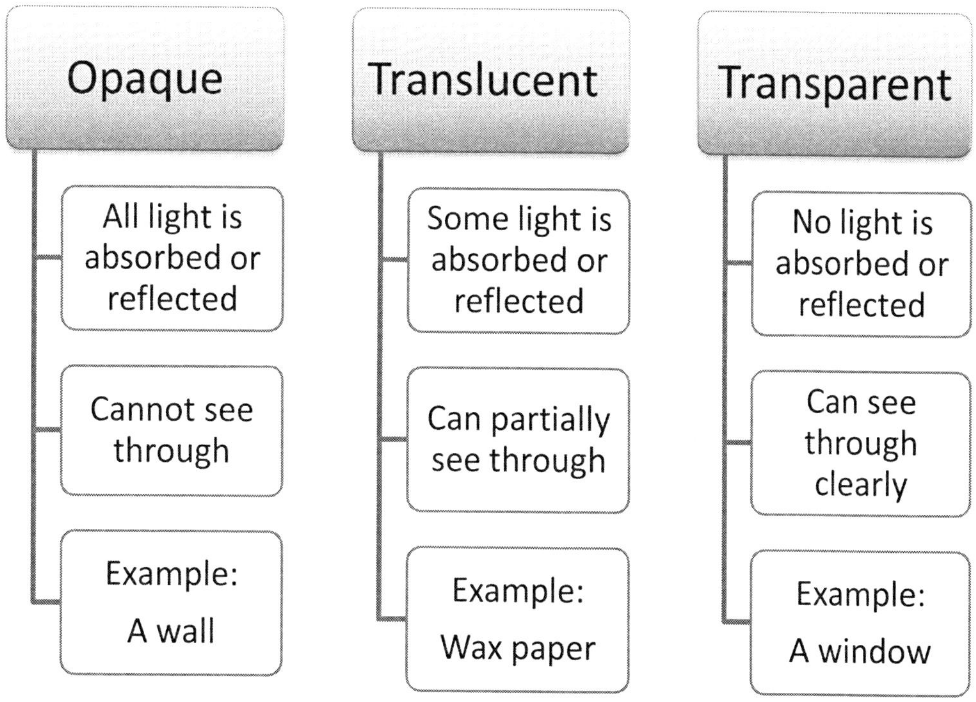

Opaque
All light is absorbed or reflected
Cannot see through
Example: A wall
Translucent
Some light is absorbed or reflected
Can partially see through
Example: Wax paper
Transparent
No light is absorbed or reflected
Can see through clearly
Example: A window

Figure 11.5: Comparison--The Venn Diagram: (Mayans and Aztecs)

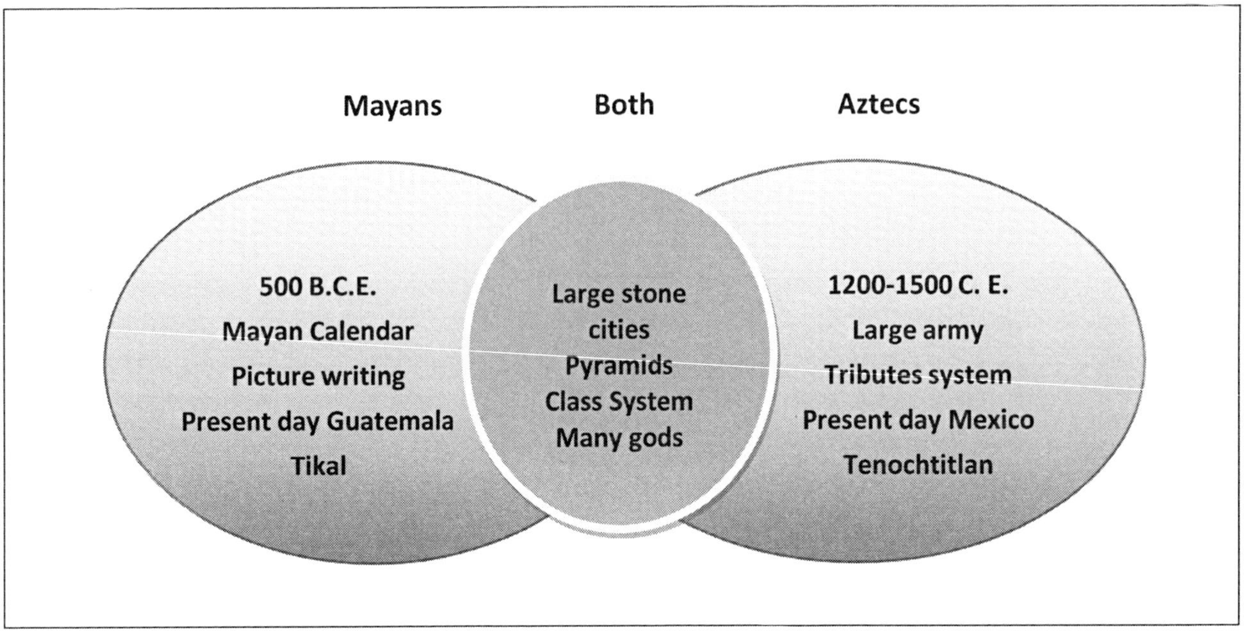

Each of these graphic organizers can be endlessly adapted for different grade levels and different content. Eventually, after students have been working with these diagrams for a while, you will be able to use prompts like, "which organizer fits this text best" to help students become adept at identifying expository text structures.

Comprehension Skills for Intermediate Readers

Learning and applying expository text structures will help intermediate readers better comprehend the nonfiction that begins to make up the bulk of their reading material, but this is only one set of strategies for helping students to comprehend. Recall again the three-legged literacy stool, and remember that leg number two is labeled comprehension. Just as with vocabulary and word attack skills, many techniques you used for teaching comprehension to younger readers can be adapted to older readers. But let's discuss here some additional comprehension strategies especially applicable for content area reading.

Perhaps the most important strategy to teach older readers has to do with the concept of metacognition which we first discussed in Chapter 7. Remember that put into simple terms, metacognition means to think about your thinking. In the case of a reading assignment for example, it is as if an outside observer is standing in your brain and watching how well you comprehend what is read. This monitor keeps asking questions to determine how things are going, and if it decides you have not understood a section well, it directs you to take some sort of action to correct this. The RAND Reading Study Group (2002) found that students who were able to employ the techniques of metacognition were better able to comprehend and remember what they read.

Probably you have had the common experience of reading a page in a textbook, getting to the end, and discovering that you do not remember anything you just read. This is an example of both metacognition and the lack of it. Thankfully, at the end of the page, your metacognitive monitor woke up, alerted you to your lack of comprehension and directed you to read the page again. Unfortunately, your monitor was asleep for too long and allowed you to read a whole page before intervening. As a teacher, you will want to teach your students strategies for staying active in their reading thereby saving them from long pages of passive incomprehension. There are many ways that students can remain active readers. One way, the use of graphic organizers, we have already discussed here, and you should also look back in Chapter 7 for the techniques given there. Here are a few more ways to help students remain focused:

- *Text Attack Skills*. Most intermediate readers have very little idea of how to "attack" a page of nonfiction text efficiently. Teachers have taught them word attack skills like phonics, but they have not had similar assistance in **text attack skills**. Instructing students to take a **text walk** (similar to a picture walk) in which they skim the text briefly looking at the headings and getting a general idea of the content is a good start. Next, teach students to constantly pose questions about what they are reading. For example, students might ask themselves questions like, "What does that new word mean" or "Did I understand that part" or "How does this new information fit in with what I already know?"

  Finally, the use of constant internal questioning will alert students to comprehension problems and teachers can teach them to employ what Reutzel & Cooter (2012) call "fix-up strategies". Readers who detect a comprehension problem should be taught to think about how to fix this problem. Common fix-up strategies good readers employ include re-reading a passage, looking up a word in the dictionary, using accompanying graphic material and asking someone for assistance.

  It often helps students to have a way to remember these text attack skills, and a tried-and-true mnemonic device is SQ3R(Robinson, 1961). The characters stand for Survey, Question, Read, Recite and Review, and you will recognize these actions as the very ones good readers employ when they try to comprehend difficult material. Many other mnemonic devices have been proposed since SQ3R was designed, and any of these could also be chosen, or you could make up your own. The point is to give older students some specific system for attacking a text and to help them remember this system.

Figure 11.6 Sample Text Attack Skills

Text Walk (Survey headings and illustrations)
Questioning (Turn headings into questions)
Answering Questions (Read sections to answer heading questions)
Fix-up Strategies (Do whatever is necessary if questions remain)

- *Writing to Learn Strategies*. The fourth mode of communication in the Blessing Chart (Figure 3.1 and Figure 8.8), writing, will become ever more useful as students become more literate. Now that your intermediate students can read and write passably, they will need to learn specific ways to use writing in order to learn. One such technique it to have students complete some sort of learning log to help them organize what they are learning. A double-sided journal is often helpful for this with one side containing the questions students want to answer from their reading and the other side including what they discovered as they read. An ongoing log is especially helpful for learning that extends over the course of several weeks, such as in a unit on electricity. (See also Chapter 8.)

  A further writing technique that is helpful for students is note-taking. To assist students in learning how to take notes, it is helpful to provide them with a blank format for note-taking, perhaps a simplified outline. Then model the technique by doing a think-aloud as you fill out the blank format together. Teach students to pay particular attention to key terms which are often highlighted in textbooks. Also teach students to look for main ideas (often the first line) and supporting details for each heading.

  A final writing technique that is helpful to students as they read and comprehend content materials is **summarizing.** A summary is simply a more concise way of presenting the material in the textbook. Students, though, often have very little idea how to get to this shorter version. Teaching students to focus on key terms and concepts and to delete less important ideas or examples are corollary skills to note-taking, and a good summary can often come from the outline completed during note-taking practice. Again, use think-aloud and modeling to help students sort essential from nonessential information and to construct competent summaries. Marzano (2010) found that being able to summarize their reading helped students to better comprehend and remember what they read. (See also Chapter 7.)

- *Graphic Materials Learning*. Young students are accustomed to poring over the pictures in their books to extract every ounce of meaning. Unfortunately, this attention to visual representations somehow goes by the wayside when students become older and are faced with new ways to visually represent information. Textbooks, depending on their content, may include maps, graphs, charts, tables, time lines, diagrams and figures. And each of these specialized graphics will come along with specialized terms and skills needed to make use of them. For example, maps use terms like legend and scale and compass rose, terms that are especially confusing to students who know other definitions of these terms from other contexts.

  The result of this information overload is that students often just skip over the graphic materials in the text thereby missing important information. To help students focus on these materials, choose just one type at a time (a map for example), teach the skills needed to read this graphic (legend, scale, compass rose, coordinates, etc.), and then ask students to connect what this graphic portrays to what the text says. Focusing frequently on graphic materials in context will allow students to gain confidence in using these materials.

- *<u>Research Aids Techniques</u>*. Textbooks and nonfiction books contain a whole host of additional materials designed to make these books more accessible. Such **research aids** may include a table of contents, an index, a glossary, a bibliography or reference list, and a list of additional resources. Just as they do with the graphic materials in textbooks, students faced with these unknown aids tend to just skip them. Again, it is best to teach these aids in context as they are needed to study a text. For example, as students are studying a chapter on the water cycle in science, the teacher could ask them to look up an unknown term in the glossary, or use the index to find other places in the text that discuss the water cycle or refer to the additional resources list to do further research on the topic. Eventually, through consistent use, students will begin to see these research aids as valued additions to their textbooks.

Let's Talk Teaching

All of the preceding sections focus on specific ways to integrate reading instruction into the content area classroom. This section will examine two generalized ways to do this. The first is the Directed Reading Lesson mentioned in Chapter 2, and the second is the use of thematic units.

The Directed Reading Lesson in the Content Areas

You may want to refer back to Chapter 2 where the Directed Reading Lesson (Cooper, et al., 1979) was first presented and remember that this method is based on the early work of Betts (1946). The method contains three components, pre-reading, directed reading and post-reading. In Chapter 2 we saw this method used with first graders using the book, *If you Give a Mouse a Cookie* (Numeroff, 1985). Now let's follow the same method in a content area lesson by looking again at the opening vignette for this chapter. Ms. Morgan actually followed a DRL format in her lessons. Here are the steps she took:

PREREADING:

1. Provided background knowledge by reading *Esperanza Rising* (Ryan, 2000).
2. Introduced vocabulary words using an **advance organizer** worksheet.
3. Discussed and defined vocabulary in context.
4. Put new vocabulary words into word banks.
5. Used *Esperanza Rising* to awaken schema by making lists.
6. Further activated background knowledge with a **quickwrite**.

DURING READING:

1. Began with text walk as a preview of chapter in textbook.
2. Used headings to focus attention by turning these into questions to be answered.
3. Used Bloom's Taxonomy to include questions at all levels in the chapter discussion.
4. Reviewed all learning through the end-of-chapter questions provided.
5. Taught the reading skill of reading a bar graph in context and connected this to another curricular area.

POSTREADING:

1. Offered extension activity choices which all included writing or other graphic representations.
2. Extended learning to other texts by providing various trade books at different reading levels on the topic of immigration.
3. Used two kinds of assessment to determine if teaching goals about immigration had been met.

It is clear from Ms. Morgan's lesson that she was primarily focused on her social studies content. She had goals and standards relating to the topic of immigration that she wanted to meet. But concurrently with this emphasis on social studies content, Ms. Morgan also included good reading instruction for her students. So at the same time as they were learning facts about immigration, they also improved their reading skills by working with vocabulary, learning comprehension techniques, learning specialized skills like graph-reading and extending their knowledge using writing. All of these are literacy skills that enhanced Ms. Morgan's lessons on immigration immeasurably and provided her students with the literacy tools they needed to be successful in social studies.

Thematic Units

As students get older their classrooms become progressively more departmentalized. In second grade, for example, the same teacher will likely teach her students language arts, mathematics, science and social studies. By fifth grade, though, students may have four different teachers instructing them in these four areas, and this can easily lead to fragmentation of the curriculum. Students will learn better and retain more, however, if content is integrated for them. This is often done using a thematic unit which is a teaching unit organized around a curricular theme.

One method for designing a thematic unit is to start with a piece of literature and organize other curricular areas around this book. For example, the teacher could choose the book *Dear Mr. Henshaw* by Beverly Cleary (1983) which is a book about a boy who writes to an author to try to cope with numerous issues in his life. The teacher would then organize lessons in language arts, mathematics, etc. to teach skills in these areas by relating them to this unifying book. See Figure 11.7 for an example.

Figure 11.7: Curriculum Map for *Dear Mr. Henshaw:*

Language Arts	Mathematics	Social Studies	Science
• Letter Writing • Writing to author • Journaling • Symbolism	• Weight • Distance • Time	• Family Structure • Bullying • Maps/map reading • Careers	• Butterflies • Electricity • Nutrition • Alarm systems

Another way to organize a thematic unit is to start with a concept that is taught at your grade level and then integrate numerous texts and curricular areas around this central concept. An example of a thematic unit organized around the concept of the U. S. Civil War is in Figure 11.8.

Figure 11.8: Curriculum Map for Unit on U.S. Civil War

The U. S. Civil War

Social Studies

Time lines
Map study
Venn of N/S
Slavery
Geography
Underground Railroad
Laws enacted
Major issues

Science

Sky for Underground Railroad

Industrialization in North

Agriculture in South

Cotton gin

Books

Lincoln: A Photobiography

Slave Dancer

Pink and Say

Jip, His Story

Language Arts

Biographies
Vocabulary study
Writing assignment: Journal of a soldier
Emancipation Proclamation
Debates
Gettysburg Address
Point of View

Mathematics

Bar graphs
Circle graphs
Population
Dates and Times
Miles between battles

Websites

www.cobblestonepub.com

civilwar150.longwood.edu

www.nps.gov/hps/abpp/civil/htm

Misc.

Decision-Making; Debates

Music of the era

If you plan to do thematic teaching in your classroom, it will be important for you to know of a great many trade books at different reading levels that pertain to your content area. Moving beyond the exclusive use of a textbook in the content areas means you will need a long list of other children's books to draw upon. This can be a challenge. Luckily, many of the content area professional bodies publish lists of good trade books in their areas. The website information for several of these professional bodies is provided in Figure 11.9.

Figure 11.9: Websites of Content Area Professional Associations

Mathematics	www.nctm.org
Social Studies	www.socialstudies.org
Science	www.nsta.org
English	www.ncte.org
Reading	www.reading.org

Summing Up

The main point to keep in mind from this chapter is that all teachers are literacy teachers. As students move beyond the beginning literacy stage, their needs change and the emphases of their instruction change. Still, literacy is a primary task of their teachers. For one thing, if literacy instruction stops at third grade, we run the risk of producing readers who remain with third grade reading skills. Additionally, if content area teachers do not give students the specific tools needed to be literate in specific content areas, students may remain generally literate but unprepared to cope with the special literacy demands of a field. Either way, by considering reading instruction some other teacher's job, you have failed to teach your students what they need to be successful.

This chapter discussed many ways, such as text attack skills, graphic organizers, directed reading lessons and thematic teaching to help students with literacy in content areas. Remember that even older, fairly literate students still need a teacher of reading because the text demands of the intermediate grades are so much more rigorous. Be that teacher.

Chapter 12
Making Lifelong Readers

We first met Collin as a preschooler in Chapter One. Remember that back then he was bent on getting French fries. This motivation encouraged him to learn the word McDonalds™, and then many other necessary words, holistically as sight words. After he had developed a rather large bank of personally selected and useful words by asking any adult at hand to write down words for him, he rather belatedly began to figure out letters and sounds by using the same method of adult badgering. As a result of this single-minded effort on his part (and the parts of all the beleaguered adults around him), Collin crossed over into Literacy Land before he entered kindergarten.

His kindergarten teacher noticed this and excitedly reported it to his parents at their first parent conference. Collin's teacher was delighted, but since most of the activities taking place in kindergarten were concrete, hands-on lessons, Collin's reading skills were neither help nor hindrance, and he continued his happy journey through Literacy Land pretty much on his own.

In first and second grades, the focus in the classroom was much more on becoming literate, but there seemed to be no space for a child who already was. Collin dutifully practiced initial consonants, filled out countless worksheets, and read faithfully in his grade level reading group. At home, though, he finished the entire Laura Ingalls Wilder Little House series and disgusted his mother with ideas for cooking worms after reading Thomas Rockwell's book, *How to Eat Fried Worms* (1973).

For Collin, school and reading began to be disconnected in this way early, but things did not get ugly until third grade. Then for the next two years, Collin tuned out school and developed some unfortunate reading habits. For example, he stopped conscientiously filling out worksheets in class (grades fell, parents were contacted), and instead focused on assigning himself interesting books to read at home, complete with self-designed extension activities. He finished off *A Wrinkle in Time* (L'Engle, 1973) this way, and also *The Giver* (Lowry, 1993).

He stopped paying enough attention during round robin reading to do his part mostly because he always had another book he was reading hidden on the lip of his desk. He was especially proud in fourth grade to read *The Yearling* (Rawlings, 1938) in this way not because it was such a difficult book to read but because it was so thick and took tremendous resourcefulness to hide. Clearly, for Collin, literacy and school were no longer connected concepts. School seemed to just be a waiting game. Then Collin walked into Mr. Scott's fifth grade.

Books everywhere! Books on shelves. Books on windowsills. Books in what used to be the cubbies. Stacks of books on the floor. Tubs of books on the tables. And these weren't textbooks. They were good books! Some he had already read like *Wrinkle in Time*, but some he had only heard of but thought sounded good like *Johnny Tremain* (Forbes, 1943). What could this mean? Would the kids be allowed to read these books or were they just for decoration? It all looked very promising.

As the weeks wore on, this early promise came true, and Mr. Scott's classroom became reading heaven for Collin. In addition to the multitude of great books available, Mr. Scott helped his students choose good books to read and then gave them lots of time to read them. He held reading conferences with each student to talk about their reading, and he encouraged them to share their thoughts with each other. Oh sure, there were some mini-lessons over literacy skills, and Mr. Scott demanded lots of writing, but mostly the students spent their time reading and responding to good literature. Reading heaven!

Making Lifelong Readers

Early in this book you will recall we used the metaphor of the three-legged stool to explain a balanced reading program. Leg One referred to reading skills like phonics, morphology and sight words. Section Two of this textbook focused on these skills of reading. Leg Two referred to reading comprehension which was the focus of Section Three of this textbook. The third leg—reading volume, or reading a lot—has been woven into many of our preceding chapters, but it is time now to focus directly on this last leg. For a teacher who conscientiously gives students all the skills they need to become readers, but then never compels them to read widely is in danger of producing alliterate readers, that is students who can read but never do.

You were introduced in Chapter Two of this textbook to the work of Keith Stanovich (1986) who coined the term "Matthew Effect." This term, which referred to the biblical story in which the rich get richer, described what happened to students who had more or less reading volume as they progressed through school. Readers who read more became better readers and continued to read more. The rich got richer. Unfortunately, students who read little, became less able readers and then they read even less becoming even poorer readers. Numerous studies are cited in Krashen (1993) that indicate this is just what happens. These studies support the need for that strong third leg on the balanced reading stool.

Krashen estimated that reading volume must begin by mid-first grade if a new reader is to become a competent reader someday. So the information in this chapter is applicable even to our youngest students. However, by third grade when children have attained the skills of reading well enough to have developed some independence, it is absolutely imperative that students spend increasingly large chunks of time reading **connected text**. **Reading volume**, then, must begin early and increase significantly as the school years go by.

In this chapter, reading volume does not refer to the skills-based literacy activities done in Language Arts, Science or Social studies, though those activities are valuable and they were discussed in Chapter 11. Rather, reading volume here refers to the extended periods of time students spend reading connected text

Sidebar 12.1: Key Terms

Book Talk: An introductory talk about a book given by a teacher or knowledgeable student in order to entice others to read the book.

Connected Text: Authentic writing done in sentences and paragraphs as opposed to the short writing found on worksheets.

Genre: A category of literature, such as historical fiction or fantasy.

Literature Circle: A book discussion technique in which students lead the discussion about a book they have all read.

Literature Unit: A curricular unit built around a piece of literature or a group of books. Sometimes called a thematic unit.

Reading Volume: The amount of reading done by a person.

Trade Book: A book written primarily for enjoyment or information as opposed to a text book written primarily to instruct.

for enjoyment or information. This is sometimes termed "free reading." (See also Chapter 6.)

While it may indeed be free, this activity has enormous value in your classroom, and you bear the responsibility for making sure it attains its maximum value. Chambers (1991, in Gamble & Yates, 2008, p. 8) explains your role as that of the "enabling adult." According to Chambers, a knowledgeable adult can guide students in their book selection, can provide precious time for reading and can help students respond to what they have just read.

Let's look now at three broad areas through which you should plan to be that enabling adult to help students strengthen their reading volume leg. These three areas are: Motivation, Materials and Responses.

Motivation

Perhaps the most important factor in motivating students to read is an enthusiastic teacher. You cannot give what you do not have, so commit now to reading widely in the best children's literature and developing a respect and enthusiasm for these books. A teacher who enthusiastically discusses with students a new book she has found or who wonders aloud with students who have also read *The Giver* (Lowry, 1993) whether Jonas lives or dies, has already implanted in students' minds the idea that reading is a worthwhile and exciting endeavor. This will happen rather naturally as students and an enthusiastic teacher coalesce into what Hepler and Hickman (1982) call a community of readers.

You can go even further to motivate students to read by planning shared reading activities or book talks. You are, of course, still reading good literature aloud to your students each day, and you can use this shared reading time very intentionally to motivate students by mentioning other books on the same topic or by the same author. Or you can periodically do a **book talk** on a book you love, telling students why you think this book is so great, and perhaps reading a particularly enticing page or two. If you lead students toward books in these ways, it pays to have multiple copies of the highlighted book available. Enthusiasm is catching!

Besides personal enthusiasm, your room can also serve as implicit motivation to read. When Collin, in the opening vignette, walked into Mr. Scott's room, he had entered a place in which every inch of space said, "READ!" Chapter two in this textbook discusses how to create an environment that is literacy rich. As mentioned in that chapter, it is important to have comfortable spots for reading (bean bag chairs, sofa, bath tub), but more important than this physical environment is to have a classroom that is obviously devoted to reading. Mr. Scott has done this. Besides the shelves and shelves of books, he has an author study area in one corner. He has current newspapers on the back table. He has a writing center, and a books-on-tape area, and a display of new fantasy titles. Of course, if all these opportunities go unused, all Mr. Scott has done is create an inviting (and cluttered!) classroom space. A literacy rich environment is only a first step toward helping students read more.

The next step to motivating readers is to provide time for them to actually read. *Becoming a Nation of Readers* (Anderson, 1985), the landmark study by the National Institute of Education, recommended that students must read at least two hours per week in order to become skilled readers. Since recent research reveals that most students today read very little outside of school, it is obvious that most of this time spent on reading volume will need to take place in school. This means that teachers need to plan a minimum of about 25 minutes of free reading per day for their students.

This time should be considered paramount, and should not be muscled out by other "work" that is considered more important. Indeed, according to Krashen (1993) and others, this time is the most important work of the day. And while it is wonderful for students to use spare bits of found time (if they finish a task early, while they are waiting for the bell, etc.) to read, this must not take the place of regularly scheduled time for reading volume. In order for Mr. Scott's carefully designed space to become more than a literacy showplace and book depository, Collin is going to need to start reading some of those enticing books,. For students like Collin, time to do so may be all the motivation they need. For reluctant or challenged readers, though, time will be important, but the other motivational tools listed earlier will also probably be necessary until these readers develop the intrinsic motivation to read and the habit of diving into a book.

A final motivating factor in turning students into lifelong readers is the matter of choice. Nearly everything students do in school involves very little choice for them. They must do the assigned reading; they must complete various written assignments; they must stick to the topics in the assigned curriculum. All of this is fine, but assignments do not motivate most students to read. This is especially true if students are consistently assigned to read out of their reading level about topics which do not interest them in genres they do not prefer.

In order for students to embrace reading as a worthwhile and enjoyable activity to pursue even when they are not assigned to do it, students will need to have the freedom to sometimes choose their own reading. The time set aside for free reading is the place to start encouraging this choice. A student who has been consistently controlled in his reading selections, however, will not magically be able to make his own choices all at once.

Matching students to materials will place enormous responsibility on the teacher even if completely free choice is allowed to students. In order to knowledgeably help students make good choices, you will need to know both your students and your books. To know your students reading habits, you might give a written survey to your students asking such questions as what book they read last, their favorite book or what they like to watch on TV. A student interview, such as the one Mrs. Carpenter gave Nicholas in the vignette for Chapter 9 can also help you determine a student's reading tastes. And, of course, you will need to keep in mind reading level and difficulty of materials that a student can read independently. The Five-Finger Method mentioned in Chapter 6 may help students with this.

Beyond this knowledge of each student, a teacher must have broad knowledge of children's literature in order to know which books to recommend to individual students. Let's do a quick overview of children's literature now to prepare you for this task.

Materials

The field of children's literature is vast. It covers books meant for infants all the way up to books designed for high-school students, where the name of the literature changes from children's literature to young adult. Just focusing on books meant for elementary-school students still yields a dizzying array of new and classic books. Some experts estimate that there are at least 5000 children's books published each year in the United States. These books come in all the genres available in adult literature, and these genre designations are a good way to begin categorizing this huge collection of books.

A **genre** in literature just means a type of book. Books may be written in either prose or poetry style. They may be about things that really happened which is termed nonfiction, or they can be about things that never really happened which is termed fiction. Within these broad genres of nonfiction and fiction there are many sub-genres. Figure 12.1 details the subgenres of nonfiction and figure 12.2 details the subgenres of fiction. Take a moment to look at these now.

Figure 12.1: Subgenres of Nonfiction

Subgenre	**Definition**	**Examples**
Biography/Autobiography	Provides accurate information about real people. An autobiography is a book written by the person themselves.	*Lives of the Athletes* (Krull, 1997) **The Cat with the Yellow Star* (Rubin, 2006)
Informational Book	Provides accurate factual information about a range of topics, such as dinosaurs or World War II.	*Black Potatoes* (Bartoletti, 2001) **The Sun*(Simon, 1996)
Concept Book	Teaches a specific concept, such as the concept of alphabet or numbers	*Mad as a Wet Hen and Other Funny Idioms* (Terban, 1987) **Ten Black Dots* (Crews, 1986)

Figure 12.2: Subgenres of Fiction

Subgenre	Definition	Examples
Historical Fiction	Realistic fiction set in the past. May use some actual people or events for authenticity, but story is fiction.	*Goodnight, Mr. Tom*(Magorian, 1981) **Pink and Say* (Polacco, 1994)
Realistic Contemporary Fiction	Fiction set roughly in the present. Realistic enough to have been able to happen though it never really did.	*The Great Gilly Hopkins*(Paterson, 1978) **Owl Moon* (Yolen, 1987)
Traditional Literature	Fantasy literature coming from an ancient oral tradition. So old that the original author is not known and there are usually many variants.	*Ella Enchanted* (Levine, 1997) **Princess Furball* (Huck, 1989)
Contemporary Fantasy	Fiction with unrealistic story elements or characters. Written by known authors.	*The Tale of Despereaux* (DiCamillo,2003) **Tuesday* (Wiesner, 1991),
Mystery	Books in which clues are planted by the author to help characters (and readers) solve a question or puzzle.	*The London Eye Mystery*(Dowd, 2007) **Black & White*(Macaulay, 1990)
Poetry	Books written in some poetic style rather than in prose style.	*Love That Dog* (Creech, 2001) **Fold Me a Poem*(George, 2005)

A special genre for children's literature that is not usually found in adult literature is the genre of picture books. Picture books can fall into any of the sub-genres listed in Figures 12.1 and 12.2. The examples with an asterisk given in these tables and all the other ones in this chapter are picture books. Teachers of young children automatically use picture books in their classrooms, but these books should not be overlooked by intermediate grade teachers. Often the brevity and clarity, not to mention the helpful illustrations, of these books are useful to illuminate difficult concepts. And their beauty, in both language and artwork, can encourage older reluctant readers to take another look at reading.

It will be important that you have a wide variety of books from every genre at various reading levels. It will do little good, though, to have huge numbers of low-quality selections. Our students will find their own ways to mediocre literature, such as books based upon the latest TV shows, formulaic series books and books designed to sell products. The books you provide in your classroom must be high-quality literature. Many sources recommend that you consider the following criteria when evaluating books for your classroom:

- *Literary elements*. Are attributes like setting, plot, characters and theme well-done? Do the characters come to life? Is the plot interesting, creative and complete with no loose threads of the story left dangling at the end? Is the theme worth teaching children, and is it developed within the plotline without moralizing?

- *Language*. Is the language in the book fresh and rich? Is it age-appropriate, yet also challenging? Does the dialogue between characters sound authentic?
- *Illustrations.* If the book has pictures, are they well-done and aesthetically pleasing? Do they match the written text while also extending it? Are they accurate where necessary?
- *Integrity*. Does the author treat readers with respect, not talking down to them? Is there an absence of stereotypes? Are the ethics and morals of the book ones we want children to develop? Is the book satisfying?

These quality markers are the ones to keep in mind as you read any children's book in preparation for including it in your classroom collection. It may be helpful to design a brief form on which to make your notes. Figure 12.3 has an example of what such a form might look like, or you can make up your own form.

Figure 12.3: Sample Form for Critiquing a Children's Book

Children's Literature Critique

Title: ______________________________ Genre: ______________________

Author: _____________________________ Age Level: ___________________

<u>Writing:</u>

Strong story elements
High-quality language
Appropriate level
Understandable
Accurate

Comments______________________________
____

<u>Illustrations:</u>

High-quality pictures
Style complements words
Appropriate number
Creative
Accurate

Comments______________________________
____

<u>Integrity:</u>

Honest presentation
Respect for audience
Healthy values
Lack of stereotypes

Comments______________________________
____

<u>Match to Child</u>

Age appropriate
Region
Ethnicity
Interests

Comments______________________________
____

Rating: (Circle) Excellent Good Fair Poor

Besides using quality markers to make your own decisions about books, there are two other ways you might go about focusing on quality children's literature. The first of these ways is to stick with authors whose work has already proven to be excellent. While some of any author's books will necessarily be better than others, and while an author will sometimes write a book not to your taste, past quality is still a reliable indicator of present and future quality. A short list of authors and illustrators who can be counted on to produce high-quality books is provided in Figure 12.4. There are many other great authors and illustrators, though, so let this list be a start but not a limitation as you design your own classroom collection.

Figure 12.4: Short List of High-Quality Children's Authors and Illustrators

Eve Bunting	Kristine O'Connell George	Robert McCloskey
Judy Blume	Susan Goldman-Rubin	Scott O'Dell
Jan Brett	Nikki Grimes	Katherine Paterson
Eric Carle	Kevin Henkes	Patricia Polacco
Beverly Cleary	Karen Hesse	Pam Munoz Ryan
Andrew Clements	Pat Hutchins	Cynthia Rylant
Sharon Creech	Ezra Jack Keats	Maurice Sendak
Donald Crews	Madeleine L'Engle	Seymour Simon
Karen Cushman	Anita Lobel	Mildred Taylor
Russell Freedman	Lois Lowry	David Wiesner

The second way to look for high-quality children's literature is to focus on a few of the awards given in the field. Figure 12.5 provides a handful of the biggest awards, but there are many other smaller or specialized awards. When a book wins an award, you can be fairly sure it is good quality literature. What you cannot know is whether the book is appropriate for your students or whether they will like the book. The awards will not tell you these things, but the winners of these awards will at least serve as a beginning place for your own reading and selection.

Figure 12.5: Important Children's Literature Awards

AWARD	REASON GIVEN	EXAMPLE
Newbery Medal	Author of most distinguished American book for children	*Number the Stars* (Lowry, 1990) *A Single Shard* (Park, 2002)
Caldecott Medal	Illustrator of most distinguished American picture book	**The Three Pigs* (Wiesner, 2002) **Rapunzel* (Zelinsky, 1998)
Coretta Scott King Awards	Author or illustrator of children's book by or about African Americans	*One Crazy Summer* (Williams-Garcia, 2011) **Dave the Potter* (Hill, 2011)
Pura Belpre Award	Latino/Latina author or illustrator of children's book celebrating Latino culture	*Esperanza Rising* (Munoz Ryan, 2000) **Just a Minute* (Morales, 2003)
Orbis Pictus Award	Distinguished nonfiction book for children	*Children of the Great Depression* (Freedman, 2006) **When Marian Sang* (Munoz Ryan, 2003)
Christopher Award	Children's book affirming highest values of human spirit	*Frindle* (Clements, 1996) **Hero Cat* (Spinelli, E. 2007)

In looking at Figure 12.5 and considering these major awards, it is obvious that some of the awards are for books by or about specific cultures or ethnicities (Coretta Scott King Award, Pura Belpre Award), and this should alert you to the need for diversity in the books you select for your classroom. The landmark study reported by Nancy Larrick in 1965 as "The All White World of Children's Literature" illuminated the shameful fact that nearly all of the characters in children's books at that time were white with *Snowy Day* by Ezra Jack Keats (1962) being a notable exception as the first children's book with an African American main character to win a major award. From Larrick's consciousness-raising article came the Coretta Scott King Award which was established to encourage African American authors and illustrators to create books for children.

The work of Bishop (1990) highlights why diversity in books is important for all children, not just African American children. Bishop uses the metaphor of windows and mirrors to explain why all children need diverse literature. For some students, this literature will allow them to look in the mirror and see themselves better. For other students, this literature acts as a window to a different world, broadening their limited experiences and encouraging understanding and empathy. Using this metaphor as a guide, it will be important for you to provide diverse literature in your classroom. And diverse literature must go beyond cultural and ethnic diversity to broadly embrace all types of diversity, such as gender, religion, region and ability.

The major awards given for ethnically diverse books, such as the Coretta Scott King and Pura Belpre are good places to start. But obviously, major awards will not be enough to ensure you have the very broad range of diverse books needed to provide windows and mirrors for all. There are no major awards, for example, for children's books which specifically show girls and women in non-traditional and self-determined roles. In order to define diversity broadly and select a wide variety of books, you will need to go beyond the major awards and evaluate books yourself in terms of their quality. Huck, el al. (2004, p. 23) recommend that you consider the following guidelines in selecting diverse books:

- Select a broad range of diverse titles. Have lots of books with a variety of ways in which different ethnicities, genders and abilities are presented.
- Avoid all stereotyping. Be especially alert for signs that indicate that everyone of a particular culture or gender thinks or acts in the same way. Even if the description is not negative, portraying everyone as the same is inaccurate and misleading for children.
- Pay particular attention to language. Consider the use and effect of any derogatory terms to decide whether the book should even be used. Discuss different dialects found in the books.
- Evaluate the books' perspective. Consider whether a book is an authentic representation of the experiences of people like those in the book. This often means you will need to ask insiders of a group whether the behaviors, dialogs and experiences portrayed in the book ring true for them.

In creating lifelong readers by encouraging reading volume in your classroom, select a wide range of books and other reading materials, and try to make your classroom look a lot like Mr. Scott's classroom in the opening vignette. Using the ideas already given in this chapter will guide you, but if you want more help, the websites listed in Figure 12.6 are good sources for additional information. Once you have a motivating classroom with lots of books and lots of time to read them, you are ready to help your students begin to respond to what they read.

Figure 12.6: Children's Literature Websites

Site	Explanation
www.ala.org	American Library Association
www.cbcbooks.org	Children's Book Council
www.reading.org	International Reading Association
www.ncte.org	National Council of Teachers of English
www.acs.ucalgary.ca/	Children's Literature Guide
www.carolhurst.com	Reviews of children's books

Responding to Literature

Think back to the very first vignette in this book when we met Collin and Whitney as pre-readers. While these children learned to read in radically different ways, both had as their guiding motivation the ability to communicate with others. This push toward communication began for these little ones with the oral skills of listening and speaking, then it progressed to the written skills of reading and writing. Figure 3.1

in Chapter 3 (The Blessing Chart) displayed these skills separately as oral or written, receptive or expressive, but they are intimately related and supportive of each other. Apply this knowledge now as you consider how to make lifelong readers of your students. If the true motivation to read involves communication, then any program which encourages reading, but limits responding to this reading, will fall short.

The research which guides much of this work is the Reader Response Theory which was articulated by Rosenblatt (1978). This theory, which we first discussed in Chapter One of this book, envisions reading as a transaction between the reader and the writer. Hickman (O'Sullivan, 2007) further encouraged teachers to let readers bring their own experiences unhindered to a story before the adult enters in and makes the text into a teaching tool. The point is that students do not come as blank slates to their reading, and they don't leave as blank slates either. Students bring their own backgrounds, experiences, and problems into the mix as they read. These combine with what the author presents in the book to form new insights and thoughts in students. Naturally, students will wish to convey these new ideas to someone. There are many ways in which this can happen.

The most common way that teachers ask for students to respond to reading is to ask them questions either orally or in writing. This has some value. Asking students to respond in a discussion to high-level questions calling for critical thinking will allow their new insights to come forward. Testing students over the literal elements of a book will allow the teacher to know whether students at least understood the rudimentary structure of the book.

Testing and class discussion, then, have a place in your classroom. But if these are the only ways in which you ask students to respond to reading you will probably not motivate your students to read more. Indeed, a study by Pavonetti, Brimmer and Cipielewski (2002/2003) on Accelerated Reader (a computer program which tests student knowledge of books and offers rewards) found that this read-then-test program did not motivate students to become lifelong readers. You will need to progress far beyond discussion and test methods to really allow students to respond to what they read.

One of the broad ways in which students can respond to literature is through their writing. Chapter 8 lists many ways in which writing, the fourth mode of communication in the Blessing Chart, can be incorporated into the classroom. Use of journals is particularly helpful and teachers use journals in many ways. For example, you could ask students to keep a double-entry journal in which a character's actions are listed on one side and the reader's thoughts are listed on the other. Or you and your students could engage in response journals in which you dialogue with each other in writing about a particular book. Or students could keep a reading log in which they list all the books they have read along with reactions to these books. However you incorporate writing into your students' responses to reading, you are encouraging them to share their thoughts and insights about books with others and at the same time strengthening that fourth mode of communication.

Finally, there are numerous creative ways that go beyond reading and writing in which students can respond to books. The arts are a particularly fruitful place for reader response. Using music, visual art, drama and dance opens the possibilities for ways in which students can respond to books. Or connecting their responses to technology by creating blogs or computer presentations may appeal to some students. These more creative response methods are often particularly valuable for students who struggle with reading and writing and for those English language learners who are learning to express themselves in a new language.

The bottom line is that in order to make lifelong readers out of your beginning and intermediate readers you will need to pay particular attention to motivation techniques, to the selection of strong materials, and to opportunities for students to read and respond to books during the school day. One staple of this lifelong reader classroom is Sustained Silent Reading (SSR) which was discussed in Chapter 6. Allowing time for free reading is essential, but there are also additional methods you can use to get your students into books. The next section contains several of these.

Let's Talk Teaching

Here are four methods which go beyond SSR or free reading for incorporating **trade books** into your reading program.

- *Reading Workshop.* Reading workshop (Atwell, 1998) functions in much the same way as the Writing Workshop discussed in Chapter 8. Reading workshop focuses on individual student reading and response, but it also includes other features. In a typical reading workshop day, the teacher may begin the session by briefly sharing information from his own reading. He would then follow this with a mini-lesson focusing on a reading or writing skill the students need. The bulk of the time in the reading workshop is then devoted to the students' own self-selected reading. This portion might last up to 40 minutes and besides silent reading could also contain conferences with the teacher and work on written or other responses to reading. At the end of the workshop, a few minutes are set aside for student sharing. Reading workshop is actually the method Mr. Scott used in our opening vignette to organize his literacy instruction.

  Reading workshop is nearly all student-directed, but this does not mean the method is effortless for the teacher. In fact, reading workshop places tremendous demands on a teacher to keep track of where each student is in his reading. Keeping an individual log for each student, as well as a class chart for the entire group, is imperative for organization. Assessing students to determine the skills to be covered in the mini-lessons must also take place. And, of course, the teacher must have a deep knowledge of children's literature in order to guide her students' choices. Yet, even with all these demands, reading workshop is an extremely valuable piece of any reading program.

- *Book Clubs and/or Literature Circles.* Classroom book clubs operate in much the same way as adult book clubs always have. Students come together in a small group to discuss a book they have chosen to read. These discussion groups are around a self-selected book, and are also student-directed. The focus in the discussion is on going beyond literal understanding of the book to deeper levels of insight. Sometimes just reading the same interesting book and being allowed the time to talk about it with peers is enough to result in a fruitful discussion. Often, though, students have very little idea how to run or contribute to a student-directed book discussion. This is where the method of Literature Circles is helpful.

Literature Circles are essentially just a book club discussing a self-selected book, but in order to guide students into a better discussion, each student is assigned a particular role in the group. Daniels (1994) delineated several possible roles, such as Discussion Director, Literary Luminary and Illustrator. Teachers often add other roles of their own choosing. Since a Literature Circle group commonly contains 3-6 students, not all roles are used for every discussion. Figure 12.7 explains the most common Literature Circle roles.

Figure 12.7: Literature Circle Roles

Discussion Director	This person selects questions to ask to begin the discussion and keep it going smoothly.
Literary Luminary	This person finds quotations in the book that they deem valuable.
Summarizer	This person offers a short summary of what was read and also summarizes the discussion.
Connector	This person finds connections between the reading material and something else like another book, a TV program, or personal experience.
Illustrator	This person draws a picture or other graphic representation of the reading material.
Wordsmith	This person finds new or important vocabulary words that should be discussed.

In order to incorporate Literature Circles into your classroom, have students select an interesting book to read, assign the various roles and allow time for the groups to meet. As students get more adept at self-directed discussion, the assigned roles may become less necessary. At some point, it is advisable for a literature circle to also share a bit about their book with the larger class.

- *Literature Units and Core Books*. Two examples of thematic or **literature units** were given in Chapter 11. These units focused on either a core book (*Dear Mr. Henshaw,* 1983) or they focused on a topic (Civil War). Other ways in which to focus a literature unit are around a genre (i.e. historical fiction), an author (i.e. Katherine Paterson), or a theme (i.e. coming of age). O'Sullivan (2004) suggested focusing literature units around character traits we would like children to develop, such as courage or caring. However you include directed literature study in your classroom, you will certainly be bringing additional good literature beyond the basal reader to your students.

  One drawback of teaching a core book or a class novel is that you have removed the element of student choice so necessary for motivation. No book, no matter how well-written, will appeal to all students, and often core books are dictated by the school district making this choice even further removed from the student. So as a complete reading plan, literature units will be limited. This does not mean you should never use them, however. Roe and Smith (2012) recommend that you teach core trade books as you would any other reading material using pre-reading, during reading and post-reading activities. Be careful, though, not to "basalize" your trade books, teaching them so endlessly that the life is drained from them.

  Another way to include class novels in your reading program and still provide for some student choice is to encapsulate the core text into a bigger literature study. For example, in an author study of Beverly Cleary, all students could read and respond to *Dear Mr. Henshaw* (1983), then each student would choose one or two other Beverly Cleary books to read and add to the response mix of the class.

- *Home-School Connection*. Children spend only about 14% of their time in school with the other 86% of their time doing various activities out of school (Donovan, Bransford, & Pellegrino, 1999) Couple that fact with research that finds strong home-school partnership to be important to the literacy success of children (Morrow, 2010) and you can easily see why it will be important for you to establish a good home-school connection for building reading volume.

  Parent communication is one important avenue to building this connection. Either through conferences or through regular newsletters you can address such topics as what your class is reading right now, suggestions for additional books students might read at home, or the importance of library visits. Parent education workshops are also a good forum for building home-school connections. Discussing read-aloud techniques and why reading out loud is important even for parents of older students would make a good workshop topic as would specific ideas for encouraging children to write at home.

  Finally, regular routines can connect home and school to encourage reading volume. Many teachers manage a book bag program in which they send students home with bags containing a carefully selected book to read with parents. Teachers also ask students to read for a specified amount of time (maybe 20 minutes) at home and record this reading on their reading log.

Parents can be invited to school as guest readers or for an author tea when students are ready to share a finished writing project. And parent volunteers can manage much bigger literacy projects, such as an in-school publishing company for student work. Big or small, parent involvement is very important in helping students become lifelong readers and should be encouraged whenever and wherever it is possible. The final message, then, is that you are not in this alone. Teachers, parents and the community all have a stake in making sure children become fully literate.

Summing Up

This chapter dealt with the third important leg of the balanced reading stool—reading volume. We discussed the importance of wide reading, and the elements of motivation, materials and response for encouraging this reading volume. Motivation included such considerations as a literacy rich environment, the enthusiasm of the teacher, and ample time for student-selected reading. During our discussion of materials, we looked at the major genres, authors and awards in children's literature and also considered the need for including diverse types of books in your classroom. Finally, we discussed several teaching methods, such as reading workshop and literature circles for responding to literature.

Moving On

And that brings us to the end of this textbook on teaching a child to read. While this was a *Just the Bones* introduction to this important topic, you now have lots and lots of ideas for the best ways to teach reading. So this ending is really just your beginning. Now take all these ideas into your classroom and help your children cross over into Literacy Land and learn to prosper there!

Bibliography—Academic References

Adams, M., Foorman, B., Lundberg, I., & Beeler, T. (1998). *Phonemic awareness in young children.* Baltimore: Paul H. Brookes.

Allington, R. (2002). *Big brother and the national reading curriculum: How ideology trumped evidence.* Portsmouth, NH: Heinemann.

Anderson, R. C., Heibert, E.F., Scott, J. A., & Wilkinson, I A. (1985). *Becoming a nation of readers.* Washington, DC: National Institute of Education.

Arya, P., Martens, P., Wilson, G.P., Altwerger, B., Lijun, J., Laster, B., & Lang, D. (2005) Reclaiming literacy instruction: Evidence in support of literature-based programs. *Language Arts*, 83 (1), 63-72.

Ashton-Warner, S. (1963). *Teacher.* New York: Simon & Schuster.

Atwell, N. (1998). *In the middle: New understandings about writing, reading, and learning* (2nd ed.). Portsmouth, NH: Heinemann.

August, D., & Shanahan, T. (Eds.). (2006). *Developing literacy in second-language learners: Report of the National Literacy Panel on language-minority children and youth*. Mahwah, NJ: Erlbaum.

Bell, P. (2013, April). *A little PDA goes a long way: Strategies for content literacy.* Paper presented at the Annual Conference of National Science Teachers Association, San Antonio, TX.

Bettelheim, B. & Zelan, K. (1982*). On Learning to Read.* New York: Knopf.

Betts, E.A. (1946). *Foundations of reading instruction.* New York: American Book.

Bishop, R. S. (1990). Mirrors, windows, and sliding glass doors. *Perspectives* 6, ix-xi.

Bloom, B.S. (1964). *Stability and change in human characteristics*. New York: John Wiley & Sons.

Bloom, B. S., Englehart, M. D., Furst, E. J., Hill, w. H., & Krathwohl, D.R. (1956*). The taxonomy of educational objectives. Handbook I: Cognitive domain.* New York: David McKay.

Bond, G.L., & Dykstra, R. (1967/1997). The cooperative research program in first-grade reading instruction. *Reading Research Quarterly*, 2(4), 1-142. (Reprinted in *Reading Research Quarterly*, 32(4)).

Bormuth, J.R. (1968). The cloze readability procedure. In *Readability in 1968*, J.R. Bormuth, Ed. Champaign, IL: National Association of Teachers of English.

Calkins, L. (1994). *The art of teaching writing*. Westport, CT: Heinemann.

Center for the Improvement of Early Reading Achievement (CIERA) (2001). *Put reading first: The research building blocks for teaching children to read*. Jessup, MD: National Institute for Literacy.

Chall, J. (1967). *Learning to read: The great debate.* New York: McGraw-Hill.

Chambers, A. (1991). *The reading environment.* Stroud: Thimble Press

Clay, M., (1985). *The early detection of reading difficulties: A diagnostic survey with recovery procedures.* Portsmouth, NH: Heinemann.

Clay, M.M., (1991). *Becoming literate: The construction of inner control.* Portsmouth, NH: Heinemann.

Clay, M. (1993). *An observation survey of early literacy achievement.* Portsmouth, NH: Heinemann.

Clymer, T. (1996). The utility of phonic generalizations in the primary grades. *The Reading Teacher*, 50, 182-187.

Cook, L. K., & Mayer, R. E. (1988). Teaching readers about the nature of science text. *Journal of Educational Psychology, 80(4),* 448-456.

Cooper, J. D., Kiger, N. D., Robinson, M. D., & Slansky, J.A. (2012). *Literacy: Helping students construct meaning.* Belmont, CA: Wadsworth.

Cooper, J. D., Warncke, E., Shipman, D., & Ramstad, P.A. (1979). *The what and how of reading instruction*. Columbus: Merrill.

Cullinan, B. (1993*). Pen in hand: children become writers*. Newark, DE: International Reading Association.

Cummins, J. (1981). The role of primary language development in promoting educational success for language minority students. In Office of Bilingual Bicultural Education, *Schooling and language minority education: A theoretical framework* (pp. 3-49). Sacramento, CA: State Department of Education.

Cummins, J. (2001). *Negotiating identities: Education for empowerment in a diverse society* (2nd ed.). Los Angeles: California Association for Bilingual Education.

Cunningham, A. E., & Stanovich, K. E. (1998). What reading does for the mind. *American Educator,* 22, 8-15.

Cunningham, P. (2013). *Phonics they use: Words for reading and writing* (6th ed.). Boston, Pearson.

Cunningham, P., & Allington, R. (2011). *Classrooms that work* (5th ed.). Boston: Allyn & Bacon.

Daniels H. (1994). *Literature circles: Voice and choice in the student-centered classroom*. New York: Stenhouse.

Dewitz, P., Jones, J., & Leahy, S. (2009). Comprehension strategy instruction in core reading programs. *Reading Research Quarterly*, 44(2), 102-126.

Dolch, E. W. (1936). A basic sight vocabulary. *Elementary School Journal, 36,* 456-460.

Donovan, M.S., Bransford, J.D., & Pellegrino, J.W. (Eds.). (1999). *How people learn: Bridging research and practice.* Washington, DC: National Academies Press.

Dorr, R. E. (2006). Something old is new again: Revisiting language experience. *The Reading Teacher,* 60, 138-146.

Duke, N. & Pearson, P.D. (2002). Effective practices for developing reading comprehension. In *What research has to say about reading instruction*, A. Farstrup & S. J. Samuels (eds.). Newark, DL: International Reading Association, 205-242.

Dunsmore, K. & Fisher D. (Eds.). (2010). *Bringing literacy home*. Newark, DE: International Reading Association.

Durkin, D. (1978). What classroom observations reveal about reading comprehension instruction. *Reading Research Quarterly*, 14(4), 482-533.

Feldhusen, J., Van Winkle, L., & Ehle, D. (1996). Is it acceleration or simply appropriate instruction for precocious youth? *Teaching Exceptional Children, 28(3)*, 48-51.

Flesch, R. (1955). *Why Johnny can't read—and what you can do about it*. New York: Harper.

Fountas, I.C. & Pinnell, G. S. (2006*). Leveled books, K-8: Matching texts to readers for effective teaching*. Portsmouth, NH: Heinemann.

Friend, M. (2008). *Special education: Contemporary perspectives for school professionals* (2nd ed.). Boston: Pearson/Allyn & Bacon.

Fry, E. (1977). Fry's readability graph: Clarifications, validity, and extension to level 17. *Journal of Reading 21*, 249.

Fry, E. (2004). *1000 instant words*. Westminster, CA: Teacher Created Materials.

Gamble, N. & Yates, S. (2008). *Exploring children's literature*, (2nd ed). Los Angeles: Sage

Garan, E. M. (2002). *Resisting reading mandates: How to triumph with the truth.* Portsmouth, NH: Heinemann.

Genesee, F., Lindholm-Leary, K., Saunders, W., & Christian, D. (2006). *Educating English language learners.* New York: Cambridge University Press.

Gentry, J. R. (1982). An analysis of GNYS at WRK. *The Reading Teacher* 36 (2), 196-200.

Gibson, S. (2008/2009). An effective framework for primary grade level guided reading instruction. *The Reading Teacher, 62(4)*, 324-334.

Goldenberg, C. (2012). Improving achievement for English learners: Conclusions from recent reviews and emerging research. In R. D. Robinson, M. C. McKenna & K. Conradi (Eds.), *Issues and trends in literacy education*. New York: Pearson. 133-152.

Goodman, K. (1973). Reading: A psycholinguistic guessing game. In R. Karlin (Ed.), *Perspectives on elementary reading.* New York: Harcourt Brace Jovanovich.

Goodman, K. (1986). *What's whole in whole language?* Portsmouth, NH: Heinemann.

Goodman, Y. (1978). Kidwatching: An alternative to testing. *Journal of National Elementary School Principals,* 57(4), 22-27.

Graves, D. H. (1983). *Writing: Teachers and children at work*. Portsmouth, NH: Heinemann.

Graves, M. F. (2006). *The vocabulary book: Learning and instruction.* New York: Teachers College Press.

Graves, M., Juel, C., Graves, B. & Dewitz, P. (2011). *Teaching reading in the 21st century: Motivating all learners.* Boston, MA: Pearson.

Green, J. E. (October 14, 2002). *Accountability run amok.* 2002-2003 Author Seminar Lecture Program. Bloomington, IN: Phi Delta Kappa Educational Foundation.

Halliday, M. (1978). *Language as social semiotic: The social interpretation of language and meaning.* Baltimore: University Park Press.

Hasbrouck, J., & Tindal, G. (2006). Oral reading fluency norms: A valuable assessment tool for reading teachers. *The Reading Teacher*, 59(7), 636-645.

Hepler, S. I., & Hickman, J. (1982). The book was okay. I love you: Social aspects of response to literature. *Theory into Practice, 21*, 278-283.

Huck, C. S., Kiefer, B. Z., Hepler, S., & Hickman, J. (2004). Children's literature in the elementary school (8th ed.). New York: McGraw Hill.

International Reading Association. (2007). *Teaching reading well: A synthesis of the International Reading Association's research on teacher preparation for reading instruction*. Newark, DE: Author.

Juel, C. (1988). Learning to read and write: A longitudinal study of 54 children from first through fourth grades. *Journal of Educational Psychology*, 80, 437-447.

Juel, C. (1994). *Learning to read and write in one elementary school.* New York: Springer-Verlag.

Kame'enui, E., Simmons, D., & Cornachione, C. (2001). *A practical guide to reading assessments.* Eugene: University of Oregon, National Center to Improve the Tools of Educators.

Kamil, M. L., & Bernhardt, E. B. (2004). Reading instruction for English-language learners. In M. F. Graves, C. Juel, & B. B. Graves, *Teaching reading in the 21st century* (3rd ed., pp. 496-541). Boston: Allyn & Bacon.

Kohn, A. (2001). Fighting the tests: A practical guide to rescuing our schools. *Phi Delta Kappan,* 82(5), 348-357.

Kozol, J. (Speaker, 2001). *National Conference on Education Keynote Address* (Cassette recording No. AASA01-01. Orlando, FL: American Association of School Administrators.

Krashen, S. (1982). *Principles and practice in second language acquisition*. Oxford: Pergamon.

Krashen, S. (1993). *The power of reading: Insights from the research*. Englewood, CO: Libraries Unlimited.

LaBerge, D., & Samuels, J. (1974). Toward a theory of automatic information processing in reading. *Cognitive Psychology*, 6, 293-323.

Larrick, N. (1965, September 11). The all-white world of children's books. *Saturday Review* 63-65.

Lee, J., Grigg, W. & Donahue, P. (2007). *The nation's report card: Reading 2007* (NCES 2002-496). Washington, D.C.: U.S. Department of Education, National Center for Educational Statistics, Institute of Educational Sciences.

Mariotti, A. S., & Homan, S. (2010). *Linking reading assessment to instruction*. New York: Routledge.

Marzano, R. J. (2010). Summarizing to comprehend. *Educational Leadership* 67, 83-84.

Marzano, R.J., Pickering, D.J., & Pollock, J.E. (2001). *Classroom instruction that works: Research-based strategies for increasing student achievement.* Alexandria, VA: Association for Supervision and Curriculum Development.

McGuffey, W. (1835). *McGuffey's Eclectic Readers.* Cincinnati, OH: Truman & Smith.

Morrow, L. M., Mendelsohn, A.L., & Kuhn, M. R. (2010). Characteristics of three family literacy programs that worked. In K. Dunsmore & D. Fisher (Eds.) *Bringing literacy home*, (pp. 83-103). Newark, DE: International Reading Association.

Mullis, I., Martin, M., Kennedy, A. & Foy, P. (2007). *IEA progress in international reading literacy study in primary school in 40 countries.* Boston: TIMSS and PIRLS International Study Center, Boston College.

National Commission of Excellence in Education. (1983). *A Nation at Risk.* Washington, D. C.: author.

National Early Literacy Panel. (2008). *Developing early literacy: Report of the National Early Literacy Panel.* Washington, DC: National Institute for Literacy.

National Institute for Literacy. (2010). *Early beginnings: Early literacy knowledge and instruction.* Jessup, MD: Author.

National Reading Panel. (2000). *Report of the National Reading Panel: Teaching children to read.* Washington, D.C.: National Institute of Child Health and Human Development.

No Child Left Behind Act of 2001. Public Law No. 107-110. Stat. 1425 (2002).

Oczkus, L. (2003). *Reciprocal teaching at work: Strategies for improving reading comprehension.* Newark, DE: International Reading Association.

Ogle, D. M. (1986). K-W-L: A teaching model that develops active reading of expository text. *The Reading Teacher* 39, 564-570.

Olness, R. (2005). *Using literature to enhance writing instruction: A guide for K-5 teachers*. Newark, DE: International Reading Association.

O'Sullivan, S.L. (2007). *A festival of talent: Wisdom from the first decade of the Charlotte S. Huck Children's Literature Festival.* Dubuque, IA: Kendall-Hunt.

O'Sullivan, S.L. (2004). Books to live by: Using children's literature for character education. *The Reading Teacher* 57(7), 640-645.

Padak, N., & Rasinski, T. (2008). *Evidence-based instruction in reading: A professional development guide to fluency.* Boston: Allyn & Bacon.

Palincsar, A. S. & Brown, A. (1984). Reciprocal teaching of comprehension-fostering and comprehension-monitoring activities. *Cognition and Instruction*, 1, 117-175.

Pavonetti, L. M., Brimmer, K. & Cipielewski, J. F. (2002/2003). Accelerated Reader: What are the lasting effects on the reading habits of middle school students exposed to Accelerated Reader in the elementary grades? *Journal of Adolescent & Adult Literacy,* 46, 300-311.

Pearson, P. D. & Gallagher, M.C. (1983). The instruction of reading comprehension. *Contemporary Educational Psychology,* 8, 317-344.

Piaget, J. (1955). *The language and thought of the child*. New York: World.

Pressley, M. (2006). *Reading instruction that works: The case for balanced teaching*. New York: Guilford Press.

RAND Reading Study Group. (2002). *Reading for understanding*. Santa Monica, CA: RAND.

Rasinski, T.V. (2003). *The fluent reader: Oral reading strategies for building word recognition, fluency, and comprehension.* New York: Scholastic.

Renzulli, J., & Reis, S. (2003). The schoolwide enrichment model: Developing creative and productive giftedness. In N. Colangelo & G. Davis (eds.), *Handbook of gifted education* (3rd ed., pp. 184-203). Boston: Allyn & Bacon.

Reutzel, D. R. (2006). Hey teacher, when you say fluency, what do you mean? Developing fluency and meta-fluency in elementary classrooms. In T. Rasinski, C. Blachowicz, & K. Lems (Eds.), *Fluency instruction: Research-based best practices* (pp. 62-85). New York: Guilford Press.

Reutzel, D. & Cooter, R. B. Jr. (2012).*Teaching children to read* (6th ed). New York: Pearson.

Robinson, F. P. (1961). *Effective study*. New York: Harper & Row.

Robinson, R.D., McKenna, M.C., & Conradi, K. (Eds.) (2012). *Issues and trends in literacy education*. 5th ed. New York: Pearson.

Roe, B. D., & Burns, P. C. (2011). *Informal reading inventory* (8th ed.). Belmont, CA: Wadsworth.

Roe, B. D., & Smith, S. H. (2012). *Teaching reading in today's elementary schools* (11th ed.). Belmont, CA: Wadsworth.

Roehler, L. & Duffy, G. (1991). Teachers's instructional actions. In R. Barr, M.L. Kamil, P. Mosenthal, &P.D. Pearson (Eds.), *Handbook of reading research* (Vol. 2, pp. 861-883). White Plains, NY: Longman.

Rosenblatt, L. (1978). *The reader, the text, the poem: The transactional theory of the literary work*. Carbondale: Southern Illinois Press.

Routman, R. (2003). *Reading essentials: The specifics you need to teach reading well.* Portsmouth, NH Heinemann.

Rubin , R., & Carlan, V. (2005). Using writing to understand bilingual children's literacy development. *The Reading Teacher, 58(8)*, 728-739.

Samuels, J. (2004). Toward a theory of automatic information processing in reading, revisited. In R. Ruddell and N. Unrau (Eds.), *Theoretical models and processes of reading (5th ed.).* Newark, DE: International Reading Association. 1127-1147.

Silvaroli, N.J.,& Wheelock, W. H. (2004). *Classroom reading inventory (*10th ed.). New York: McGraw Hill.

Smith, N. B. (2002). *American reading instruction*. Newark, DE: International Reading Association.

Stanovich, K. E. (1986). Matthew effects in reading: Some consequences of individual differences in the acquisition of literacy. *Reading Research Quarterly*, 21, 360-407.

Teale, W.H., & Sulzby, E. (1991). Emergent literacy. In R. Barr, M. Kamil, P.Mosenthal, & P.D. Pearson (Eds.), *Handbook of reading research* (Vol. 2, pp. 418-452). New York: Longman.

Temple, C., Nathan, R.I., Burris, N., & Temple, F. (1993). *The beginnings of writing* (3rd ed.). Boston: Allyn & Bacon.

Tierney, R.J., & Shanahan, T. (1991). Research on the reading-writing relationship: Interactions, transactions, and outcomes. . In R. Barr, M.L. Kamil, P. Mosenthal, & P.D. Pearson (Eds.), *Handbook of reading research* (Vol. 2, pp. 246-280). White Plains, NY: Longman.

Truss, L. (2003). *Eats, shoots & leaves: The zero tolerance approach to punctuation*. New York: Penguin.

Van Allen, R. (1976). *Language experiences in communication.* Boston: Houghton-Mifflin.

Vygotsky, L. (1986). *Thought and language.* Cambridge, MA: MIT Press.

Watt, M. (2005). *Standards-based reforms in the United States of America: An overview.* (ERIC Document Preproduction Service No. ED 490562).

Woods, M. L., & Moe, A.J. (2011). *Analytical reading inventory* (9th ed.). Boston: Pearson.

Yopp, H.K. (1988). The validity and reliability of phonemic awareness tests. *Reading Research Quarterly*, 23, 159-177.

Yopp, H.K. (1995). A test for assessing phonemic awareness in young children. *The Reading Teacher*, 49(1), 20-29.

Bibliography—Children's Literature References

Bartoletti, S.C. (2001). *Black Potatoes*. NY: Houghton Mifflin.

Bunting, E. (2002). *One Candle*. NY: HarperCollins.

Cleary, B. (1968). *Ramona the Pest*. NY: Avon Books.

Cleary, B. (1983). *Dear Mr. Henshaw*. NY: HarperCollins.

Clements, A. (1996). *Frindle*. NY: Scholastic.

Coerr, E. (1977). *Sadako and the Thousand Paper Cranes*. NY: Dell.

Creech, S. (2001). *Love That Dog*. NY: HarperCollins.

Crews, D. (1986). *Ten Black Dots*. NY: Greenwillow.

DiCamillo, K. (2003). *The Tale of Despereaux*. Cambridge, MA: Candlewick.

Dowd, S. (2007). *The London Eye Mystery*. NY: Random House.

Finchler, J. (2000). *Testing Miss Malarkey*. NY: Walker & Company.

Forbes, E. (1943). *Johnny Tremain*. NY: Dell.

Fox, P. (1973). *The Slave Dancer*. NY: Bantam Doubleday Dell.

Fradin, J. & Fradin, D. (2008). *Droughts*. Washington D.C.: National Geographic.

Freedman, R. (1980). *Immigrant Kids*. NY: Scholastic.

Freedman, R. (1987). *Lincoln: A Photobiography*. NY: Clarion.

Freedman, R. (2006). *Children of the Great Depression*. NY: Clarion.

George, K. O. (2005). *Fold Me a Poem*. NY: Harcourt.

Giff, P. R. (1997). *Lily's Crossing*. NY: Random House.

Greene, B. (1973). *Summer of My German Soldier*. NY: Bantam.

Gwynne, F. (1976). *A Chocolate Moose for Dinner*. NY: Simon & Schuster.

Hill, L.C. (2011). *Dave the Potter: Artist, Poet, Slave*. NY: Little, Brown.

Huck, C. S. (1989). *Princess Furball*. NY: Greenwillow.

Hunt, I. (1964). *Across Five Aprils*. NY: Grosset & Dunlap.

Hutchins, P. (2000). *Ten Red Apples*. NY: Greenwillow.

Keats, E. J. (1962). *The Snowy Day*. NY: Viking.

Keats, E. J. (1964). *Whistle for Willie*. NY: Viking.

Krull, K. (1997). *Lives of the Athletes*. NY: Harcourt Brace.

Lai, T. (2011). *Inside Out & Back Again.* NY: HarperCollins.

Lee, M. (1997). *Nim and the War Effort.* NY: Farrar, Straus and Giroux.

L'Engle, M. ((1962). *A Wrinkle in Time.* NY: Dell.

Levine, G. C. (1997). *Ella Enchanted.* NY: HarperCollins.

Louie, A. (1982). *Yeh-Shen: A Cinderella Story from China.* NY: Putnam & Grosset.

Lowry, L. (1993). *The Giver.* NY: Houghton Mifflin.

Lowry, L. (1989). *Number the Stars.* NY: Houghton Mifflin.

Macaulay, D. (1990). *Black and White.* NY: Houghton Mifflin.

Magorian, M. (1981). *Good Night, Mr. Tom.* NY: HarperCollins.

Martin, B. Jr. (1967). *Brown Bear, Brown Bear, What Do You See?* NY: Henry Holt.

Martin, R. (1992). *The Rough-Face Girl.* NY: Putnam & Grosset.

Mochizuki, K. (1993). *Baseball Saved Us.* NY: Scholastic.

Morales, Y. (2003). *Just a Minute: A Trickster Tale and Counting Book.* NY: Chronicle.

Numeroff, L.J. (1985). *If You Give a Mouse a Cookie.* NY: Harper & Row.

Numeroff, L. J. (1991). *If You Give a Moose a Muffin.* NY: HarperCollins.

Park, L.S. (2002). *A Single Shard.* NY: Random House.

Paterson, K. (1978). *The Great Gilly Hopkins.* NY: Scholastic.

Paterson, K. (1980). *Jacob Have I Loved.* NY: HarperCollins.

Paterson, K. (1996). *Jip, His Story.* NY: Scholastic.

Peck, R. (2007). *On the Wings of Heroes.* NY: Dial.

Polacco, P. (1994). *Pink and Say.* NY: Putnam & Grosset.

Polacco, P. (2000). *The Butterfly.* NY: Philomel.

Rawlings, M. K. (1938). *The Yearling.* NY: Simon & Schuster.

Rockwell, T. (1973). *How to Eat Fried Worms.* NY: Yearling.

Rubin, S. G. (2005). *The Flag with Fifty-Six Stars.* NY: Holiday House.

Rubin, S. G. (2006). *The Cat with the Yellow Star.* NY: Holiday House.

Ryan, P. M. (2000). *Esperanza Rising.* NY: Scholastic.

Ryan, P. M. (2003). *When Marian Sang.* NY: Scholastic.

Salisbury, G. (1994). *Under the Blood-Red Sun.* NY: Yearling.

Say, A. (1993). *Grandfather's Journey*. NY: Houghton Mifflin.

Simon, S. (1996). *The Sun*. NY: Morrow.

Sobol, D. (2007). *Encyclopedia Brown, Boy Detective*. NY: Puffin.

Spinelli, E. (2007). *Hero Cat*. Tarrytown, NY: Marshall Cavendish.

Terban, M. (1987). *Mad as a Wet Hen and Other Funny Idioms*. NY: Clarion.

Waber, B. (1972). *Ira Sleeps Over*. Boston: Houghton Mifflin.

Wiesner, D. (1991). *Tuesday*. NY: Clarion.

Wiesner, D. (2002). *The Three Pigs*. NY: Clarion

Wilder, L. I. (1935). *The Little House on the Prairie*. NY: Harper.

Williams-Garcia, R. (2010). *One Crazy Summer*. NY: HarperCollins.

Yolen, J. (1987). *Owl Moon*. NY: Philomel.

Zelinsky, P. (1998). *Rapunzel.* NY: Scholastic.

Index